Colleges Fail

Let Colleges Fail

The Power of Creative Destruction in
Higher Education

Richard K. Vedder

INDEPENDENT
INSTITUTE

ISBN: 978-1-59813-403-2
eISBN: 978-1-59813-405-6

Cataloging-in-Publication data on file with the Library of Congress

Independent Institute
100 Swan Way, Oakland, CA 94621-1428
Telephone: 510-632-1366
Fax: 510-568-6040
Email: info@independent.org
Website: www.independent.org

Cover Design: John Caruso
Cover Image: Stanford Oval, courtesy of King of Hearts / Wikimedia Commons / CC-BY-SA-30.0
Interior Design: Jason Sunde

10 9 8 7 6 5 4 3 2 1

Contents

Introduction

AMERICANS ARE BLESSED to be part of a national community that is exceedingly prosperous and generally considered to be a great place to live—millions want to immigrate annually to its shores—far more than the nation wishes to accept. Additionally, America's vaunted economic exceptionalism is matched by a perceived excellence in higher education: American universities dominate the rankings of the planet's greatest universities. This book concentrates on the second of these two examples of American exceptionalism. At the same time, however, I will argue that in many regards the collegiate experience in America has suffered a major decline in recent decades, and that its ability to reverse that decline is considerably weakened by massive subsidies, mostly from governments but some from well-meaning private philanthropies, subsidies that prevent corrections of poor performance and block innovation.

The American economy has flourished because of private property rights, the rule of law, and the operation of competitive markets. These have eased the entry into business by entrepreneurs with great ideas: it gave America great inventor-entrepreneurs like Eli Whitney, Thomas Edison, Henry Ford, John D. Rockefeller, Sam Walton, and, more recently, Steve Jobs, Bill Gates, Jeff Bezos, Mark Zuckerberg, and Elon Musk. But the economy has equally flourished because markets do not tolerate, at least for very long, incompetence, lethargy, and a failure to innovate to meet the changing tastes and incomes of the population. To succeed in America, businesses must respond to new technology and alterations in the economic environment or face possible extinction. Drawing on previous writings by German-speaking social scientists, including Karl Marx and Werner Sombart, the Austrian American economist Joseph Schumpeter famously introduced the concept of "creative destruction" in his 1942 book *Capitalism, Socialism and Democracy*.[1] Schumpeter observed that markets reallocate resources from unproductive to productive uses by destroying (through creative destruction) businesses whose failure to adapt to changing tastes, new technology, or altered prices of productive inputs leads to declining sales, an end to profitability, and, ultimately, bankruptcy or sale to a more dynamic and forward-thinking enterprise. American business enterprises must change with the times or face financial ruin.

Contrast businesses with universities. They too can fall on hard times if they are unresponsive to the changing demands of students, the impact of worldwide events like major wars and health pandemics, or even a waning interest in funding professorial research. But typically, third parties come to their rescue—governments allocate emergency funds, private donors respond to appeals for support. Some even have large endowment funds providing a steady income. Therefore, the "death" of a university is much less common than the "death" of a private business. This was vividly illustrated in the 2020–22 coronavirus pandemic. Many colleges faced sharply reduced tuition and other revenues and also enhanced costs, but the federal government came to their rescue, first under the Trump and then Biden administration, with large amounts of financial assistance. Indeed, universities can be considered institutions extracting what economists call "economic rents": payments beyond those necessary to have a good or service provided. We return to this theme later in the book.

What all this suggests is that reallocating collegiate resources to new providers as older ones cease operations—and thus restructuring higher education—simply does not happen very much, because unsuccessful universities rarely die. (The forthcoming chapters provide more details.) Therefore, a stagnation in the movement of resources toward new ideas and the colleges and universities espousing them, and away from the less responsive schools, slows the pace of American higher education innovation.

This book explores the reality of this phenomenon and its implications for America. Its early chapters demonstrate the many current deficiencies of American universities; later chapters expand on the concept of creative destruction. It asks questions: Why do we subsidize universities through taxpayer-provided grants or private donor gifts while we do the opposite for most producers of goods and services and actually *tax* them to subsidize so-called public goods like education delivery or military protection? Why are universities given special status not given to other providers of useful services such as used-car dealers or fast-food restaurants? Why have well-intentioned federal programs such as government-guaranteed student loans had an impact dramatically different than was intended when the legislation was passed? How have state governments responded to the public desire for higher learning? Do the amounts and methods of supporting so-called public universities vary dramatically from state to state? The answer is yes, and the implications of that deserve some explanation.

The second part of the book looks for solutions to the problems arising from a lack of needed creative destruction in higher education. It argues that if universities were more responsive to markets and less able to count on bailouts from supporters including, especially, the state or federal governments, then market-based incentives would likely prod them into more closely emulating the behavior of their private sector counterparts. Can and should universities be made at least a bit more like profit-making private sector businesses? (The short answer is yes.)

One option would be to simply create new universities to compete with existing ones; in the context of K–12 schools, Andy Smarick argues that creating new schools works better than reforming old ones.[2] That option, although sometimes useful, does not deal with the fundamental problems arising from government loan and grant programs providing bailouts. Moreover, our system of accreditation poses barriers to entry and innovation that also need to be reformed. (Do we even need accreditation?) Radical changes that amount in effect to privatizing state universities are also possible. Less substantial but still real changes could make state institutions more responsive; for example, high-tuition models could offer prospective students new forms of private financing of their education (like income-share agreements). Moving to a voucher/scholarship approach is discussed in chapter 8. In chapter 7 other measures are evaluated, including requiring universities to share in the cost of loan forfeiture if they accept a lot of mediocre students who drop out or fail to repay their student loans. In the current vernacular, schools need to have skin in the game. Other moves to restrict barriers to increased competition include reforming or even eliminating accreditation.

Reducing government bailouts would have other benefits. For example, schools would be forced to concentrate on job one (educating students and perhaps expanding the frontiers of research), thereby cutting unnecessary expenses. Salaries for diversity, equity, and inclusion bureaucrats, an expensive administrative cost, might be largely eliminated along with other forms of administrative bloat. Perhaps academic tenure would be reevaluated, along with a reassessment of capital expenditure needs or perhaps even the desirability of subsidizing intercollegiate athletics.

In short, higher education in American can be substantially changed, and where the benefits of doing so exceed the costs, it should happen. Americans, for example, on average spend sizably more educating a college graduate than do Canadians, but are American college grads markedly superior to those in our neighbor to the north? We are probably not getting as much bang for the buck as we can, and this book explores ways of altering the way we do things in order to use higher education to improve the public welfare.

This book came about after some brainstorming with a mostly like-minded group of scholars at a little retreat organized by the Independent Institute on the Monterey peninsula of California in early 2023. A small group was discussing ways to rethink higher education when I blurted out, "We should encourage Schumpeterian 'creative destruction.'" The idea resonated with the scholars present, so I announced, "I am going to write a little book about it."

This book is not my first or even second book done under the Independent Institute's auspices, the others spearheaded by the founder of that organization, the late great David Theroux. The prime movers there for this book include Graham Walker, Mary Theroux, Williamson (Bill) Evers, Rob Ade, and Christopher Briggs. Especially helpful toward the end was Phil Magness, one of the most energetic and brightest younger scholars in America today, now ensconced at the Independent Institute. Three student assistants—then 16-year-old high school student wunderkind Nicholas Jadwisienczak and Ohio University students Josiah Jennison and Elliott Winkler—did a variety of things this mostly computer illiterate writer could not do. Some marginally incoherent babble was banished from this book and immeasurably improved by copyeditor Karen Seriguchi, superbly overseen by Kathleen Curran, the Independent Institute's managing editor. And I appreciated the tolerance of Karen, my wife of fifty-six years standing, as I worked madly to complete this project.

I

Higher Education Is Failing!
Ten Cardinal Sins

WRITING A FEW years ago, I took nearly four hundred pages to describe the many problems of American higher education.[1] In this book, we will necessarily severely condense that analysis, only tangentially discussing many issues confronting colleges and universities (for example, the high cost of, and other issues associated with, intercollegiate athletics). Let's list and briefly discuss just ten of the issues ("cardinal sins") here, demonstrating that American higher learning has serious problems, ones needing addressing sooner rather than later.

The Problems of American Universities

First, enrollments have been falling (see table 1.1). Indeed, enrollments have consistently fallen since 2011, despite a slowly rising American population. This decline is unique in American history. Note the steady and substantial increase in enrollments in the last quarter of the last century and the first decade of this one. Then note the steady decline after 2010. We have annual American enrollment data since 1870, and although the declines are not unprecedented, never have the number of students *shrunk continuously for over a decade*, in a period of mostly general prosperity and no major wars requiring the military service of younger Americans. A part of the drop for a couple of years (2020–22) was related to the COVID pandemic, but a meaningful rebound did not occur as soon as the health crisis receded. A growing number of young people are "just saying no" to college, apparently believing that the gains from attending school are likely to be less than the costs. It is interesting that in the last few years enrollments were rising in Canada as they were falling in the US.

Table 1.1 US college enrollments, 1975–2022

Year	Total fall enrollment
1975	11,184,859
1990	13,818,657
2005	17,487,474
2010	21,019,438
2014	20,209,092
2019	19,630,178
2022	18,525,035

Source: National Center for Education Statistics, Digest of Education Statistics, table 303.10, accessed June 3, 2024, https://nces.ed.gov/programs/digest/d22/tables/dt22_303.10.asp.
Note: Enrollment for 2022 is estimated.

Adjusting for the growing US population, the recent decline in college attendance appears even more striking. In 1975, about fifty-one of every one thousand Americans were attending college, a proportion that grew by one-third, to sixty-eight per one thousand in 2010. The 2022 proportion was less than fifty-six per one thousand. Over 73 percent of the gain in the proportion of Americans in college between 1975 and 2010 was lost with the 2.5 million enrollment decline after that date. College enrollment rates (the percentage of recent high school graduates aged 16 and 24 in college) declined from over 70 percent in 2009 to 62 percent in 2022.[2] Moreover, the enrollment decline was concentrated largely in male students, suggesting that collegiate policies of recent vintage have turned off men in particular. Is there perhaps even a "war against men" raging on college campuses?

Although colleges attract persons of widely different ages, the overwhelming majority are younger Americans wishing to extend their education beyond high school. One popular explanation for the declining enrollments in recent years is that birth rates are falling. It is true that in some sense Americans are witnessing a "birth dearth." Yet the decline in enrollments from 2010 to 2022 is not primarily explained by that phenomenon. The majority of undergraduate students attending college in 2010 were born between 1988 and 1992, while those attending school in 2022 were mostly born twelve years later, between 2000 and 2004. In the earlier period, the annual average number of births in the United States was 4,061,000, almost identical to the number (4,060,000) in the later period.[3] To be sure, other demographic factors affect enrollment, such as the proportion of students outside the traditional 18-to-22 age group, but there is little indication that dramatic changes here are a dominant factor in the observed enrollment decline. Similarly, changes in the inflow of foreign students are only a secondary factor in the observed enrollment stagnation.

Second, public support of, and confidence in, higher education is low. Polling data from several sources consistently make this point. The most recent polling at this writing was done in early 2023 jointly by the *Wall Street Journal* and NORC (formerly, the National Opinion Research Center). A solid majority (56 percent) of respondents to the 2023 poll agreed that college was "not worth the cost because people often graduate without specific job skills and with a large amount of debt to pay off." Only 42 percent said college was worth the cost.[4]

Two additional facts make that polling data disturbing for those concerned about the future of American universities. First, the numbers highly valuing higher education have been in steady decline. In 2017, 49 percent said college was worth the cost; in 2013, a solid majority (53 percent) did while only 40 percent said it was not worth the cost. Every year, roughly 1 percent more of the US population adopt the position that college is not worth it. Additionally, younger Americans, specifically those aged 18 to 34, who have the most recent personal college-related experiences, were generally *less* likely to think college was worth it than older groups.

Polling by others is broadly consistent with the *Wall Street Journal*/NORC findings. For example, a 2022 poll by Public Agenda shows that Democrats have more positive feelings about the worth of higher education than Republicans or independents. But even among Democrats, some 40 percent agreed that "a college education is a questionable investment because of high student loans and limited job opportunities."[5] The Public Agenda study found other differences worth noting, including a sense that community colleges are better investments and create better opportunities for low-income students.

Traditionally, state colleges and universities, educating the large majority of college students, have enjoyed a fair amount of independence from supervision by the governments that at least nominally "own" them. The last several years, however, have seen a surge in state legislative efforts to impose various controls on universities. Why? I think the polling data clearly point to the answer: as satisfaction with universities declines, politicians believe they can gain popularity (and job security) by imposing constraints on what public schools do. This is particularly true in large Republican-leaning states such as Florida, Texas, and Ohio, as the data indicate that Republicans tend to be particularly skeptical of the positive benefits of contemporary American higher education.

Third, unpopular ideas are often suppressed or ignored.[6] Universities provide a presumably neutral forum for evaluating and disseminating ideas. Indeed, they are "marketplaces of ideas." Their effectiveness is severely reduced if some ideas are not allowed to be discussed, or when one feels afraid to express an opinion. In the late nineteenth and early twentieth centuries, it was widely agreed that Germany led the world in the quality of its universities because of unfettered research exploration. Yet the rise of Nazism in the 1920s and especially 1930s led to an abrupt decline, because some of the best and brightest luminaries of the German intelligentsia fled the country because it was downright dangerous to express oneself freely (of course, this was particularly true of Jewish scholars). Consequently, Germany went into a serious scholarly decline. Is something similar happening in the United States? Stories of the oppression of ideas on American campuses are many—let me illustrate with just four celebrated examples from the last decade.

Beginning in the 2015–16 academic year at Yale, students participated in a Halloween celebration. A politically correct university apparatchik sent out a message to students urging them not to wear offensive costumes, such as feathered headdresses or turbans. Erika Christakis, an associate master at Silliman College who was also a liberal Democrat, sensibly argued: "Whose business is it to control the forms of costumes of young people?" This led to an uproar, especially among minority students demanding the resignation of Ms. Christakis and her distinguished husband, Nicholas, the master of

Silliman and a physician and sociologist. The spineless Yale president, Peter Salovey (still reigning many years later), met with a group of protesters, where he allegedly proclaimed, "We failed you." After some more harassment, the Christakis couple resigned their positions at Silliman College (although Nicholas continues to work at Yale). Free expression lost out to wokeness.

Amy Wax is (as of this writing) the tenured Robert Mundheim Professor of Law at the University of Pennsylvania Law School. Penn wants to fire her.[7] Is she incompetent or guilty of such clear transgressions as a theft of property, a failure to teach classes, or sexual harassment? No. The holder of degrees from Harvard, Yale, Columbia, and Oxford, Professor Wax is both a lawyer who has appeared at least fifteen times before the US Supreme Court and a physician. She once won a prestigious prize for teaching. She is being censured for her opinions—her right to free expression. She has glorified the values of Western civilization as well as those of mid-twentieth-century America. She has made uncomfortable observations, such as that black law students on average do poorer in class than white ones. In short, she is an outspoken conservative woman. Law School dean Ted Ruger told a group of students that "she pisses me off." So he initiated a move to fire her (not fully resolved at this writing). Professor Wax appears to be being punished for holding views outside the currently fashionable woke academic mainstream.

Moving to the West Coast, the Stanford University chapter of the Federalist Society invited US Court of Appeals judge Stuart Kyle Duncan to speak at an event in early 2023. At that event, a diversity, equity, and inclusion (henceforth DEI) administrator spoke up and egged on protesting students who decided that this presumably conservative-oriented jurist should not be allowed to speak and prevented him from talking—the modern collegiate cancel culture, or "heckler's veto," at work. The administrative apparatus at Stanford effectively suppressed free speech and expression. To be sure, Stanford's president apologized and said it was unacceptable conduct, but the damage was done, and wokeness and the suppression of ideas triumphed over free inquiry and expression.

Let's move to the Midwest and away from elite schools. In April 2023, Professor Scott Gerber of Ohio Northern University was accosted by campus security officers while teaching, hauled out of his classroom, and asked to leave campus. He was told to resign or face being fired for lack of "collegiality."[8]

Professor Gerber was easily the most noted scholar at the Ohio Northern law school and has been a popular teacher as well. Although not told what was really wrong with him (other than allegedly possessing a feature shared by many professors, a lack of collegiality), he has in fact been publicly criticizing many actions within the university, such as its overt disdain for intellectual diversity. He apparently just does not fit in with the opinions of the Ohio Northern administration.

All these incidents and others have led students with a right-of-center orientation increasingly to self-censor: to keep quiet to avoid being ostracized or harassed by left-leaning students or faculty.[9]

Fourth, intellectual diversity is declining. Not only are the opinions of a considerable number of academics being suppressed, the very community of academics is increasingly less diverse in its perspectives on life.[10] In particular, the overwhelming majority of faculty teaching in fields where public policy issues are an important part of the intellectual milieu (the social sciences in particular, but also some of the humanities and fine arts disciplines) are on the left politically. That is not a new phenomenon, but one that has markedly intensified over time. It is not uncommon to find English or sociology departments, for example, where 100 percent of the faculty are registered Democrats. I once met an Ivy League sociologist who said he was a Republican and was so surprised that I asked for his autograph! A recent survey of over three hundred faculty in five academic units at Yale University (the departments of economics, political science, history, and philosophy, and the law school) showed almost *twenty-four times* as many registered Democrats as Republicans—two of the five surveyed departments (economics and philosophy) had no Republican professors.[11] A 2021 survey revealed that "fully 7 in 10 conservative American academics say they self-censor in their teaching, research or academic discussions."[12] Professors are afraid to be heard.

In occasional meetings of conservative-oriented professors, I often hear and also give this advice: Don't be too vocal in expressing your opinions until you get tenure. Publish relatively noncontroversial research that does not call too much attention to your conservative orientation. In effect, for career advancement many conservatively oriented professors feel a need to self-censor, to keep their opinions to themselves, an extremely regrettably circumstance in academic communities that flourish from a free and civil exchange of ideas.

Surveys by organizations like the Higher Education Research Institute at UCLA and others show a marked leftward shift in the faculty, increasing the reluctance of the few conservative or libertarian faculty to speak up.

I would note here that faculty members are increasingly wards of the state. Governments heavily subsidize universities, including so-called private ones, and thereby the salaries of the faculty, providing incentives for faculty to generally favor bigger government. Moreover, particularly when Democratic administrations dominate at the national level, top government officials are often chosen disproportionately from the faculty and administrative ranks of top universities, with elected politicians depending on those faculty for advice. These faculty members and administrators typically also make meaningful financial contributions to political campaigns.

Colleges and universities, of course, could mitigate the lack of intellectual diversity on campus if they wanted to. In the long run, that would involve ending the harsh discrimination against certain viewpoints—not letting the political orientations of prospective faculty members deter them from being hired—and indeed, considering a greater political diversity in the faculty as a virtue needing addressing. Also, campuses could enormously increase their intellectual diversity by welcoming visitors with myriad points of view. Instead, lectures by conservative spectators are sometimes disrupted by protesters trying to suppress alternative viewpoints. Administrators should, but seldom do, harshly discipline those trying to impose their views on others inappropriately.

Fifth, the cost of college is extremely high for both students and the broader society. From about 1840 to perhaps 1978, the tuition of American college students rose roughly 1 percent a year annually after adjusting for inflation. Commentators during that period and later noted that higher education is a service industry with a large highly skilled labor component that cannot easily be replaced with machines, as was the case in industries like auto manufacturing. As labor productivity in America generally rose over time, so did wages, including those of professors. According to this view, higher education is inherently subject to rising costs even after adjusting for general inflation.[13]

But even if this is true, it does not explain the sharp acceleration in tuition fees in the four decades after 1978—to roughly 3 percent a year after inflation adjustment. As a consequence, college costs went from slowly falling as a proportion of family income (say between 1940 and 1978) to increasing as a burden on family finances. In the earlier period, inflation-adjusted college costs rose 1 percent in a typical year, but incomes rose 2 percent because of productivity advances in the economy. College became a lesser burden, so college enrollments soared. In 1940, only about 5 percent of adult Americans had college degrees, whereas four decades later the proportion had about tripled. In recent decades, however, as tuition fees rose 3 percent a year and incomes were still rising only 2 percent annually, tuition and related fees became a growing proportion of family spending.[14]

A newer, and to my mind a better, explanation for the more modern rise in the costs of college was provided by a former US secretary of education, William Bennett, in a *New York Times* op-ed in 1987.[15] The Bennett hypothesis, as it is sometimes known, asserts that the huge growth in federal student financial assistance programs have led to a sharp increase in college costs. As schools see that their students, even relatively low-income ones, can easily borrow the money needed to pay tuition fees, they aggressively raise their prices. Without this federal assistance, sharp increases in fees would lead to a large decline in applications for admission, something schools felt they wanted to avoid. With federal assistance, student demand grows and becomes less sensitive to fee changes (in economist parlance, "demand becomes more inelastic"). Some research suggests than perhaps 60 to 65 cents of every new dollar of federal aid was captured by the schools through higher tuition fees.[16] These revenues helped fund a huge surge in administrative personnel at schools, discussed below.

As the demand for higher education among prospective students fell for a variety of reasons in the last decade, the ability of colleges to raise fees has weakened, perhaps reversing the forty-year trend toward reduced college affordability. The COVID pandemic of 2020–22 dramatically affected demand, and unusually high federal subsidy payments have further blurred what the current long-term trends are. Nonetheless, as of this writing, college is costly by historical or international norms.

Sixth, college students often do not learn much. Colleges sometimes fashion themselves as "learning communities," places where students leave with greater knowledge, maturity, leadership qualities, and virtue than when they entered. Colleges are where boys become men, girls become women. But above all, colleges are where students *learn*: at the conclusion of their university education they should know more about the world than when they entered.

Despite their role in measuring and increasing knowledge, colleges typically know (or at least report) relatively little about their success in enhancing academic achievement. Nonetheless, some data suggest that not much learning is going on. Roughly 40 percent of those entering college full time fail to graduate in six (not four) years. Time-use surveys suggest college students spend remarkably little time on academic pursuits.[17] Some testing results suggest shocking deficiencies in literacy among college students. The lack of standardized testing at the time of graduation is unfortunate but perhaps reflects the desire of the educational establishment to disguise the meager gains in knowledge over costly college careers. Decade-old data suggest that the critical learning and writing skills of college seniors are little better than those of freshmen.[18]

Seventh, colleges are overwhelmed by administrative bloat. Pick fifty college professors randomly from the thousands of colleges in the United States. Some will come from elite private schools, some from research-starved community colleges, others from typical midquality state universities. Almost certainly nearly all of them would agree on one thing: there are too many college administrators, to the point they impede the ability of faculty to effectively teach and do research. Historically, it made sense for specialists to deal with the needed functions that college administrators performed—keeping and validating college transcripts, registering students for courses, disciplining unacceptable student behavior, maintaining the buildings and grounds, and so forth.

Over time, the ratio of administrators (broadly defined to include most nonteaching white-collar campus personnel) to faculty has risen substantially, reducing the proportion of resources going to job one—the dissemination and creation of knowledge. I once got remarkably good statistics for my own typical state university, Ohio University, and noted that in the 1970s, when the data began, it employed about twice as many faculty members as administrative personnel. Today, there are more administrators than faculty. That has been the trend nationwide, as is demonstrated in greater detail in a later chapter. At least in part, the growth in administrative staff may reflect an overproduction of PhDs: some who are unable to get teaching positions simply became administrators, often in newly minted DEI or student affairs positions.

Aside from the issue of inappropriate resource allocation, I sense that control over university activities has moved away from heavy faculty involvement; instead, the faculty at many schools are merely hired hands. Even though a university is utterly impossible without faculty, it can exist (perhaps not optimally) with only a modest administrative staff. The administrative staff often lack the dedication and sometimes even the competence to deal with the main function of institutions of higher learning: the creation and dissemination of knowledge.[19]

Two groups of administrators in particular have contributed to the fundamental problem of a decline in the free-wheeling expression of ideas on campus: DEI personnel and those associated with student affairs offices. As stated above, they often operate in direct opposition to the principles of supporting a vigorous and free-ranging discussion of alternative viewpoints in an atmosphere of civility. Fifty years ago, most schools had only a handful of what we today call DEI administrators, if any. A recent survey of sixty-four schools, mostly public, that are members of the Power Five athletic conferences, showed that the average school had over forty-five DEI personnel—the University of Michigan had 163![20] Similarly, massive numbers of student service personnel and Title IX administrators have contributed immensely to widespread reports of the denial of due process and basic fairness to students accused of sexual misconduct.[21]

Eighth, access to higher education among the poor has declined. Federal financial support for America's colleges and universities has seen an explosive growth over the past half century or so, a majority of it related to allegedly promoting greater access to higher education. The vast federal assistance programs—subsidized student loans, Pell Grants, PLUS loans for parents of students, work-study programs, and so on—are almost always touted as promoting greater access to higher education for those from lower-income groups. Racial preferencing in various forms, especially admissions and outsized grants for HBCUs (historically black colleges and universities), has been designed to promote access given the lower average incomes of major racial minorities such as African Americans and Hispanics.

Yet for all that, the proportion of Americans attending college coming from the bottom quartile of the income distribution is likely less than it was in 1970. In forthcoming chapters, I talk about how the federal college student financial assistance programs, especially student loans, have led to higher tuition fees, with the colleges and their staffs capturing the majority of the benefits ostensibly designed to help lower-income students wanting to attend college. High sticker prices have scared off many low-income students, but fewer high-income ones, from applying for college.

Raj Chetty, a Harvard professor who won a MacArthur "genius" grant and received tenure at the age of twenty-eight as well as the prestigious John Bates Clark Medal from the American Economic Association, has, in association with others at top universities (especially recently John Friedman and Nathaniel Hendren), studied the impact of colleges on income mobility and equal opportunity. Chetty and several associates have concluded that, contrary to what many proponents of government support envision, many of the so-called elite schools are heavily dominated by students from wealthy families and higher education does not serve as a great catalyst for income mobility and achieving the American dream.[22]

Although many other things have changed as well, standard measures of income inequality suggest a widening of that inequality during the past four decades—a period of enormous growth in higher education participation. The proportion of adult Americans with college degrees has nearly tripled. At the same time, the proportion of income held by the top 5 percent of earners has increased. This is consistent with the notion that higher education promotes an aristocracy of sorts. Rather than help the poor rise up the economic ladder, government subsidies arguably work to diminish the American dream by expanding a rent-seeking class of affluent academics and their friends.

Ninth, the rate of return on college investments is decreasing. Although academics love to argue that colleges serve the broader society, most students expect that the considerable financial cost they incur will be worth it. In part, of course, going to college has a "consumption" dimension: students look forward to having fun, making new acquaintances and having experiences that make the college years among the best in a long lifetime. Still, surveys show that students and their parents look at college as a tool that helps assure a comfortable middle-class (or better) life. In the parlance of finance, college attendees expect a reasonably high rate of return on their considerable investment.

On the face of it, the evidence seems to suggest that getting a college degree is probably a good investment. After all, the median earnings of adult graduates with a four-year (bachelor's) degree in America are about twice as high as for those with just a high school diploma.[23] Over a lifetime of work, college graduates on average earn roughly a million dollars more than those with just a high school diploma—far more than the costs associated with getting a college degree.

Yet those statistics disguise some inconvenient truths that indicate college is a distinctly riskier investment than the rosy earnings data suggest. First, I repeat that close to 40 percent of college students attending school full time fail to graduate in *six* years. Moreover, statistics compiled by the Federal Reserve Bank of New York suggest that close to 40 percent of recent college graduates are "underemployed," meaning they work in relatively low-skilled jobs typically filled by high school graduates—as home health care aides, baristas in coffee shops, workers in discount retail stores, and the like.

Moreover, the use of averages disguises the reality that not all college graduates are "average." Students in differing majors earn vastly different salaries. A recent study showed that four years after getting a bachelor's degree, majors in computer science or operations research averaged over $100,000 in earnings, while the average chemistry major earned a much more modest $56,168, and music majors a meager $34,643—less than $18 an hour for someone working a full 2,080-hour year.[24] Almost as important as the field of major study is the school attended. The average graduate of an Ivy League school earned well over double the earnings of graduates of many lower-reputation state universities or liberal arts colleges.

Moreover, while most discussion of the advantages of college stress the *income* advantages of a college degree, the rise in income for college students has been accompanied by rising student debt—not faced by those with just a high school education. As a consequence, the *wealth* advantages (wealth being the accumulation of assets—what you are worth) of a college degree have been declining.[25]

Tenth, colleges are bad at optimally using the human and physical resources at their disposal. I am writing this late on a Wednesday morning in May. Of the thirty-two faculty and graduate student offices on the floor of my academic building, just three (including mine) are occupied—less than 10 percent. By four o'clock, I expect the number will be one (me). This is not atypical of American academia. Students go to school at most thirty-two weeks a year. What happens to classrooms and lecture halls the other twenty weeks? To put it mildly, they are vastly underutilized. Schools have library stacks that are rarely visited, dormitory rooms that are empty about four months each year, and so on. And many football stadiums get perhaps ten days annually of significant use, as the teams today often practice in indoor air-conditioned facilities rather than on the playing field.

But the underutilization of resources is not confined to the physical plant. Even more egregious is the underutilization of staff. I would note that faculty members at my school are grumbling because they are expected to teach up to six classes a year (three each semester). They may be in class for nine hours weekly for thirty or so weeks a year—less than three hundred hours. Add in several hours weekly for class preparations and grading papers and examinations, and a bit more for student advising. The typical faculty member can do all that in thirty-five hours weekly for thirty to thirty-two weeks a year, maybe eleven hundred hours total—far less than the typical full-time professional worker averages in the American economy. My colleagues will scream: we are doing research! That is true to some extent for many, some of whom do put in long hours in laboratories or libraries. But a large number are working maybe forty weeks a year for thirty-five hours a week, much less than the typical doctor or lawyer spends on professional activities. And a majority of faculty, despite protests to the contrary, do not produce more than one article or project or so a year.

Perhaps the ultimate and most important underutilization of resources is that of students. Because of grade inflation and other modern academic mishaps, students don't study very hard, and they take four years to complete a bachelor's degree that in many places (such as Oxford and Cambridge Universities) is finished in three. Society loses one year of valuable human resources (college grads) because of the leisurely pace they take to earn a bachelor's degree.

In this author's judgment, American campuses these days exhibit a pronounced anti-male sentiment.[26] Enrollment statistics seem to support that. Although sixty-two of every hundred persons of college age are attending institutions of higher education, only about fifty-seven men do, compared with sixty-six women.[27]

Moreover, many campuses fail to maintain their buildings—paint is peeling, windows and roofs need replacing, and so on. Why? Faculty and staff want resources to spend on themselves, but buildings cannot speak, so their needs often go unattended, which ultimately proves costly as they then need to be replaced or remodeled in a much more expensive way than if they had been conscientiously maintained. Building maintenance is boring, unexciting, while planning and building new structures is bold and exciting.

Conclusion

This tour d'horizon of American higher education is necessarily incomplete. I could spend far more time lamenting the peculiar American tradition of spending billions of dollars on collegiate ball-throwing contests having little to do with higher learning. I could have lamented how the granting of academic tenure is often exceedingly costly and prevents needed resource reallocation. I ignored professional and graduate education. Why do we have humanities students spending six or eight years obtaining a PhD only for them to get a low-paying job having little to do with their field of study? Virtually all the basic subjects in law (e.g., torts, administrative procedures) are taught in two years—so why do we require three years for law school? Why don't we completely redo the way we assess educational quality, doing away with accrediting bodies that try to enforce academic cartels that are monopolistic and anti-innovation?

Enough for now of complaining about the deficiencies of contemporary American colleges and universities. Although a more detailed analysis of the status quo is needed, we also need to start thinking about how we can do things differently to get better results. The next several chapters contrast capitalism with non-market-oriented higher education, first by showing how creative destruction is a necessary although not sufficient prerequisite for a vibrantly performing economy. We even question whether the government has a role in higher learning at all and show how the differential policies in our fifty states can be used to identify changes that would improve the system. In the last six chapters, we explore how a market-based use of creative destruction can be useful in reforming a system in bad need of repair.

2

Capitalism Succeeds by Allowing Failures via Creative Destruction

WHEN WE THINK of the business enterprises that succeed in the American economy, we see a constantly changing list over time. US Steel was the most heavily capitalized company in America when Andrew Carnegie, working with J. P. Morgan, created it out of many smaller firms in 1901. Although it still exists today (although at this writing it might be sold to Japanese interests), it is far overshadowed by any meaningful measure by literally hundreds of other companies. At this writing, its market capitalization (the value of all its stock) was $7.24 billion; Apple Computer's worth was $2.69 *trillion*—well over three hundred times greater. Enron and Eastman Kodak were major names until the beginning of this century. Today Enron is gone and Kodak (having gone through bankruptcy once and whose capitalization at this writing is a mere $329 million) is a shadow of its former self. By contrast, Apple and Microsoft did not exist a half century ago, but today are by any measure at or near the top of any assessment of America's most successful companies. New companies emerge with changing circumstances: Zoom became a household name almost overnight during the COVID pandemic.

Contrast that with America's universities. Defining and measuring the greatness of universities is much harder without a clearly defined and universally accepted bottom line. Nonetheless, virtually everyone would agree that Harvard has been at or very near the top of any list of the best universities, not only in 2024 but also a hundred years ago in 1924, or two hundred years ago in 1824, or even three hundred years ago in 1724. The great American universities are pretty much the same today as they were a generation or two ago.

My assistant obtained the list of the twenty-five top national universities as determined by *U.S. News & World Report* in the year 2000 and again twenty-two years later, and compared that with the twenty-five top American corporations as listed by *Fortune* magazine in its Fortune 500 rankings based on corporate sales. Of the top twenty-five universities on the list in 2000, all but one (the University of Virginia) were in the top twenty-five in 2022 (and Virginia ranked twenty-sixth in 2022, with New York University joining the top twenty-five), and most schools changed little in rank (Harvard went from second to third, for example).

Contrast this with the largest corporations. Only six of the top twenty-five in 2000 were still in the top twenty-five in 2022. And many companies merged or divided. Hewlett-Packard, for example, split into two companies, apparently thinking that the optimal size and scope of its businesses had changed. Roughly three-quarters of the top companies in 2000 had either died or undergone significant change.

All this may seem to suggest that American businesses are fragile, unstable, maybe even weak, while our universities are paragons of strength, stability, and permanence. Yet that would be a fundamentally wrong assessment. American businesses generate the bulk of the output of goods and services produced in the largest economy in the world, and they provide incomes that allow hundreds of millions of Americans to have the highest standard of living of any large nation. Moreover, this achievement is all the more remarkable when one considers that two or three hundred years ago, the United States and its predecessor colonies were not only much smaller and poorer, but had much less material abundance than other nations such as Great Britain.

With Economic Freedom Came Prosperity and Affluence

At the time of America's Declaration of Independence in 1776, the output of the average American was at most probably around $2,000 annually measured in dollars of current purchasing power. Today, it is well over thirty times that amount, meaning that Americans today produce per person more in two weeks than Americans in 1776 produced in a year. The population has soared from perhaps 2.5 million to more than one-third of a billion, in large part because of the largest international migration of peoples this planet has ever seen.

Indeed, I find it interesting to compare probably the two most publicized examples of wall building by nations over the last century. In 1961, the East Germans, supported by their Russian masters, built the Berlin Wall to keep East Germans from leaving that poor Marxist hellhole—to eliminate out-migration. Contrast that to the wall the United States partially constructed in the past decade between the US and Mexico—designed to eliminate *in*-migration—keeping people out of the US.

Yet the American economic success is not the consequence of a single dynamic entrepreneur's vision or technological advance. It reflects millions of decisions and actions of diverse economic actors rather than a single government. And in the achievement of progress, old methods of making goods and services were replaced by new modes of production and even new goods and services to produce. Resources are constantly being redirected to different, generally better ways of doing things.

An immigrant to America from his native Austria, Joseph A. Schumpeter, understood this well and coined the term *creative destruction* to describe progress or economic advancement in capitalist systems. Writing in 1942, Schumpeter, drawing on earlier writings by Karl Marx and the economist-historian Werner Sombart, said that a "gale of creative destruction" characterizes the "process of industrial mutation that continuously revolutionizes the economic structure within, incessantly destroying the old one, incessantly creating a new one."[1]

Adam Smith, Economics, and Higher Education

Schumpeter built his economic insights on earlier writings of great economists. In *The Wealth of Nations*, Adam Smith brilliantly explained how persons in the pursuit of their own self-interest often advanced a goal unintentionally, namely, the betterment of material welfare for all humankind.[2] Smith showed that voluntary trade between individuals benefited both buyers and sellers and, by extension, the broader society. The division of labor and product specialization that trade promotes increases "the wealth of nations." Smith also perceptively noted the differences between free-market exchanges among individuals and the practices of universities, a major theme of this book.

Smith asserted, no doubt correctly, that when professors collected some or all of their compensation direct from the students rather than from university endowments, they worked harder and tried to please their customers, the students: "The endowments . . . of colleges have necessarily diminished . . . the necessity of application in the teachers."[3] Smith noted that at Oxford the faculty received compensation from the school, not direct from the students, and as a consequence "in the university of Oxford, the greater part of the publick professors have, for these many years, given up although even the pretence of teaching."[4] The incentives to excel at disseminating ideas through teaching diminished sharply when the professors no longer had "skin in the game."

Smith's insights, like Schumpeter's, are enormously perceptive. Market economies work well because there are incentives to please the customer. Both the teacher and the student are better off if the student finds the professor prepared, insightful, and knowledgeable—as happens when the professor's income is based on voluntary market exchange occurring when the student pays tuition direct to the professor. But if some third party (the University of Oxford from its endowments, or modern universities from their state subsidies, private donations, or endowments) is paying the professor, incentives to excel as a teacher decline dramatically. Justin Strehle and I, looking specifically at American university endowments, found that only a modest proportion of endowment funds directly benefited students through improved instruction or lower tuition costs.[5] A big proportion of the funds provided extra income (what economists call "economic rents") to the faculty and administrative staff.

Smith's insights suggest that *markets make colleges more effective and efficient.* Teaching was better at Oxford when there was a direct monetary exchange between the professor and the student customer. This Smithian insight, along with Schumpeterian creative destruction, points the way to reforming universities and potentially reducing, if not eliminating, many of the "sins" outlined in chapter 1.

University vs. Corporate Behavior: The Compensation of Leaders

One indicator of the difference between higher education and for-profit private enterprise is how each rewards top performers. I compared the compensation of the chief executive officers (CEOs) of the ten largest companies based on stock market valuations with the compensation of the CEOs (usually president) of the ten highest-ranking universities.[6] The median 2022 compensation of the heads of the ten largest companies was slightly over $21 million, typically a small proportion of which came in the form of salary (a regular paycheck), with most of the rest in profits from stock options or in bonuses arising from a good job performance in the previous year or so. Only two of the top ten made under $20 million, and both of them (Amazon's founder Jeff Bezos and Berkshire-Hathaway's Warren Buffett) were multibillion-dollar owners of a significant chunk of their own company, so they were compensated through stock appreciation not measured in standard compensation surveys.

Contrast this with the presidents of the top ten American universities. The median pay was under $1.6 million—the average top college president took over a year to earn what the most valuable corporations' presidents made in a month. Former Harvard president Claudine Gay made less than $900,000 annually. The highest-paid president, Ronald Daniels of Johns Hopkins, made $3,289,817 in total compensation, truly high by university standards but still a small fraction of private corporate CEO pay. I suspect that President Daniels's relatively high pay in part reflected the influence of Johns Hopkins's largest private benefactor by far, Michael Bloomberg, himself a longtime beneficiary of huge financial rewards for shrewd private enterprise innovation and stewardship.

The same pattern holds for the top subordinate officers at for-profit corporations and universities. High-level corporate officials like the chief operating or chief financial officer at the most valuable corporations typically make several million dollars annually (up to $10 million), while the equivalent university officials, such as the provost (chief academic officer) or the chief financial officer typically make well under $1 million annually.

However, not all important university personnel are low paid. First, intercollegiate athletics is strongly market based. Sports revenues for several dozen schools that enroll a sizable minority of American college students are enormously impacted by television contracts, ticket revenues, and ancillary income (e.g., parking lot fees, royalties for use of the university name on sweatshirts), all derived from market-driven activity. A successful football coach could add millions of dollars of revenue to a university. Accordingly, good football coaches are highly paid, more so than the presidents who are nominally their bosses but who work in a far less market-driven environment where institutional revenues are not so clearly impacted by performance.

My assistant ferreted out the pay of presidents and head football coaches at five universities highly successful at football: the Universities of Georgia, Alabama, and Michigan, as well as Texas Christian University and Ohio State University. A majority of the football coaches earned about $10 million, the lowest paid, at Texas Christian, earning $6 million. Even the top assistants, specifically the offensive and defensive coordinators, often made seven-digit salaries, making more than the university president. The presidents of these five schools earned between $300,000 and $975,000 annually, in every single case less *than 10 percent* of what the head football coach earned. Where else can you find the bosses earning less than a tenth of what at least one of their subordinate employees earns?

A second area where university officials occasionally earn pay more comparable to that of top employees in the private for-profit sector is in investments. The top investment officials at very rich, mostly private universities have billions, and sometimes tens of billions, of endowment dollars that they manage, so they sometimes reap a multimillion-dollar annual compensation to keep them from going to work for private financial service corporations. The late David Swensen ran the Yale endowment for years after a similarly successful Wall Street career, receiving an annual bonus in the $3 million range near the end of his life—a multiple of that of Yale president Peter Salovey.

Private enterprise relies on clear bottom line measures of success: profits and stock prices. A successful company makes lots of profits that increase in most years, thereby leading to a substantial stock price. Companies will pay dearly to the executives at least partially responsible for that success. But what is the bottom line in higher education? Was Harvard or Slippery Rock State University successful last year? How would you know? We know how many students attended and graduated, but we have only the vaguest idea of what they learned and whether that learning increased or decreased over time. We have statistics on what graduates are earning, but even they are highly imperfect. We know how observers such as media sources such as the *Wall Street Journal, U.S. News & World Report*, and *Forbes* rank them, but those assessments differ. So we are not clear on how successful top university officials are. We have some useful information (e.g., new donations, changes in enrollments and endowments, measures of incoming student quality) but no universally accepted indicators denoting a clear bottom line. We *do* have a "bottom line" for the football team, denoted by a win-loss record and revenues gained and expenses incurred in achieving that record. Hence, we have to pay the football coach a salary up to the estimated incremental revenue associated with his coaching success. The university, with no well-established bottom line (with a couple of exceptions), does not even vaguely know the value of the marginal contributions to revenues and performance made by most members of the staff.

Ironically, American higher education is often said to be "corporatized," less devoted to "education." Yet universities are far less disciplined by market activity than private business is—precisely the reason they are viewed as overcome by administrative bloat and other cost-enhancing maladies.

Prosperity Arising from Market-Based Freedom

When people are able to "do their own thing" with respect to their economic activity, they tend to be more highly productive. People are far more prosperous in societies where they can operate without many constraints on their behavior imposed by outsiders, especially governments. Several organizations have measured the degree of economic and other forms of freedom in different countries, one of them being the Canadian-based Fraser Institute working with the Washington-based Cato Institute. Their Economic Freedom of the World project—led by the late James Gwartney of Florida State and coauthored by some of my former students like Robert Lawson of Southern Methodist University and Joshua Hall of West Virginia University—ranks nearly 180 countries on a variety of government-imposed constraints on freedom, such as taxes, economic regulations, and other fiscal controls. I took the most recent rankings and looked at forty-five countries from the 176 countries surveyed, and divided them into three groups: the fifteen most free countries, the fifteen least free countries, and fifteen countries right in the middle—the median group.

The median gross domestic product (GDP) per capita among the fifteen most free nations was that for Australia, $60,443 in 2021 (the freest nation of all, Singapore, had a GDP per capita of $72,794). For the fifteen countries ranking in the middle in terms of freedom, namely, those ranked 81 to 95, the median GDP per capita was $3,266 (for the Philippines). For the fifteen least free nations, the median GDP per capita was a near starvation level of $1,774 (for Zimbabwe). Economic prosperity shows a striking decline as one moves from countries with very high levels of freedom to lower levels. Economic freedom includes such components as a solid right for private citizens to own and profit from property free of excessive taxation or theft by criminal elements, a reliable and strong rule of law, a reasonably stable currency, and so on. Loss of those attributes comes at a high price.

Resources used by the private sector have much larger payoffs in the production of goods of services—and in the incomes of those responsible for that production—than do resources directed centrally by government entities. Private businesses seeking profits have every incentive to minimize their costs by raising the productivity of the inputs used to make goods and services, be they workers or machines (capital), and to enhance their revenues by making better quality or wholly new products that consumers want to buy. Government bureaucrats have no such incentives. Universities, often government owned and operated, generally lack strong incentives to improve outcomes and lower the costs of operations. The rewards to employees are meager in large part because they are hard to measure. Hence "free" countries, where private market forces tend to dominate, are much more productive than unfree nations—or universities.

But there is more to life than making money. Perhaps governments provide things that enhance the quality of life, for example, via tax and spending policies that reduce income or racial inequality, or through environmental regulatory policies that improve the quality of the air we breathe and the water we drink. Maybe in some of the lower-income countries the population has more leisure time, less workplace stress, and so on. Income or output statistics may not pick up these factors adequately.

Fortunately, we have a great laboratory in the United States to explore some of this: fifty states with different levels of economic freedom for their citizenry. Let's look at where people move within the United States. Presumably people generally move to a different locale hoping to improve the quality of their life—to be, generally speaking, happier. Therefore, I looked at the migration within the United States of native-born Americans over the period July 1, 2021, through June 30, 2022, as estimated by the US Bureau of the Census.

To keep the analysis easily understandable by the less statistically oriented readers, I decided to look at migration behavior with respect to the movement into or out of the nine American states that do not generally tax people's income at all, compared with the forty-one other states and DC, where the government taxes the income of the citizenry. Six of the nine no-income-tax states—Alaska, Florida, Nevada, South Dakota, Texas, and Wyoming—have absolutely no tax on any form of income, while New Hampshire and Tennessee tax only investment income such as dividends. Contrast that to the other forty-one states, where high marginal tax rates (peaking at 13.3 percent for high-income earners in California and at over 14 percent in New York City) sometimes exist. A wealthy individual with an income of $25 million in California would probably pay $3 million more in income taxes annually than the same individual living in Florida or Texas. Probably that played some role in Elon Musk's decision to move his residence from California to the vicinity of Austin, Texas.

The nine no-income-tax states had net in-migration of 659,312 persons in 2022—more than one person every minute.[7] By contrast, almost the same number on net left California and New York, states with high income taxes. California, America's fastest-growing large state for many decades, actually lost a seat in the House of Representatives as a result of its low population growth between 2010 and 2020. And the migration data cannot be explained by climate, when Sun Belt states Florida and Texas had big influxes while California had massive out-migration (and it is hard to explain meaningful in-migration into relatively frigid but no-income-tax South Dakota or New Hampshire on climatic grounds).

The Census Bureau estimates that in a single year, between July 1, 2021, and June 30, 2022, New York City had a population decline of 123,104, or 1.5 percent. Simultaneously, seven of the ten urban areas in the United States with the biggest population increase were in no-income-tax Florida, with the biggest percentile gain at The Villages, a community of mostly retired persons where in a single year the population grew 7.5 percent. The evidence suggests that people seeking economic freedom (keeping more of the income they earn) are voting vigorously with their feet.

Creative Destruction and the Widening Gap between Firms and Colleges

I have argued that where individual freedom generates Schumpeterian creative destruction and a robust private sector operates, output and incomes expand over time, in marked contrast to how universities operate as a government-dominated sector without strong incentives to improve outcomes or increase worker productivity. A little empirically based exercise can show how and why the gap between the highly productive free-market private sector and universities has grown. Bottom line: profit-motivated entrepreneurs in the private sector have constantly increased productivity—output per unit of input—while that has almost certainly not happened in higher education.

I calculated the change in labor productivity (specifically, output per hour of work) in the business sector of the economy as estimated by the US Bureau of Labor Statistics from the half century from 1972 through 2021. As can be seen in figure 2.1, output increased about 2.5 times. If a worker made two widgets per hour in 1972, she would have made about five per hour in 2021 if productivity in widget-making rose at the average rate for the American economy. This increase resulted from more capital (machines) but also *better* capital—inventions arising from technological advances like computers and maybe in future years AI (artificial intelligence).

I then estimated the productivity of workers in our universities. This is difficult to do because universities produce many kinds of goods and services. In addition to teaching, they do research, they run entertainments (e.g., football games), they serve food, house people (mainly students), and at many schools run hospitals and clinical operations that are sometimes sizable. However, we do have good information on the size of university staffs and on university enrollments, so we can calculate the ratio of students per staff person over time, which is what I did in figure 2.1. It shows a *decline*: it took more staff (including faculty) to educate a single college student in 2021 than it did in 1972.

Figure 2.1 suggests that productivity in the market-based economy that governs the production of most goods and services was rising smartly—between 1 and 2 percent a year. Meanwhile, productivity, so measured, is falling in higher education—where the discipline and incentives of markets are largely absent. This calculation is necessarily crude. For example, the research output in higher education could have risen as an increasing proportion of faculty devoted more effort to it, including at university-based medical centers. But some indicators suggest that learning by students has *declined* over time.[8] And much research "output" of faculty probably has little real value to society or even to academic specialists. The 20,000th paper written in modern times (and there have been far more than that) on William Shakespeare probably added little to our insight of the Bard that had not been accomplished in the previous 19,999 papers.

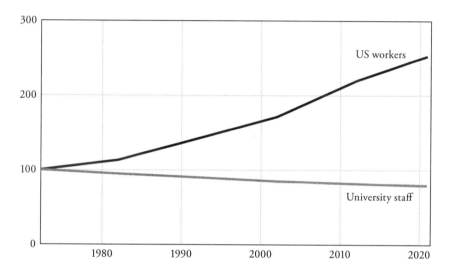

Figure 2.1 Productivity in the US economy vs. higher education, in worker output per hour, 1970–2020

Sources: US Bureau of Labor Statistics, March 2023, Table B-32, https://www.govinfo.gov/content/pkg/ERP-2023/pdf/ERP-2023.pdf; National Center for Education Statistics, 2022, Table 315.10, https://nces.ed.gov/programs/digest/d22/tables/dt22_315.10.asp; author's calculations.

If the results suggested by figure 2.1 are even remotely correct, then the basic point of this book is supported. If higher education can somehow change its ways and better emulate the market-oriented private economy dominating American life, it would improve some of the maladies facing it (e.g., stagnant public support and enrollment, many mediocre vocational outcomes, and rising costs) and possibly even deal with what I now view as the greatest problem: a shocking decline in intellectual diversity and a worsening environment conducive to free expression and civil debate of the issues of the day.

Conclusion

Where there is an ability "to do your own thing" and where the rule of law and private property rights allow human economic flourishing, people generally prosper and people move to join in the economic success. Most economic activity occurs in a market-based environment where goods and services are sold by private producers, be they farmers growing wheat, firms making computer chips, or beauticians styling people's hair.

Higher education is different. To be sure, there are some privately owned for-profit colleges, but they are a small factor in American higher education, as we shall see later. Colleges and universities are dominated by people operating outside the normal profit-oriented private market economy, substantially subsidized by governments (state, federal, and even some local). *Universities are largely wards of the state.* They depend on high tuition fees made possible by large federal student loans, direct government subsidies, substantial research grant support, and so forth. Even private philanthropic support is aided by tax breaks that the government provides donors.

Economies tend to be larger and more prosperous where the government's share of activity is low. People move to jurisdictions where the private sector role is relatively large and the public sector is modest. Yet universities are heavily "owned" and financed by government. Large and small private businesses alike pay taxes to help fund universities. The sector with creative destruction—private business—funds a sector with very little "destruction" but that nonetheless shows signs of decline and stagnation: falling enrollments, for example, and polls that indicate waning public support. Should we be moving to change that—making universities more responsive to market forces, more subject to creative destruction? I think the answer is yes, and most of the remainder of this book builds a case for that position.

3

Why Are Universities Subsidized,
but Firms Taxed?

IN THE LAST chapter, I argued that universities are wards of the state: if not formally part of government, heavily dependent on it. I have also argued that where resources are largely controlled by governments—where individual freedom is minimal—we have greater poverty and an out-migration of citizens. North Koreans, with almost no individual freedom and living in great poverty, risk their lives trying to get to the free and prosperous South Korea, but no South Koreans attempt to flee to the North.[1] Yet in the United States, the private firms battling it out for consumers are burdened by governments to pay taxes, while universities are *subsidized* by the tax monies provided by private businesses as well as their owners and employees. We tax the efficient engines of our prosperity to subsidize relatively inefficient universities. Why?

The Rationale for Government Subsidies of Higher Education[2]

The notion that education in general and universities in particular have special qualities that make them distinctly different from most other human endeavors is not a modern idea. In the heart of the Victorian era, an extraordinary theologian and polymath, John Henry Newman, wrote this: "University training is the great ordinary means to a great but ordinary end; it aims at raising the intellectual tone of society, at cultivating the public mind, at purifying the national taste, at supplying true principles to popular enthusiasm . . . at giving enlargement and sobriety to the ideas of the age, at facilitating the exercise of political power, and refining the intercourse of private life."[3]

Newman was implying that universities confer on society goodness that goes beyond the learning acquired by their students. A century or so later, writing in 1962, Milton Friedman issued a libertarian manifesto, *Capitalism and Freedom*, which generally extolled the virtues of free markets while deploring the impact of governmental intrusions, but held that education, including in its highest (university) forms, was an exception.[4] He argued that universities have positive neighborhood or spillover effects, what economists call "positive externalities." Universities improve the lives not only of those attending college, but also of those surrounding them, by leading by example. Less educated persons take cues from the college-educated citizens surrounding them, often serving under them. Philosophers as far back as Plato opined that the best and brightest among us have better human capital skills and thus should be our leaders ("philosopher kings"). Even in seemingly routine work, in a factory context, for example, the hard work, problem-solving skills, and leadership of a college-educated manager inspire less educated workers to become more productive. The educated leaders provide productive "learning by doing" to their associates, raising the living standards and quality of life for all of society. The college-educated are also more civic minded, helping the less fortunate through philanthropy, and because they also have low rates of unemployment, they reduce the raiding of the public purse that funds such income assistance schemes as unemployment compensation.

But Friedman argued that even if you accept the notion that universities produce positive spillover effects, it does *not* necessarily mean governments should *own and run* schools. Instead, Friedman advocated giving vouchers (scholarships) to students and allowing them to pick the school of their choice, introducing an element of competition for students and in so doing to emulate some of the efficiencies of markets.

However, Newman and Friedman in the mid-twentieth century could not anticipate the changes occurring in higher education in the late twentieth and early twenty-first centuries. Even Friedman thought the vocational dimensions of higher education should not be funded by governments, because they provided private benefits to the student but not the positive benefits of a general education grounded in the sciences, humanities, and mathematics. As Friedman put it: "Public expenditures on higher schooling can be justified as a means of training youngsters for citizenship and for community leadership—though . . . the large fraction of current expenditures that goes for strictly vocational training cannot be justified. . . . Restricting the subsidy to schooling obtained at a state-administered institution cannot be justified on [any] grounds."⁵ Although Friedman did not put it this way, he seemed to advocate supporting the general education of the citizenry in literature, mathematics, and written communication but not, for example, the public financing of an accounting or finance degree that would help earn a student a CPA designation or a shot at a remunerative Wall Street job.

Higher education grew enormously and changed dramatically, not all for the good, in the several decades after Friedman wrote *Capitalism and Freedom*. In 2003 I asked him if he still believed that some government subsidization of higher education was justified. He replied: "I have not changed my view that higher education has some positive externality, but I have become much more aware that it also has negative externalities. I am much more dubious than I was when I wrote *Capitalism and Freedom* that there is any justification at all for government subsidy of higher education. The spread of PC [political correctness] right now would seem to be a very strong negative externality, and certainly the 1960s student demonstrations were negative externalities. . . . A full analysis . . . might lead you to conclude that higher education should be taxed to offset its negative externalities."⁶ In light of more recent student demonstrations (some reportedly calling for the genocide of Jews) and even more importantly collegiate attempts to suppress free expression by students and faculty, I am certain that, had Friedman lived to the present, he would even more forcibly reinforce his 2003 recommendation of *taxing* universities.

The negative spillover effects of higher education go further. To cite one example, the leftish domination of universities has led to graduates who have fostered declining objectivity and viewpoint diversity in the media, leading to a less vibrant and responsible press. Another: many graduates of colleges in woke majors like gender studies are underemployed, becoming more of a net burden than a contributor to society. If we tax businesses whose activities do much to enhance our material abundance and promote general prosperity, why shouldn't we also tax the universities and certainly not subsidize them?

If you buy an iPhone or an automobile, you pay sales tax on the purchase; why shouldn't students or the universities have to pay sales tax on tuition fees?

The Dominance of Government Subsidies

My claim that universities are wards of the state is supported by an examination of data on university revenues. I had my assistant gather data on university revenues received during the last predominantly pre-pandemic year, 2019–20. Where do American schools get their funds? Figure 3.1 is revealing. Looking at all university revenues (except those related to university hospitals and medical center operations, which are fundamentally health care facilities), we learn that almost precisely one-half of revenues came direct from governments, roughly one-quarter from student tuition fees, and one-quarter from "other" sources, including room and board charges, conference center operations, research grants, endowment income, intercollegiate athletics, and so on. Interestingly, further exploration of the data shows the proportions were relatively similar forty years earlier. The prime customers (the students) pay less than half of what governments do to fund colleges and universities. Moreover, Friedman's admonishment that where government subsidies are made, they should go direct to the students in the form of tuition vouchers rather to institutions has been ignored. Additionally, governments, in years of substantial financial adversity for universities, often provide special incremental support, such as occurred in the 2021 and 2022 academic years when enrollments were depressed by the COVID pandemic (which cut tuition fees) and by pandemic-enhanced expenses.

To be sure, there are enormous variations among institutions. Some schools are much more tuition dependent, especially a small category of for-profit institutions, discussed later in this chapter, that get perhaps 95 percent of their income from tuition fees, much of that income however financed through student loans supported by the federal government. A number of very wealthy private schools derive 40 percent or more of their funds from investments owned by the school, far more than they receive in tuition fees. A few schools, such as the nation's military academies, receive nearly 100 percent of their revenue from the federal government. Many people employed in higher education claim that "government financial support of higher education is

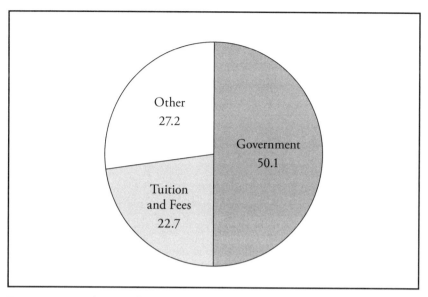

Figure 3.1 Distribution of US university revenue in percentages, 2019–2020

Source: US Department of Education, National Center for Education Statistics, 2022, Table 333.10, https://nces.ed.gov/programs/digest/d22/tables/dt22_333.10.asp?current=yes%5C.

falling," a mostly fallacious claim that is dealt with in greater detail in coming chapters.

Why College in America Is So Expensive: Changes over Time and Space

The dominance of government in higher education funding has grown dramatically over time. You might think greater government financial support would reduce the need to rely on students and their families for tuition payments. Yet the opposite is the case. Not only have tuition fees risen as government support expanded, but college has become *less* affordable. Let me give you two examples from my personal experience, one using an elite private university, the second a typical public state institution. In 1958, when I first attended Northwestern University, the tuition was $795 a year. At the time, the per capita income in the state of Illinois, where Northwestern is located and where I lived, was $2,463. In other words, it took 32.28 percent of the annual income of an average resident of Illinois to pay one year's tuition at

Northwestern. Fast-forward to 2022. Tuition at Northwestern was $62,391, which was 90.66 percent of annual personal income per capita in Illinois, nearly triple the proportion observed sixty-four years earlier.

At Ohio University, where I began teaching in 1965, the proportion of family income absorbed by in-state tuition fees also increased over time, albeit not nearly as sharply. In 1965, in-state tuition fees of $450 were 15.63 percent of personal income per capita in Ohio. By 2022, that had increased to 23.07 percent, a 48 percent increase in the proportion of personal income absorbed by tuition fees. The burden of attending the school, a typical state university, had risen meaningfully. To be fair, over time price discrimination (charging customers different amounts) in higher education expanded considerably, so the true burden for many did not grow quite as much as those numbers indicate. But the price of virtually anything else you can name, with the possible exception of medical care, rose *less* than incomes over time, and many goods (e.g., automobiles, television sets, medical care) saw dramatic qualitative improvement not obviously apparent in higher education. The burden of buying bread, blue jeans, air travel, or appliances had fallen, often dramatically, while university fees were absorbing more of the family budget. In the 1950s and 1960s, many college students largely financed their college expenses through earnings in part-time jobs when school was in session and through full-time summer employment. That is rare today.

At the same time, the cost of educating a student in American universities has risen sharply, even after adjusting for overall inflation (see figure 3.2). Spending per student more than doubled in the half century between 1970 and 2020. More personnel is needed get a student through school today than half a century ago, and that staff receives higher compensation. So it is no wonder that tuition fees soared so much. The typical student attends college perhaps 220 or so days a year, so it costs on average roughly $200 per day to finance the college education of an average student.

Apologists for the collegiate status quo would be contemptuous of any claim that figure 3.2 had public policy implications, on several grounds. First, they would argue that "teaching students is only one of many things universities do: they conduct life-saving research, they enrich the lives of people with things like sporting events, theatrical productions, and concerts; they operate

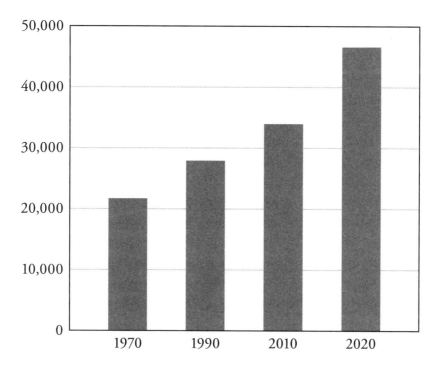

Figure 3.2 University expenditures per full-time student in constant 2020 dollars, 1970–2020

Sources: National Center for Education Statistics, Digest of Education Statistics, 2022, https://nces.ed.gov/programs/digest/2022menu_tables.asp; author's calculations.

hospitals and clinics, which literally save lives," and so on. Yet a large portion of government and private-donor grants to universities is made ostensibly with the education of students in mind. Universities have lowered the teaching load of professors to promote research not because that was a public mandate or even a request by private donors, but simply because they decided to do so—doing research seems more prestigious, important, and even fun than merely educating young adults. Moreover, in an academic "publish-or-perish" world, getting an article in the *Journal of Last Resort* is more remunerative and fulfilling than teaching dozens of mostly uninformed and indifferent freshmen or sophomores. Emphasis on research as manifested in lower teaching loads occurred mostly because the faculty, not the broader society, wanted it.

Some might argue that we provide a higher-quality education today. I don't believe it. To be sure, students live in nicer accommodations on average than students did fifty years ago, with air conditioning, somewhat more food choices, nicer recreation facilities, and fancier classroom buildings, often with atriums. They have computers that were unavailable a half century ago. But the most relevant bottom line is: Are they learning more? Are they more virtuous? Are they better prepared to face the challenges of the next generation than were their predecessors? Perhaps even, are they having more fun? These are difficult things to measure to be sure, but the rudimentary evidence I see (mainly on learning outcomes, critical thinking abilities, and the like) shows no improvement over the past. Students spend far less time on academics than their predecessors did a couple of generations ago, for example.[7] And is the explosion in administrators per student something that improves educational outcomes for students? I think not—indeed, the growing administrative presence has led to a downplaying of the very academic values that are the core of the rationale for public university support.

Is the US Spending More than Other Countries?

Another way of approaching the issue of the appropriateness and efficiency of spending on American universities is to compare American universities and their spending with that of similar schools in other countries. The Organisation for Economic Co-operation and Development (OECD) represents over thirty of the world's most advanced nations economically, and it has collected statistics on average spending per full-time-equivalent university student in all of the OECD countries. Easily, the highest-spending country on a per-student basis is the United States (see figure 3.3).

Spending in the United States is over 50 percent more per student than in our adjoining neighbor Canada and at least 20 percent higher than in Britain, which, adjusting for population, has at least as many top-flight universities (based on international rankings) as the United States. For example, at this writing the most recent *Times Higher Education* world rankings had sixteen US universities in the top twenty-five and only four British institutions, but since the population of the US is about five times that of the United Kingdom, on a population-adjusted basis Britain ranked slightly above the US.

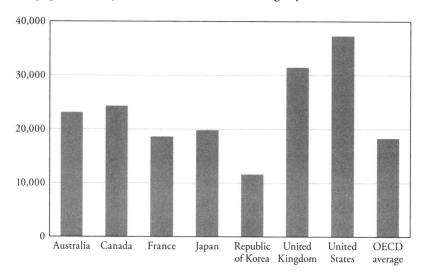

Figure 3.3 Expenditures per full-time university student in constant 2021 dollars, selected countries, 2019

Source: National Center for Education Statistics, Digest of Education Statistics, 2022, Table 605.20, https://nces.ed.gov/programs/digest/d22/tables/dt22_605.20.asp.

This book is not meant to be an exhaustive examination of *international* higher education, so I will leave it to others to more intensively explain the US differences with other countries. My guess is that academic salaries in the US are higher than in almost all the other countries examined because of generally higher productivity in the overall American economy, but that the ratio of employees to students is not lower in the US than in most of the other OECD countries, meaning per student college labor costs are higher. The fixation on DEI issues in the US in recent years does not seem to be nearly as much an international phenomenon, so associated increases in relative administrative costs in the US may also now be contributing to the high cost of educating American students. International differences can also be observed regarding such things as teaching loads, retirement policies, and tenure provisions, which also affect a nation's spending.

Federal Student Loans and the Law of Unintended Consequences[8]

For the first three hundred years of higher education in America, up to World War II, federal involvement in US higher education was negligible. As I have elsewhere observed, even the much-heralded creation of "land grant" universities with the Morrill Act in the 1860s (passed only when thirteen Confederate states were not in Congress) did not lead to substantial federal support of higher education.[9] As late as 1940, more Americans attended private colleges and universities than government-provided schools (mostly universities owned by states). The federal government's involvement in directly financing student college education began in 1944 with the Servicemen's Readjustment Act (the GI Bill), which provided large tuition relief for some returning veterans of World War II.

The modern era of generalized federal support began relatively slowly in the late 1950s, when in response to American worries about falling behind in science after the Soviet Union launched the first satellite (Sputnik) in 1957, the federal government started to provide aid for students in the STEM (science, technology, engineering, and mathematics) disciplines. The real substantial growth, however, begins with the Great Society programs of the 1960s, when the modern federally guaranteed student loan programs began in earnest, along with other efforts, including what became known as Pell Grants and federal work-study programs.

These programs were conceived as a way of removing financial barriers to higher education, especially for Americans of modest means. They were enormously expanded, however, in the late 1970s, making middle-income Americans eligible for assistance. Much of this financial subsidy became incorporated in the Higher Education Act, first passed in 1965 and since revised, designed to "strengthen the educational resources of our colleges and universities and to provide financial assistance for students in postsecondary and higher education." That legislation has been continuously updated, always in a more expansive fashion (although a renewal of the legislation is overdue). In the late 1970s, when student aid eligibility grew dramatically, the US Department of Education was also created in spite of significant Republican and Democratic opposition, to oversee and administer federal assistance and regulatory programs.

In my opinion, American higher education is not as good today as it was in 1980, when the Department of Education was getting started, and the federal government deserves most of the blame for that, especially its financial assistance programs. As one early reader of these words has commented, those new government subsidies "created a moral hazard problem: recipients of federal money could spend it on degree mills with substandard programs." This also led to the pernicious growth in the de facto regulatory powers of accreditation agencies that have become obstacles to innovation. In the last three decades of the twentieth century and the first decade or so of the twenty-first century, federal student-assistance programs grew almost exponentially. Even in this century, when enrollments have declined in most years, student loans have grown substantially (see figure 3.4). Putting it bluntly, federal student lending has been an unmitigated disaster, which became apparent to parents and students alike around 2010 and after, leading ultimately to declining student enrollments and, with that, declining student lending.

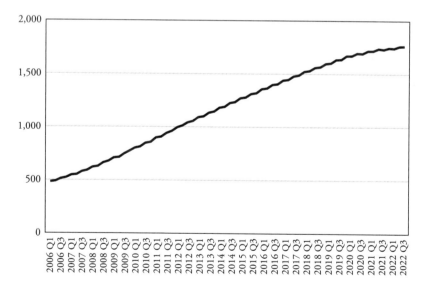

Figure 3.4 US student loan debt in billions of dollars, 2006–2022

Source: Board of Governors, Federal Reserve System, "Student Loans Owed and Securitized," accessed June 10, 2023, https://fred.stlouisfed.org/series/SLOAS.

Writing a few years ago, I outlined eight problems with the federal financial assistance programs. Let me repeat them here. First, as Education Secretary Bill Bennett articulated in 1978, they enormously raised the cost of college to students, as universities took advantage of the new source of funding to aggressively raise tuition fees. Instead of rising maybe 1 percent annually after inflation adjustment before 1978 or so, after the vast expansion of federal lending, fees rose for roughly four decades around 3 percent a year.

Second, and arguably most fundamentally, the rapidly rising fees scared off many potential low-income students, so a smaller proportion of recent college graduates appear to come from the bottom quartile of the income distribution than was true in the mid-1970s before the explosion in loans. [10]

Third, for many students, college has become a risky investment: even if they graduate there is still a good chance they will be underemployed for a period of time—meaning they will be unable to get a high-paid job traditionally filled by degree holders. The growing realization of this phenomenon is probably a major cause in the decade-long decline in overall college enrollments.

Fourth, these programs have imposed a serious cost on taxpayers. The government used to claim that it made money on student loans: it borrowed money, sometimes from foreign lenders, at relatively low interest rates (i.e., 3 percent) by issuing bonds, and then lent the proceeds of the bonds to student borrowers at higher rates (i.e., 6 percent), thereby making a profit. Yet the Government Accounting Office and others have estimated the programs have imposed a meaningful cost to taxpayers, in part because many borrowers fail to repay their loans, or, especially in the Biden years, because the government has initiated pauses on loan payments or, more controversially, outright forgiveness of large amounts of student debt, which continued in slightly modified form even after the Supreme Court ruled it unconstitutional. Also, beginning in the Trump administration but greatly expanded in the Biden years, new income-repayment schemes have become so generous that large numbers of donors with modest postgraduation incomes will effectively see much of their loan obligations forgiven. I believe many of these efforts are illegal, immoral, illogical, even politically stupid. [11] Moreover, almost certainly many longstanding recipients have simply stopped making payments, anticipating ultimate loan forgiveness by the federal government.

Fifth, a good bit of the qualitative decline in American higher education in my judgment is attributable indirectly to the student loan program. Students whose capacity to learn is highly questionable, judging from their high school experience and, even in some cases, from evidence of modest intellectual capacity, have been enticed to go to college. Grade inflation has blossomed to keep colleges from flunking out embarrassing proportions of their students. And the evidence shows that student work effort has precipitously declined.

Sixth, I think that the financial burden of college, as manifested in student loans, has indirectly contributed to the decline in birth rates, family formation, and home purchases. Tens of millions of Americans have student debt, averaging over $30,000, and that burden leads them to delay forming new family units, sometimes literally living in their parents' basements. Birth rates have plummeted and the population will start declining unless immigration remains robust.

Seventh, these programs are historically plagued with high delinquency rates—people not meeting their legal agreements. This has consequences regarding the respect of property rights and the sanctity of contracts but also reflects the noncommercial nature of the programs. High-risk individuals have the same borrowing rights and pay the same interest rates as low-risk individuals likely to get good high-paying jobs.

Eighth, although the savings rate is difficult to measure and arguably even to define, Americans are not prodigious savers and almost certainly put aside a smaller proportion of their income than either Americans did a half century or more ago, when college lending was of minor significance, or counterparts in other industrialized countries. Savings provide the resources to finance new investments—machines, tools, structures—that are critical to long-term gains in productivity, income, and, ultimately, our ability to consume goods and services—our standard of living. Before federal student loans became available, families planning on sending kids to college typically saved for years. Today, a large portion of families fail to do that, assuming their children can finance their schooling by federal borrowing. Hence the propensity to save has declined.

If the student loan programs have raised the costs to students and have had a plethora of probably unintended but very real consequences, who has benefited from them? I think the answer is clear: the rent-seeking employees of universities. The growth in student loans has been associated with a continued robustness in the number of college staff, particularly administrators who administer the financial assistance programs along with a whole host of new employees financed through the higher tuition fees. It was not state appropriation increases that financed the addition of a triple-digit numbers of employees at the University of Michigan or Ohio State (and vast numbers elsewhere) to handle diversity and inclusion efforts, for example, not to mention increases in other administrative areas.

I think a better-than-decent case can be made that the administrative bloat of the modern university was largely funded by the student loan program, and that the dilution of the faculty role in university governance that accompanied the growth in administrators has contributed mightily to universities losing their way, losing sight of their very raison d'être. The emphasis on both disseminating and creating knowledge has decreased, and universities have tried to assert a role inappropriate to their mission: trying to pressure America into adopting policies inconsistent with the factors that made the United States the land of opportunity, the greatest and most prosperous large nation in the world.

The discussion above does not consider all the implications of the 2021–24 efforts by the Biden administration to effectively forgive student-loan indebtedness or to make loan-repayment terms so lenient as to effectively provide de facto partial loan forgiveness to numerous borrowers. Such moves were grossly unfair to the many similarly financially situated Americans who did not attend college and thus never got what turned out to be gifts from the taxpayers. Nor were they fair to the millions of responsible Americans who repaid their loans. The federal policies created an environment where loan repayments were not viewed as a moral obligation to be taken seriously.

Protecting Consumers or Eliminating Competition? For-Profit Education

This book has argued that the competitive market system has served the nation well and that higher education should try to emulate it to a greater extent. Yet there is already a for-profit higher education sector, schools that sell their services in the marketplace, conferring degrees and certificates that most enrollees presumably use to advance themselves in the labor market. These for-profit schools suffer from some inherent disadvantages. They receive no direct government subsidies, unlike their nonprofit competitors, but have to pay taxes (again, unlike the competition).

Figure 3.5 shows that in the late twentieth century and the first decade of this century, for-profit schools grew enormously in popularity, peaking at around two million students, nearly 10 percent of total college enrollments in the United States by 2010. Since then, however, enrollments have declined dramatically, indeed accounting for a significant portion of the decline in total college enrollments in the US.

Although these schools, like not-for-profit ones, have (or had) varying missions, a large portion of them mainly serve adults seeking to gain credentials that can advance employment opportunities. The for-profits are not in the business of providing postsecondary socialization opportunities to predominantly middle- or upper-class Americans. They disproportionately serve low-income individuals, many of them minorities. On-campus sites are typically located in suburban office buildings with parking, but no recreational centers or even dormitories for student housing. Much instruction is online. Many classes are held in the evenings or on weekends to accommodate the schedules of working students. Some of them have a narrow vocational orientation, such as training court reporters or culinary arts employees.

Although these schools are privately owned and "for profit," they are heavily dependent on federal student loan programs. Because most of the students are relatively poor, often working mothers or fathers, student loans are often the primary financing vehicle. Indeed, it is no coincidence that the rise of this industry in the closing decades of the twentieth century and the first decade of this one occurred during the period of robust expansion of federally subsidized student loans. Similarly, the decline in for-profit enrollments coincides with a decline in the proportion of Americans having federal student loans. The decline in the for-profits has had other effects, leading to what Phil Magness calls an "adjunct crisis."[12] For a more comprehensive assessment of the for-profit sector, I recommend a fine analysis by Jayme S. Lemke and William F. Shughart II.[13]

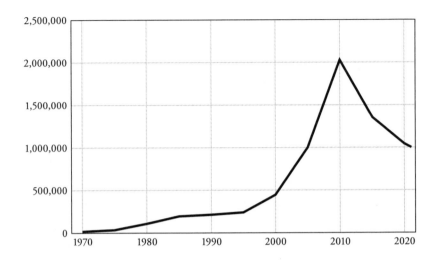

Figure 3.5 Private for-profit university enrollment in the US, 1970–2021

Source: National Center for Education Statistics, Digest of Education Statistics, 2022, Table 303.10, https://nces.ed.gov/programs/digest/d22/tables/dt22_303.10.asp.

I visited a number of for-profit schools and met with their leaders during the heyday of the industry in the first two decades of the twenty-first century. As in any other business, some shady operators, "diploma mills" almost, had a negative impact on the very concept of "for profit" colleges. Some of these schools used misleading advertising and high-pressure tactics to sign up students and get their federally provided (via loans) tuition dollars. But some people of integrity provided students with a good education and did so at markedly lower cost than traditional state universities. For example, rather than owning expensive real estate that remained empty much of the time, the for-profits typically rented functional but not opulent space that was occupied by students far more frequently than the buildings owned by not-for-profit state schools. When enrollments rose, the for-profit schools leased more space, and, conversely, during enrollment declines they let leases expire, avoiding the huge mismatch of space and students common in not-for-profit institutions. Teachers were paid to teach, not to do research of dubious value. Teachers who were disasters in the classroom tended to be eased out. The big summer or weekend drop-off in campus activity characterizing state universities was largely absent. The for-profit motive incentivized schools to operate with notably more efficiency than found in traditional state or nonprofit private universities.

The decline at the for-profits in enrollments after 2010 resulted mainly from an extremely hostile regulatory environment imposed by the federal government. What is particularly objectionable was that many examples of inadequate performance in for-profit higher education were found in government-owned or government-subsidized universities as well, and even in private not-for-profit universities, but they were often exempted from regulatory actions. Some observers even suggested that certain politically unfavored for-profit schools were targeted by a federal regulatory jihad.[14]

The regulatory environment toward for-profits became hostile with the ascension of the Obama administration in 2009. Democrats controlled all the executive and legislative branches of the federal government, and some of them thought it was philosophically wrong for people to profit from something that in their judgment should be a free or low-cost service provided or controlled by the government. Senators Tom Harkin of Iowa and Dick Durbin of Illinois were notable leaders in articulating this point of view; especially important in the administration was President Obama's deputy undersecretary of education, Robert Shireman. Shireman pushed for an aggressive application of a largely dormant provision of the Higher Education Act, calling for "gainful employment" regulations especially directed at for-profit programs with students receiving federal loans (which were also put under more direct federal control rather than administered through private banking organizations as had been done previously, again largely thanks to Shireman).

The concept of a gainful-employment rule seemingly makes a lot of sense, but the devil is in the details. Most Americans would agree that colleges should be providing students with skills that offer them opportunities to earn more money after college. If the earnings of a large portion of graduates of a college are lower than the average for high school graduates, students are not "gainfully employed," and it therefore seems sensible that such schools should not receive public support.

However, there is one *huge* flaw in the gainful-employment rule as it is applied by the US Department of Education: with relatively minor exceptions, *it applies only to for-profit universities.* Miguel Cardona, the US Secretary of Education, made that explicit in May 2023 during an announcement of the newest proposed regulations: "I think most taxpayers agree that federal financial aid dollars should not be given to pad the profits of colleges peddling useless programs."[15] What angered Secretary Cardona the most, apparently, was that those colleges made a profit, considered in the broader American economy to be an appropriate compensation for the capital investments, managerial expertise, and innovative ideas they implemented. Why is education any different?

Compare the University of the District of Columbia—a public university essentially immune from the gainful-employment regulations of the US Department of Education—with Strayer University's District of Columbia campus, located only 3.3 miles away. Strayer is a large for-profit school. Neither school has a successful record of graduating students—the College Scorecard of the US Department of Education suggests that fewer than one-fourth of them graduate within *eight* years of entering either school. Both schools have exactly the same reported median earnings of students ten years after first entering: $43,000 a year. Two schools with nearly identical student performance records are located a few minutes apart in the same city. One, Strayer, is subject to the gainful-employment rules, while the other is not. Why? The political answer: some politicians want to put out of business universities that are organized around the competitive free-market principles that govern most of the American economy.

Table 3.1 lists a number of schools that, despite abysmal performance records, are not subject to closure because of a denial of federal student loan assistance, unlike for-profit schools. The for-profits have plenty of company among conventional government or private not-for-profit schools whose contribution to society is questionable. Perhaps it is time for creative destruction to eliminate all of them—regardless of their ownership structure.

Additional insight regarding gainful-employment regulations is provided by the Federal Reserve Bank of New York underemployment-rate data. As indicated in chapter 1, the defined underemployment rate has been around 40 percent. An "underemployed" person doing a job typically held by high school graduates would generally not be "gainfully employed." The definition of *gainful employment* as implemented is unfair and discriminatory, even though in principle it is a legitimate concept.

Table 3.1 Examples of schools with low student-performance records

School	State or district	Graduation rate (%)	Median earnings ($)
University of the District of Columbia	District of Columbia	24	43,000
Southern University at New Orleans	Louisiana	35	35,000
Sinte Gleska University	South Dakota	14	22,000
Mississippi Valley State University	Mississippi	38	30,000
Central State University	Ohio	28	33,000
Texas Southern University	Texas	33	36,000
Bethesda University	California	22	41,000
University of Alaska Fairbanks	Alaska	34	46,000

Source: US Department of Education, College Scorecard, 2023, https://collegescorecard.ed.gov/search/?state=OH&page=0&sort=threshold_earnings:desc.

How Majors Materially Matter

The emphasis in this chapter has been on variations among universities in performance. But something more important is usually ignored: the differences in the marketability of students in diverse majors. To illustrate that, my assistant dug up data on earnings by major at an Ivy League university, Columbia. The US Department of Education's College Scorecard at this writing shows median earnings of all Columbia students ten years after attending of $98,000 and an impressive 94 percent graduation rate. But the data in table 3.2 shows *vast* differences by major. The gainful-employment regulations discussed above are formulated by college. What if we had gainful-employment regulations classified by *major*? Graduates of Columbia in a low-paying major such as literature or the arts are typically not "gainfully employed." One might ask: Why should students be able to get a large student loan at Columbia to earn a degree paying less than what an unskilled high school graduate could earn? If the gainful-employment concept is applied in higher education to encourage training in those fields that society values the most, why not make distinctions based on what students study and their subsequent earnings potential rather than on a school's ownership structure? It is worth noting that the importance of the field of study is even more pronounced at the master's and PhD levels; postgraduates in highly employable disciplines tend to earn salaries multiple times that of those with graduate degrees in the humanities, fine arts, gender studies, and the like.

Table 3.2 Salaries of Columbia University graduates, by highest- and lowest-paying majors

Major	Median starting salary ($)
Highest paying	
Computer science	96,400
Nursing (registered, administration, research, and clinical)	85,600
Operations research	79,000
Economics	75,300
Engineering (electrical, electronics, and communications)	74,200
Lowest paying	
Rhetoric and composition/writing studies	19,700
Visual and performing arts	21,800
Fine and studio arts	33,100
Anthropology	35,100
Biology	39,400

Source: US Department of Education, College Scorecard, 2023, https://collegescorecard.ed.gov/search/?state=OH&page=0&sort=threshold_earnings:desc.

Conclusion

This chapter introduces arguments challenging the special status conferred by American governments on universities. The common view that universities provide a positive common good that should be subsidized is questioned, and evidence is presented regarding areas that the government operates to subsidize universities and make them wards of the state. I argue that American universities have become more costly and unaffordable over time and relative to universities in other advanced nations. One huge factor in the dysfunctionality of the ivory tower in America is the disastrous federal student financial assistance programs that have contributed to high costs and low learning while reducing educational opportunity for low-income Americans, among other things.

For-profit universities are more in keeping with the American tradition with respect to the production of goods and services and, despite huge advantages given to government-subsidized schools, were gaining popularity and market share until, probably mainly for ideological reasons, the federal government attacked them in various ways, most importantly in so-called gainful-employment regulations. These rules were theoretically designed to eliminate government support for schools whose students show no greater contribution to the economy (as measured by their earnings) than typical high school graduates. But since these rules are not applied to the over 90 percent of students attending publicly supported universities (including so-called private universities operating on a not-for-profit basis), they are actually harmful, favoring an inefficient government-based approach to higher learning over alternative approaches incorporating market principles.

4

Creative Destruction and Laboratories of Democracy

AMERICA'S FOUNDING FATHERS did many wondrous things, including creating a constitution that has served the nation well for nearly one-quarter of a millennium. Particularly relevant for this exercise, however, the founders also created a vibrant federal system of government, permitting what Supreme Court justice Louis Brandeis called "novel social and economic experiments" that allow the various states to pursue different paths to governance in what he called "laboratories of democracy."[1] By exploring differences in the way the fifty states handle higher education, we can perhaps find approaches to collegiate learning that work reasonably well and identify those that are less successful. In particular, we can see if states with a high level of government involvement in the affairs of the citizenry attain more higher education. Does big government favor the creation and expansion of universities?

The American constitution does not even mention education (primary or higher) or the role that governments play in it, if any, and early attempts to create a national university went nowhere. At the time, all of the nine colonial colleges were what today we would call "private." To be sure, Rutgers and the College of William and Mary are today what we would call "state schools." Even Harvard's charter is codified in the Massachusetts constitution (although not in an interventionist way). The University of Pennsylvania was for a time considered a state university when it was chartered in the early years of constitutional government but has reverted to essentially private status.[2] Generally, however, governments did not per se "own" or operate universities, a matter that became an issue leading up to a landmark Supreme Court decision several decades after the nation's founding, in a dispute effectively over the control of Dartmouth College, with the decision favoring the college's trustees, not the state of New Hampshire.[3] As Daniel Webster memorably said of Dartmouth: "It is . . . a small college. And yet, there are those who love it." The US Supreme Court would not let the State of New Hampshire take over the governance of the school, putting limits on governmental control over universities, limits that have largely stood the test of time.

That said, however, recall that I have persistently argued that universities are wards of the state. A part of "the state" is the federal government, which is increasingly encroaching on the decisions made by colleges, including so-called private ones, with few exceptions.[4] But a sizable majority of American college students still attend schools that are at least nominally owned by the individual *state* governments. To a considerable extent, it is state governments that have prevented needed creative destruction and cushioned unpopular schools from the market-based judgment that they are not economically viable. Even the conservative, relatively small-government-oriented Alabama recently approved a large financial bailout for the now closed Birmingham-Southern College, a struggling *private* school with fewer than a thousand students, heading off creative destruction, but only temporarily, apparently to appease a Birmingham-Southern alumnus who is also a powerful Republican legislator. A similar move was made in West Virginia, to save struggling Alderson Broaddus University (unsuccessful, as the school has announced its plan to close). Therefore, let's explore a bit more extensively the differences in our large republic in public support for colleges and universities, and what we can learn from the variations in that support.

Growth and Destruction in Higher Education

Let's start with figure 4.1, which looks at the number of four-year colleges and universities in the United States in recent times. Note that number grew steadily, from roughly two thousand in 1980 to about three thousand three decades later, but since around 2011 the number of schools has shown roughly a 10 percent decline. A modest amount of creative destruction seems to have occurred. But to put things in context, compare four-year universities with an important private for-profit business sector, American commercial banks. In 1980, there were nearly fifteen thousand of them, but there are barely four thousand today. And though the banking industry is on the whole faring well, mergers, a genteel form of creative destruction, has reduced the number dramatically, with an occasional big failure like Continental Bank in Chicago (1984), Washington Mutual in Seattle (2008), or California's Silicon Valley Bank and New York's Signature Bank (2023), showing that brutal destruction is always a threat, keeping even the most prudent and profitable banks on their toes. Nearly a hundred banks with assets of one billion dollars or more have failed since the 1970s—can you name one large university?

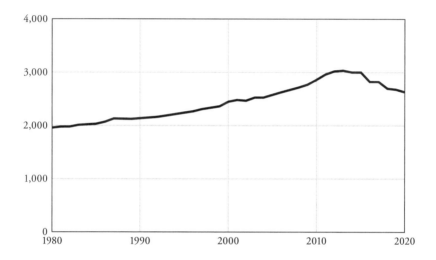

Figure 4.1 Number of degree-granting four-year institutions in the US, 1980–2020

Source: National Center for Education Statistics, Digest of Education Statistics, 2022, Table 317.10, https://nces.ed.gov/programs/digest/d22/tables/dt22_317.10.asp.

To be sure, in our vast country are big demographic variations: some states have had big changes in the population of college-age students, while others have not.[5] As figure 4.1 shows, the number of four-year universities in the early twenty-first century grew in some states, but declined in quite a number of others. With the decline in enrollments nationally after 2011, economic forces increased the pressure to close schools, in spite of some state bailouts and the monumental federal pandemic assistance to schools in the 2020–22 period.

Although patterns of decline vary geographically, the national flight to quality in higher education is undeniable: in recent years, the enrollments of schools with a mediocre national reputation have shown a big decline, while schools with a good to excellent reputation have fared well. For my own state of Ohio, I took the four state universities (Miami, Ohio State, Ohio University, and the University of Cincinnati), which have graduation rates well above average (at least 65 percent of those entering school graduate within eight years) and compared their enrollment change from 2012 to 2022 with the enrollment change at the six schools (Central State, Shawnee State, Wright State, University of Akron, University of Toledo, and Youngstown State) where a majority of students failed to graduate. Enrollments in the first group of universities in total rose 5.97 percent, while they *fell 31.28 percent* in the poorer-performing schools. Yet no school closed: governments were able to help any school avert closure. The Ohio situation is similar to that in many other states.

Between 2010 and 2020, the total number of four-year colleges in the US fell by 8.12 percent, a noticeable figure but not the type of catastrophic change observed among American businesses at various times in our history. In fourteen states, the decline in the number of schools exceeded 20 percent, and those schools were found in both low-population states like Vermont and Wyoming and in larger ones like Michigan and Tennessee. There was no distinct trend by geographic area. Looking at schools by the type of ownership (figure 4.2), however, we see some startling differences in creative destruction, but mostly concentrated in private schools, especially for-profit ones.

Despite significant enrollment declines, traditional state-supported public universities came through the decade of the 2010s without large numbers of them dying. A few states found themselves reluctantly merging some state schools, but that was the exception, not the rule. Indeed, the total number of public universities modestly *increased despite a decline in enrollments.* Enrollment declines of more than 30 percent from the 1980s or 1990s to today are common at some public universities in slow- or no-growth states in the East and Midwest, such as Pennsylvania, Ohio, and Illinois. The enrollment decline has accelerated in the last decade. For example, in 2012, enrollment at Ohio's University of Akron was 26,930, almost the same as it was a quarter century earlier, in 1987. In the fall of 2022, ten years later, it had fallen by

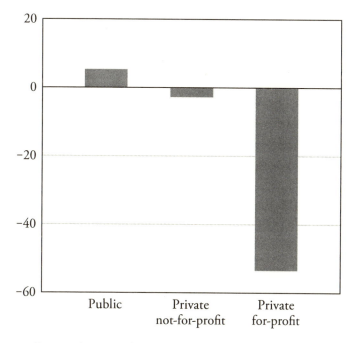

Figure 4.2 Percent change in the ownership of US four-year colleges, 2010–2020

Source: National Center for Education Statistics, Digest of Education Statistics, 2022, Table 317.10, https://nces.ed.gov/programs/digest/d22/tables/dt22_317.10.asp.

nearly a half, to 13,758. Southern Illinois University (SIU) in Carbondale went from 24,160 students in 1987 to 18,847 in 2012 and fell further to 11,107 by 2022—a decline of about 54 percent from 1987. In the Detroit suburbs, Eastern Michigan University went from 22,375 in 1987 to 20,037 in 2010, a fall of 10 percent, before beginning an accelerated plunge to 15,343 by 2022, over 31 percent lower than thirty-five years earlier. But none of those schools closed. Lots of decline, but little "destruction," creative or otherwise.

Probably nowhere was the public university enrollment decline more noticeable than in Pennsylvania, a state with a convoluted set of systems running its public universities. A major component is the Pennsylvania State System of Higher Education (PASSHE), which comprises well over a dozen schools, including Bloomsburg University, Cheney University, Slippery Rock University, California University of Pennsylvania, Indiana University of Pennsylvania, and others. The flight to quality is obvious. From 2010 to 2023, enrollment in the PASSHE schools combined declined by 30 percent, with larger declines at some campuses, finally leading to some campus consolidation under PASSHE chancellor Daniel Greenstein amid predictions of still further declines based on the smaller projected numbers of new students because of the birth dearth expected to accelerate in the next few years.[6]

Enrollment declines of these magnitudes are extraordinarily difficult to manage given the enormous fixed costs associated with large academic facilities. Does the SIU campus in Carbondale today have enormous excess capacity in classroom space? Does it have thousands of empty dormitory beds? How can it deal with expensive tenured professors on lifetime contracts? Yet it has survived these problems, probably in part because of state subsidy support.

Moreover, even the so-called private not-for-profit schools typically derive moderate to substantial government support, though indirectly, because federal student loans have allowed them to charge high tuition fees.[7] The enrollment woes of modern times forced some poorly endowed small private liberal arts colleges mostly ineligible for state government bailouts to close their doors, but the overall demise of schools was quite small.

Note, by contrast, the for-profit schools. With no private endowments or federal research support, these schools are almost exclusively tuition-dependent for revenues—they're like American businesses whose revenues are derived from product sales. There are no third parties (governments, foundations, private donors) to cushion losses in tuition fees. Creative destruction was very real, and it forced over half of them out of business, aided by a federal government whose leaders, especially during the Obama administration, were hostile to the schools on ideological grounds.

The comparison of for-profit and not-for-profit universities reminds me of an insight of Gordon Winston from a generation ago. Winston, speaking about traditional universities, notes that they are "essentially part church and part car dealer—devoted partly to charity and partly to commerce. . . . The result is a tension between doing good and doing well."[8] While this book advocates for more use of market-based approaches, the culture of higher education ("part church") often makes it difficult to effect change. As some increased creative destruction becomes part of the higher education landscape, that may, by necessity, change somewhat.

The sector least damaged by the declining demand for higher education services is the largest, state universities, and its low rate of fatalities is less an expression of efficiency, managerial competence, or innovation than it is of the nature of public subsidies. Failing public universities are bailed out by politicians seeking to maximize their own power and job security by winning votes: they can claim that "I saved XYZ State University!" In reality, *taxpayers* saved the university with resources that they could have used, via slightly lower taxes, to meet their own personal needs.

The Fifty States: Fifty Different Approaches to Higher Education

The fifty American states are part of a federation of states that collectively define its citizens as "Americans." Although Americans have common loyalties and many generally held common beliefs, their approach to government varies dramatically across the country. Because internal migration within the United States is relatively inexpensive and free of such governmental restrictions as passports and visas, Americans move frequently—we are a nation of movers. As Charles Tiebout hypothesized in a celebrated paper in 1956, Americans can and do seek out areas in which to live that most fit their personal preferences.[9] Conservatives may gather in states that seem congenial to their values, such as Idaho, Arkansas, or Texas, while persons with a progressive or liberal orientation might gravitate to New York, Massachusetts, or California.

As a lifetime student of American migration, I have noted that people are primarily swayed by economic factors when they consider moving—job opportunities, high earnings, and so on.[10] But in a nation of fifty states, multiple locations can usually meet one's financial objectives, so people also consider secondary considerations such as whether neighbors are likely to have similar values and beliefs (which has also been found to explain immigrant settlement patterns). Although I have not seen definitive evidence, I suspect that the "Tiebout effect" has strengthened over time—California, for example, has become more liberal, while Texas has become more conservative. Political philosophy and economic considerations overlap: as discussed in chapter 2, many Americans are lured by low taxes, which, in turn, are consistent with a small-government/conservative-libertarian political philosophy.

In a few swing states no one political philosophy or party seems to have a dominant role. Arizona, Georgia, and New Hampshire are good examples. In order to assess the degree to which a state is "blue" (Democratic) or "red" (Republican), my assistant and I concocted a rating that ranges in value from zero to 6. We assigned a value of 1 if Donald Trump, the Republican, received the most votes for president in 2020 in that state. If the governor was a Republican, the state received another 1 added to its score. The same was true for the US Senate and House—we gave a 1 if the majority of the state's representatives in each body was Republican, a zero if Democrat. For the US Senate, if one senator was a Democrat, and the other a Republican, we gave a 0.5 score. We did the same for the majority representation in the state's house and senate (giving two votes to the majority party in Nebraska's unicameral legislature). The calculations were based on the party affiliation of officeholders as of late 2023.[11] Any state with a total score between zero and 1.5 was adjudged to be a blue state, with a score of 4.5 to 6 being a red state, and a value of 2 to 4 a swing state (see table 4.1). By this measure, there are twenty-five red states, twenty blue ones, and five swing states.

An observant reader might legitimately ask: So what? Surveys show that attitudes toward higher education vary significantly by political orientation (something not the case a generation ago, perhaps making it harder to reach political consensus on university appropriations). As indicated briefly in chapter 1, Democrats or progressives are a good deal more sympathetic and positive toward higher education, and the gap between groups based on political affiliation has grown dramatically. A 2023 Gallup poll showed that only 19 percent of Republicans have "a great deal" or "quite a lot" of confidence in higher education, a dramatic decline from the 56 percent in 2015.[12]

A reviewer raises a fascinating point: if state political environments vary so widely, why is there seemingly *less* diversity within universities, with most having a prominently left-progressive political orientation? Many factors are no doubt at work: accreditation plays a pernicious role, DEI bureaucracies try to instill a woke ideology, schools try to imitate the reputational leaders that are uniformly leftish, and so on.

By contrast, a majority of Democrats (59 percent) still had relatively high confidence in higher education, a far less dramatic decline from 2015 (when it was 68 percent). Thus we might surmise that blue states might have higher

Table 4.1 Political orientation of the fifty states, 2023

Blue (20)	Red (25)	Swing (5)
California, Colorado, Connecticut, Delaware, Hawaii, Illinois, Maine, Maryland, Massachusetts, Michigan, Minnesota, Nevada, New Jersey, New Mexico, New York, Oregon, Pennsylvania, Rhode Island, Vermont, Washington	Alabama, Alaska, Arkansas, Florida, Idaho, Indiana, Iowa, Kansas, Kentucky, Louisiana, Mississippi, Missouri, Montana, Nebraska, North Carolina, North Dakota, Ohio, Oklahoma, South Carolina, South Dakota, Tennessee, Texas, Utah, West Virginia, Wyoming	Arizona, Georgia, New Hampshire, Virginia, Wisconsin

Sources: Wikipedia; author's calculations.

levels of higher education participation than red ones. I would surmise that the growth after 2010 of "wokeness" and racial preferencing via DEI practices in higher education (perhaps reduced by the Supreme Court's 2023 decision in *Students for Fair Admissions v. Harvard*) might have turned off a growing number of persons, but especially Republicans.

In figure 4.3, I compare those attaining at least a bachelor's degree in the adult (over 25 years old) population for the three categories of states outlined in table 4.1, taking the average of the states in computing a statistic measuring central tendency. Note that in the blue states a higher proportion of adults are college graduates (and most college graduates included in this comparison finished school before the vast political differences in attitudes toward college developed in the past decade). The proportion of college graduates who are Democrats may be higher simply because universities themselves are increasingly liberal institutions. It can be argued that people like to be around those who think similarly, so colleges with predominantly liberal orientation attract liberal students and repel conservatives.

In table 4.2, we show the considerable interstate differences regarding higher education, comparing the ten states with the highest rates of educational attainment with the ten states with the lowest rates. The group of highly college-educated states are predominantly Democratic, while the states with the lowest levels of higher education attainment are predominantly Republican (although this is also partly a North/South phenomenon). The

Table 4.2 States with the highest and lowest proportions of graduates; 2019

State	Residents with bachelor's degree or higher (%)[a]	Amount spent on higher ed. per capita ($)[b]	Resident income spent on higher ed. per $1,000 ($)[c]	Per capita personal income ($)[d]	Political orientation
Most graduates per 100 residents					
Massachusetts	45.0	748.07	10.09	73,213	Blue
Colorado	42.8	1,050.70	17.19	62,124	Blue
New Jersey	41.2	836.01	11.88	68,438	Blue
Maryland	40.9	1,102.27	17.09	62,313	Blue
Connecticut	40.1	894.69	11.58	75,533	Blue
Virginia	39.8	1,044.78	17.56	59,073	Swing
Vermont	39.3	1,362.72	24.65	55,442	Blue
New Hampshire	38.1	633.10	9.98	64,747	Swing
New York	37.9	1,713.67	10.25	67,366	Blue
Minnesota	37.3	879.30	14.95	58,543	Blue
Fewest graduates per 100 residents					
West Virginia	21.5	925.34	21.90	42,951	Red
Mississippi	22.0	1,010.30	25.98	39,445	Red
Arkansas	23.2	938.49	21.05	44,324	Red
Louisiana	25.0	802.26	16.94	47,668	Red
Kentucky	25.3	885.47	20.25	43,875	Red
Nevada	25.7	585.97	11.49	52,602	Blue
Oklahoma	26.1	960.32	20.31	48,646	Red
Alabama	26.3	1,155.94	26.21	43,288	Red
Indiana	27.1	969.34	19.91	48,749	Red

Sources: [a] National Center for Education Statistics, Digest of Education Statistics, published 2021, Table 104.88–2019, https://nces.ed.gov/programs/digest/d21/tables/dt21_104.88.asp?current=yes.

[b, c] US Census Bureau, 2019 State and Local Government Finance Historical Datasets and Tables, "State and Local Government Finances by Level of Government and by State: 2019," https://www2.census.gov/programs-surveys/gov-finances/tables/2019/19slsstab1.xlsx; National Center for Education Statistics, Digest of Education Statistics, Table 334.20, https://nces.ed.gov/programs/digest/d20/tables/dt20_334.20.asp.

[d] US Department of Commerce, Bureau of Economic Analysis, 2019, Table 1, https://www.bea.gov/sites/default/files/2020-12/rpp1220_0.pdf; FRED, 2023, "Per Capita Personal Income by State; 2019," https://fred.stlouisfed.org/release/tables?rid=110&eid=257197&od=2019-01-01#.

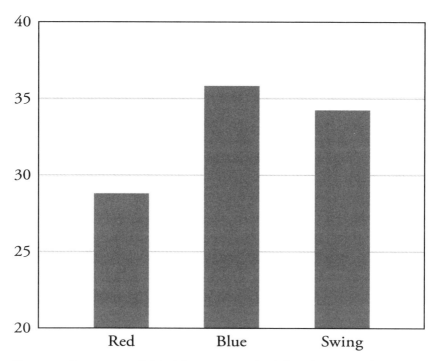

Figure 4.3 Percentages of US adults attaining a bachelor's degree in red, blue, and swing states, 2023

Source: Author's calculations.

more highly educated group of states all have incomes well above that of even the most prosperous of the less educated states.

It is interesting, however, that the ten states with the largest proportion of college graduates spend on average a *lower* percentage of their income (about a third lower) on their public colleges than the ten lowest college-educated states. And despite having much higher incomes, the low prioritization of funding state universities means that total per capita spending on higher education in the two groups of states is similar. New Hampshire spends about the lowest percentage of its income on state universities of any state in the union—yet it has the eighth-highest proportion of college graduates. State financial support for higher education and actual degree attainment are, to put it mildly, often distantly related. Why?

The states with the most college graduates have an abundance of top-flight private universities. Harvard, Yale, Princeton, and MIT, for example, are all located in one of the five states with the highest proportion of college graduates. Where private education is very strong, people are highly educated. Who needs public universities? The top public universities in states like Massachusetts (home of private Harvard and MIT), New Jersey (home of Princeton) and Connecticut (home of Yale) are schools that reputationally pale in comparison with their private school counterparts. So the notion that "very high state government support of colleges is imperative for a highly educated population" simply does not seem supported by the data.

To be sure, all sorts of conclusions could be drawn from table 4.2. Democrats might say, "The data show that Democrats are smarter and more productive—just look at the higher earnings in those states." Republicans might respond: "You have causation all wrong: Democrats have more education in part because they are richer." Or, "Higher education is a sorting device: smarter and more productive kids go to college, and those precollege attributes, not college training, are the primary reason they are both more educated and richer." But in any case, it is clear that *the incidence of college attainment is not closely related to the amount of public support at the state level.* Perhaps the law of unintended consequences is again at work, as it is with regard to federal student loans (huge federal loan spending has not led to massive increases in the proportion of low-income college graduates, and indeed has probably worked in the opposite direction). Low state spending on higher education, such as done in New Hampshire, does not lead to a much less educated populace than high public university spending in neighboring Vermont.

In a sense, the data are consistent with other political changes. In the middle of the twentieth century, Republicans were considered the rich person's party, and they had a disproportionate number of college graduates—"country club" Republicans. Democrats sent their kids disproportionately to high school and then to a factory or service job represented by a labor union, while Republican kids went into business or the professions. As colleges have become more woke, especially in this century, the tables have turned. The Democrats are the more college-educated group, and Republicans are increasingly avoiding college.

In a federal system of government with high income mobility, a lot of persons earn a degree at their state-supported university, only to move to other states. Colorado has the second-largest proportion of college graduates in the country but does not spend particularly much on its public universities, the best of which is the University of Colorado's main Boulder campus, which has a decent but not spectacular renown. But Colorado has also had a significant amount of in-migration and has many jobs of a technical nature where college degrees are required. To deal with the migration issue, almost all state universities impose much higher fees on out-of-state students (arguably a classic example of price discrimination). Indeed, some states make an effort to lure out-of-state students to augment their revenue and arguably even boost their national reputation. Prestigious schools like the Universities of Michigan, Virginia, and North Carolina or some campuses of the University of California often face political pressure from local residents because of the high proportion of out-of-state students. However, states with less stellar national reputation often depend heavily on out-of-state students as well; I think, for example, of the University of Alabama and North Dakota State University. At Alabama, a large majority of the student body is from out of state. The sticker price (published tuition fee) for out-of-state students is nearly three times that of in-state students (although there is considerable tuition discounting). If not for its outstanding football team, Alabamans might ask: Why are we subsidizing a school that has more students from other states than from Alabama? The rise in out-of-state enrollments reduces the rationale for taxpayer support of so-called state universities that are no longer primarily for residents of the relevant state.

The Great Higher Education Lie: Are States Really "Disinvesting" in Higher Education?

One reason higher education is in such disrepute with the public is that universities, supposedly the purveyor of facts and truths, consistently lie to the public they serve. I not so jokingly tell people I would rather buy a used car from a name randomly selected from the voter registration rolls than from a university president. No better example arises from the claim that "in modern times, Americans have 'disinvested' in their state universities, spending less money, correcting for inflation, than they did a decade or two ago."

A major source of this disinformation is something called the State Higher Education Executive Officers Association (SHEEO). It has concocted the Higher Education Price Index, which purports to adjust spending data for the declining value of the dollar (inflation) over time. Generally, this index assumes a higher rate of inflation than stated by government indices such as the widely used consumer price index (CPI) of the US Bureau of Labor Statistics in the Department of Labor, or the personal consumption expenditure index compiled by the Bureau of Economic Analysis in the US Department of Commerce. The latter index is closely watched by the Federal Reserve in making monetary policy, and the CPI is used to adjust Social Security benefits annually.

The SHEEO index is embarrassingly bad and highly biased toward reducing the effect of increases in state spending on universities. The index looks at spending increases at colleges and calls much of it "inflation," when at least some of what is measured results from the colleges' own rent-seeking behavior. For example, if colleges increase their employees' salaries by a generous 6 percent, that raises the SHEEO price index and reduces the purported real (inflation-adjusted) spending by states. By giving out big salary increases, universities can claim that states are reducing their support of higher education. Generally, inflation is determined by macroeconomic conditions in the broader economy, not by actions within a small subset of it.

My former student and employee Dr. Andrew Gillen of the Cato Institute has taken the dollar spending for colleges as reported by SHEEO and then used legitimate price indices to observe long-term trends. The results, best illustrated by the dotted regression line in figure 4.4 and most certainly represented by the shaded band based on multiple legitimate price indices, show an upward trend in spending of $22 to $59 per student per year over the period 1980 to 2020. (Total spending rose even more in most years, because the number of students grew in most years over those four decades.)

Conclusion

To use a French expression (proclaimed, however, by Americans more than by French), "Vive la différence!" Within America's vast geographic

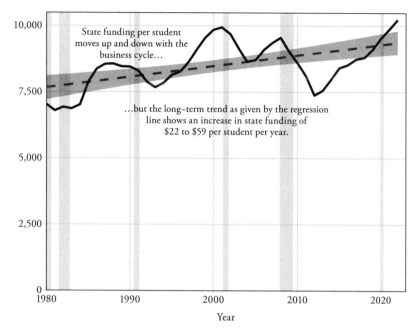

Figure 4.4 State funding of higher education per student in constant 2022 dollars, 1980–2020

Source: Reprinted with permission from Andrew Gillen, *Trends in State Funding and Tuition Revenue for Public Higher Education, 1980–2023* (Austin, TX: Texas Public Policy Foundation, 2023), figure 1.

confines and one-third of a billion people, are enormous differences that make generalizations about American higher education dangerous but not impossible. For example, few institutions of higher education have died in modern times, but those closures varied in both time (more died in the 2010s and 2020s than in the 2000s) and space (e.g., more schools have succumbed in Vermont than in Florida). One thing does stand out: schools receiving significant subsidies from third parties—governments, private donors, rich endowments—rarely die. But a meaningful group of colleges, those pursuing a profit like most American business enterprises, has been devastated, suffering an enormous amount of destruction, creative or otherwise.

It is also true that the dominant political culture or philosophy varies enormously across space—California, Illinois, and New York are far more liberal and supportive generally of government involvement than Tennessee,

Wyoming, or Indiana. Left-wing-oriented states tend to spend somewhat more on higher education than right-wing ones, with exceptions: liberal Massachusetts spends far less by any measure on colleges than conservative Alabama, for example. Overall, data maintained by the Pew Research Center support a full rebound in general appropriations after the 2008 financial crisis along with higher direct-grant programs.[13] The oft-expressed notion that Americans are abandoning their colleges and universities by providing less public funding is simply not supported by the evidence on state government support.

5

Recent Innovations in Higher Education: Good, but Not Enough

I OUTLINED IN the first chapter ten serious failings of American higher education today. Among other things, I argued that it was too expensive and provided little learning. The recent enrollment declines and reduced public support for universities are probably at least partly a consequence of a growing perception of those ten weaknesses.

This is not to deny, however, that a number of serious innovators are attempting to reform our colleges and universities. American ingenuity has been ingrained in at least some members of the academy. Indeed, many of our nation's most important inventions evolved from university research. Some higher education leaders have also had positive impacts, doing things like making a more imaginative use of new technology or finding cheaper ways of offering quality degrees. So let's explore a few recent innovative efforts or proposals, while noting that they have not collectively moved the needle a great deal—on balance, the deficiencies outlined in chapter 1 remain today. However, these innovations may help point the way to changes that will lead to more comprehensive positive reform.

Starting New Traditionally Structured Universities

Many educational reformers lament that "it is almost impossible to get meaningful productive change out of existing universities." Entrenched groups fight moves that might reduce their power or income. These include the faculty, both as individuals and as members of a campus group such as a faculty senate (or some similarly named organization) or labor union. Tenure provides faculty with protection against dismissal but makes it hard to effect needed changes on campus. Students can often be influential obstacles to change as well. Sometimes university alumni or trustees intervene to prevent changes, particularly when it comes to high-visibility activities like intercollegiate athletics. And occasionally highly paid senior administrators work hard to block reforms that might erode their power and reduce their successful rent seeking (pay that exceeds that necessary for the job performed).

Brand-new universities can avoid some of the obstacles to reform rather easily. Before instruction begins, a small group of campus founders can, for example, devise a curriculum that improves the utilization of human and physical resources by implementing year-round schooling options, including a three-year bachelor's degree. They can avoid the excessive costs of a collegiate edifice complex involving expensive underutilized buildings. They don't have battalions of powerful but unimaginative administrators who prefer the comfortable status quo to needed change.

Perhaps more importantly, new campuses can be molded to reduce the existential problems arising from "woke" ideas that have captured much of the academy. For example, they can strongly endorse from day one the concept of unfettered free expression, calling for a diversity of opinions and ideas freely articulated in a civil way in a genuine marketplace of ideas. For example, they can incorporate the so-called Chicago principles of free expression into their mission statement and charter, declaring that the institution itself will take no position on political issues of the day. They can experiment with ways other than tenure of providing an element of employment security for the faculty, while at the same time incentivizing those involved in the institution to be productive. That might mean, for example, using medium-term contracts (say three to five years) with serious review before renewal.

Above all, a new university can be constructed that is administratively lean. Fashionably woke but costly and arguably reputation-destroying practices like staffing vast DEI bureaucracies can be thwarted. No law requires having a "diversity and inclusion" operation. Why not simply declare: "We welcome students, faculty, staff, and contractors for their competence, diligence, and integrity, not for their skin color, gender, ethnicity, religion, or other group characteristic." Intellectual diversity can be attained by hiring an initial faculty of individuals with widely differing perspectives on the optimal path forward for the human race.

Why hasn't there been much new collegiate activity given the existing problems and a public perception that higher education in America is not working well? Although colleges and universities face important issues like accreditation (the universities controlling the accreditors don't want new competition, particularly competition that has advantages arising from being new), by far the biggest problem is money. A new institution of any magnitude at all requires hundreds of millions of dollars if not billions of dollars in financial support, and even smaller endeavors require a healthy amount of cash. The number of philanthropists having both the desire and the capacity to implement such innovations is limited. Still, a number of experiments are underway that deserve our respectful examination.

The University of Austin

In late 2021, an announcement was made that a new university was going to be established in or near the city of Austin, Texas, the University of Austin (UATX). Its first president, Pano Kanelos, had previously served for several years as the president of St. John's College, an old liberal arts college originally in Annapolis, Maryland, that later created a second campus in Santa Fe, New Mexico. The St. John's curriculum emphasizes the "Great Books," major classics of learning that have stood the test of time. At St. John's, Kanelos led a campaign to raise a large sum of endowment money specifically to fund substantial reductions in tuition and other fees for students.

A strong commitment to free expression is at the heart of the UATX mission. Some great academic names have had at least limited involvement in UATX, such as Ayaan Hirsi Ali, Deirdre McCloskey (once at the University of Chicago), Jonathan Haidt (New York University), Joshua Katz (once at Princeton), Tyler Cowen (George Mason), Roland Fryer Jr. (Harvard), and John Tomasi (Brown, now running the Heterodox Academy). At a UATX meeting of several dozen individuals heavily involved in higher education to which I was invited in the spring of 2023, I was astonished by the extraordinarily high quality of academic powerhouses seemingly committed to the institution, including, for example, Charles Calomiris, the Henry Kaufman Professor of Financial Institutions at Columbia University's business school, who appeared to be planning on ultimately working at least part time as a high-level administrator at UATX, and, especially important, Niall Ferguson, historian extraordinaire who has taught at Oxford, Harvard, Stanford, and other places. A lot of awfully bright, accomplished, and lively academic minds.

Ferguson said he envisioned the institution starting small, with an initial cohort of students following a common core curriculum for two years before branching off into specialized study. The school opened with a freshman class of about ninety students in the fall of 2024. The school has attracted a large number of wealthy entrepreneurs; the chair of its board, Joe Lonsdale, was a founder of software tech giant Palantir Technologies, who like Elon Musk relocated from high-tax California to the solid red, no-income-tax state of Texas. One early challenge will be how UATX deals with accreditation, as accreditors, themselves mostly controlled by the universities they evaluate, put obstacles in the way of new entrants into higher education.

UATX is potentially a great innovation, but unless it really catches fire, I suspect its short- to medium-term effects on American academic life will be limited even if it quickly raises a billion-dollar endowment and attracts many great minds. If top professors and students leave Harvard and Stanford for Austin, that might be a different story, but that now seems like a dream more than a likely reality. Nonetheless, if it is successful, it could nudge existing universities into grudgingly accepting some change in order to remain competitive. Also, I sense that while the school aspires to academic excellence, innovations in such things as the academic calendar (e.g., three-year degrees) have not been a big part of the initial discussion.

There are other efforts to create innovative schools. Ralston College in Savannah, Georgia, is a new venture whose mottoes are *Sermo liber vita ipsa* ("Free speech is life itself") and *Animus crescat* ("Let your mind expand"). Although Ralston has a number of notable names associated with it, notably the well-known psychologist Jordan Peterson, it is in an embryonic state at this writing.

Another new school is Thales College in North Carolina, the brainchild of Bob Luddy, a remarkable entrepreneur and charter school organizer, who was the prime mover behind an extraordinary small chain of charters that has been highly successful at the primary and secondary levels. The website proclaims, "Thales College is a return to what higher education was meant to be, and a fresh new take on college for the twenty-first century. The best of the past and the present is combined to prepare our students for the future." Thales offers an inexpensive degree *in three years*—with internships built in, and a classically traditional curriculum, designed to "mentor . . . students to develop the discipline and rigor necessary for professional life." Perhaps it is just hype, but as one who has lectured students at Luddy's impressive Thales Academy schools, I wouldn't bet against it. [1]

A similar effort was founded by Gordon Jones and associates in the suburbs of Salt Lake City Utah, Mount Liberty College, which at this writing has about twenty-five students and is completely government independent, not even seeking accreditation. It has a Great Books orientation.

Repurposing Older Schools

The Hillsdale–Grove City Model: Just Say No to the Federal Government

One very interesting and I think successful innovation is actually very old: some colleges have simply refused to accept the federal financial support that triggers a growing plethora of regulations from Washington. No federal student financial assistance for enrolled students, no federal research money—nothing. For nearly all schools, that seems to be too high a price to pay. But there are exceptions. I think especially of Hillsdale College in Michigan and Grove City College in Pennsylvania, two liberal arts colleges founded in the nineteenth century that resisted the federal encroachment on college policies that began in the 1960s and reached a crescendo in the 1980s. In 1984, in an important Supreme Court case, *Grove City College v. Bell*, 465 U.S. 555, the justices extended the regulatory power of the federal government over private schools whose students accept federal financial aid, later reinforced by new federal legislation. By the end of the 1980s, both Hillsdale and Grove City had essentially cut ties with the federal government and have operated without any federal aid or regulations, as authentic private schools. Both schools have a fairly strong but not dominant Protestant Christian orientation, with an emphasis on a traditional curriculum. Hillsdale's Christ Chapel (2019) is probably one of the most expensive and impressive campus religious facilities built in modern times.

The Hillsdale experience has been particularly remarkable. Under two presidents, George Roche and Larry Arnn, Hillsdale has for over fifty years become a highly successful school with an increasingly competitive student body and a host of educational initiatives beyond its initial campus. It has a roughly billion-dollar endowment for a student body on its original campus of fewer than fifteen hundred students. It has extended its outreach in ways that few if any other campuses have. Under Roche, the school started *Imprimis*, a magazine incorporating the thoughts of leading intellectuals and public officials, with a subscription list in the millions. Hillsdale ranked a solid thirty-ninth in the 2024 *U.S. News & World Report* rankings of liberal arts colleges.

Additionally, the college has expanded geographically, first with a beautiful Washington, DC, outpost (the Kirby Center) located a few blocks from the Capitol, where programs are held and students study in a master's degree program. It has newer facilities in Connecticut and California, where I suspect educational programs will be forthcoming. It has taken on an important role in the private charter school movement at the K–12 level, not only opening its own school but, far more importantly, developing model curricula for private charter initiatives around the country, ones that emphasize our constitutional heritage and the virtues of American exceptionalism. There is nothing woke about Hillsdale College. Arnn has even run Hillsdale-sponsored cruises where donors listen to lectures by Hillsdale faculty—and contribute financially to the school's mission (the endowment has exploded under Arnn's leadership).

Supporting Intellectual Diversity

Although American colleges and universities mostly have a moderately to strongly progressive "woke" orientation, a fair number of schools are decidedly not in that tradition. Some have a religious orientation, be it the conservative Protestant-leaning Bob Jones or Liberty Universities, or the über-Catholic Ave Maria University that has arisen in Florida thanks to the extraordinary financial commitment of Domino Pizza founder Tom Monaghan. Others are secular schools with a conservative orientation, like Pepperdine and Chapman Colleges in California, and Patrick Henry College in Virginia. America thus offers a good deal of diversity for students seeking a college that fits their view of the world.

Additionally, a few state governments have promoted intellectual diversity by creating state-funded research centers with a more conservative orientation. A good example is the Hamilton Center for Classical and Civic Education at the University of Florida. "The purpose of the center is to support teaching and research concerning the ideas, traditions, and texts that form the foundations of Western and American civilization."[2] Stanley Kurtz of the Ethics and Public Policy Center, working with David Randall at the National Association of Scholars and Jenna Robinson at the James G. Martin Center, has proposed a "General Education Act" that incorporates a core curriculum of forty-two semester hours including courses in world, Western, and American history, as well as American government and literature. It has received strong support in a few states.[3]

Perhaps reformers could also be inspired by foreign examples, such as the Francisco Marroquín University in Guatemala. Small institutions specializing in a few topics—perhaps a less woke version of the famed London School of Economics—would be another option.

Making Colleges Affordable: Zero- or Low-Tuition Schools

Federal data show that colleges typically spend only one-third or so of their budget directly on instruction. Moreover, faculty often claim they spend a lot of time doing research or activities unrelated to job one: teaching students material that will make them productive, knowledgeable, and virtuous adults. Also, as indicated in chapter 1, a central complaint with higher education is that it is too expensive, increasingly inaccessible to lower-income students. Yet some colleges with a good reputation make it possible for poorer kids to attend. They, generally speaking, have kept costs down by minimizing the administrative bureaucracy and have made keeping costs down to students as the single most important objective, along with offering a quality education. Interestingly, they are all private schools.

Berea College, College of the Ozarks, and Cooper Union

A small number of schools impose essentially no cost to entering students and yet offer a reasonably high-quality education. My favorite example is Berea College, located in low-income Appalachian Kentucky. Predating the Civil War, Berea was distinctive from the beginning, unique for a Southern school for being both coeducational and racially integrated in the nineteenth century. With fewer than fifteen hundred students, Berea officially charges a high tuition, but after federal and other scholarship grants, provides scholarships to all students to cover college costs. The school is aided by a large endowment (more than $1 million per student at this writing) that helps fund the extraordinary commitment to keeping the college affordable (alumni are fiercely loyal to the school). High-income students need not even apply—only relatively poor students are accepted. Students are required to work at least ten hours weekly at jobs the school has available. Although the school has many Appalachian students, it draws from a wide area, including, for that area especially, a good number of members of minority racial or ethnic backgrounds as well as international students.

A few hundred miles almost due west of Berea is a school with a similar size and mission, Missouri's College of the Ozarks, located near the Arkansas border. It too charges no tuition and expects students to work at least fifteen hours a week (its motto is Hard Work U.) It is a Christian school with a midsized endowment.

A distinctly different type of free-tuition school has been the Cooper Union in New York City, a school for architecture, art, and engineering. This small school (seven to eight hundred students) has battled to keep its no-tuition status for years, although it owns some valuable New York real estate, notably the land under the Chrysler Building. Nonetheless, for over 160 years (Abraham Lincoln spoke there while running for president in 1860), it has offered affordable high-quality education in a few specialized fields.

Perhaps the ultimate no-tuition schools are run by the federal government, namely, the nation's military academies. Students get a high-quality free education in return for hard work while undergrads and a significant postgraduation work commitment. I have often wondered if the West Point–Naval Academy–Air Force Academy model could be extended in the private sector. Could a company like, say, Google, Tesla, or Microsoft offer a low-cost bachelor's degree in three or four years to high school seniors who commit to working for the company postgraduation for at least five years at a decent salary? I think company-sponsored technical institutes offering such degree programs is a promising approach needing business support. As one who has spoken to the US Chamber of Commerce and other business groups on several occasions, I have always felt the business community has not devoted enough attention to improving the training of its most important resource: its highly skilled workers and leaders.

Using Technology to Lower Costs: Computer-Based Instruction

Until the late twentieth century, instructing college students was mostly done roughly the same way that Socrates did it: a teacher lectured to a group of students. We added blackboards, textbooks, laboratories, and maybe even an occasional video or other visual aid, but things hadn't changed much for two thousand years. In the late twentieth century, there was some hope that televised instruction would lower costs, but it was the advent of the internet as the twentieth century came to a close that led to calls for new modes of instruction using distance-learning techniques. This development led to some important changes, and computer-based instruction grew in importance, but I don't think that it has achieved the success hyped by some of its early advocates.

The COVID-19 pandemic of 2020–22 led to a dramatic overnight health-determined switch to computerized instruction that clearly led to deteriorating learning outcomes at the primary and secondary school levels, and, I would submit, at the college level as well. (I speak as one who has used both traditional teaching methods and conferencing formats like Zoom and Teams.) The pandemic experience demonstrated that computerized distance learning can transmit learning and wisdom, but also showed that on balance students usually benefit from direct contact with their professor and interaction with fellow students. However, for nontraditional part-time students with jobs or major family responsibilities, computerized instruction is the most realistic way to access higher levels of learning. Let's examine a few efforts to effectively use distance learning to provide low-cost instruction.

It is noteworthy that much of the early innovation in computerized in-struction came from the for-profit private sector, with schools like the University of Phoenix, Kaplan, DeVry, and Strayer being important and growing providers of higher education services in the first decade of the twenty-first century, often providing instruction both in person and via computer. As indicated in the previous chapter, a massive governmental attack on this sector, I think largely for ideological reasons, led to a sharp decline in enroll-ments after 2010, although it appears that some for-profits were especially attacked while others were not harassed as much. However, the not-for-profit computerized sector grew substantially, as traditional campuses offered more online courses. Arizona State University and the University of Maryland Global campus became important innovators in this space. Purdue Univer-sity bought the Kaplan for-profit operation (for a purported one dollar) and started Purdue Global.

Two especially interesting new entries were Western Governors University (WGU) and Southern New Hampshire University (SNHU), both private not-for-profit institutions. WGU was created out of a meeting of western governors in the 1990s and has grown dramatically to serve around 150,000 students today online.[4] Its fees for a year of instruction are relatively low, and in theory a bachelor's degree can be obtained for under $25,000 for a student graduating in three years (fees are assessed for six-month periods, not by the number of courses taken, incentivizing students to have a relatively heavy class load). Although created by a group of state government officials, the organiza-tion is not under formal state governmental control; affiliates of WGU have, however, been created through legislative or gubernatorial action in a number of states. At this writing, a couple of governors serve on the board of trustees, but a majority come from private business. Arguably this is the best example of a public-private partnership in higher education.

SNHU is a most unusual institution, starting as a business and secretarial training school in the 1930s, becoming New Hampshire College in the late twentieth century, and SNHU since 2001. It has always had a traditional residential campus, now serving around three thousand students. But SNHU's success is largely attributed to one scholar-entrepreneur, President Paul LeBlanc, who turned an ailing residential school into a prosperous institution by an aggressive and adroit expansion of online education, now exceeding a hundred thousand students. The school claims that a bachelor's degree in business administration can be obtained for about $40,000, less than that at other online powerhouses like Liberty University, University of Phoenix, University of Maryland Global Campus, and Capella.

Looking more broadly for data on performance at predominantly online institutions regardless of their ownership (public, private not-for-profit, private for-profit), I scoured the College Scorecard of the US Department of Education and found that graduation rates from most of these online schools are often well below 50 percent. Average earnings, ostensibly ten years after attendance, at almost all the schools I surveyed was under $50,000 a year, and often below $40,000, about the same as many high school graduates make after several years of work experience. Attending an online university to get a college credential might enhance employment opportunities, but few graduates obtain high-paying managerial or technical positions at major corporations. The excited hopes that some educational reformers and innovators had a generation ago at the beginning of the online education era have largely been unfulfilled. In theory, the best and brightest professors could give tremendous lectures online to multitudes of students at a reasonable price, an early promise of online providers such as Udacity and Coursera, but in reality that has largely not happened.[5]

Moreover, online education does not provide some of the secondary benefits of college—the socialization (including developing lifelong friends and potential business connections, not to mention maybe finding a spouse)—the learning that comes from human interactions outside the classroom. Moreover, good schools have a goodly number of professors and sometimes others that interact with students to offer advice on all sorts of noninstruction-related events critical in the transition from adolescence to adulthood. Speaking personally, I think a large proportion of the students I may have positively influenced over a long lifetime of teaching would tell you the most important interactions occurred outside the classroom—in office-hour conversations, over coffee or a drink at a local watering hole, in visits to my home, even on trips both inside the United States and abroad outside formal university involvement. Classroom instruction is important, but it is not the only thing that is important, and online education has severe limitations in dealing with the nonformal instructional dimensions of the university experience.

Free or Extremely Low-Cost Instruction

A number of efforts have been made in the past two decades, both by philanthropists and by profit-seeking entrepreneurs, to offer low-cost or even free college-level instruction. Rather than offering degrees and getting accreditation from organizations controlled by traditional universities wary of new competition, these new ventures offer college-level courses that they then induce accredited colleges to accept toward a degree, thus lowering the tuition fees the student would have to pay to the conventional accredited college or university.

Two ventures in the Washington-Baltimore area are particularly noteworthy. The Saylor Academy, founded by the philanthropist Michael Saylor, an MIT graduate with a strong entrepreneurial bent, offers as of this writing over two hundred courses for free, including free textbooks and other study materials. The standard survey courses in most popular academic disciplines are covered, as well as some advanced courses. For example, in my field of economics, Saylor offers not only the standard microeconomic and macroeconomic survey courses, but also courses in Austrian economics and monetary economics. A variety of decent-quality schools have apparently agreed to accept Saylor courses (e.g., Catholic University of America, Florida International University), including several of the aforementioned online providers like Purdue Global and SNHU as well as some foreign colleges and universities. I met with the Saylor leadership a number of years ago and was quite impressed.

In 2009, a Baltimore educational entrepreneur, Burck Smith, started StraighterLine, a business offering several dozen traditional college survey courses (e.g., English composition, microbiology, college algebra). Straighter-Line charges students by the month, not by the course, again incentivizing students to work to complete courses in a few weeks rather than several months. Students can take one course or five, finishing them in days or, theoretically, years.

Like Saylor Academy, StraighterLine itself is not accredited, nor does it offer any degrees. It has an interesting arrangement with the American Council of Education (the leading lobbyist for higher education interests in the United States) whereby ACE evaluates and recommends college credit for specific courses. Most of the major online providers mentioned above accept StraighterLine credit. A student there could easily get one-quarter or more of the credits needed for a degree, lowering the costs materially of obtaining a bachelor's diploma.

The MOOC Craze a Decade Later

A bit over a decade ago, the higher education world was agog over MOOCs (massive open online courses), ventures providing online courses for a low cost taught by superstar teachers and scholars, many from top universities like Stanford or MIT. These new ventures did not have the revolutionary impact many predicted, but are still an interesting addition to the American higher education landscape.

Coursera was founded by two computer science professors at Stanford in 2012. Working with universities and others, Coursera offers a wide variety of courses to scores of cooperating universities, some of them prestigious (e.g., University of Pennsylvania, University of Illinois). It said it had 124 million registered learners across the planet as of March 31, 2023—a vast educational enterprise. With a lot of hype, the company became a sizable for-profit venture traded on the New York Stock Exchange. It reached a market capitalization measured in the billions, for a time one of the many stars in the Silicon Valley firmament of tech-oriented companies. Its stock, selling at over $50 a share in early 2021, was at this writing three years later selling for about one-sixth of that. Why? Many factors were at work, but number one was that Coursera has never made an annual profit. Perhaps not surprisingly, the completion rate in MOOC-type instruction has also been very low.

Located a few dozen miles away in the San Francisco Bay Area is Udacity, a company founded in 2011 to offer MOOCs at low cost. It has since moved away from traditional college courses to more vocationally oriented offerings to develop employee-marketable skills. Perhaps it is on to something: it is not degrees that should matter in the long run, but rather the acquisition of knowledge and skills, inside or outside a collegiate environment. Another for-profit company that has undergone a sharp decline in its market valuation is 2U, a company that contracts not with students but with universities, including many prestigious ones, to provide educational services. It offers online services in return for a share of the revenue (the school charges its normal tuition).

A fundamental problem with many of these MOOC-type innovations: they offer courses but not degrees. As many observers have noted (Bryan Caplan being perhaps the most forceful recent critic), students want a *diploma* that signals to employers that "this student is probably at least reasonably competent with a good probability of being a good worker."

The sharp decline in the market valuations of for-profit companies with close ties to higher education is not surprising. Nationwide, enrollments are lower than a decade ago, with little prospect for expansion. The public is increasingly skeptical about the benefits of a college degree. State governments are increasingly angry at the way colleges are run. In some ways, higher education almost resembles a declining industry—sort of like the steel industry. Not many people are clamoring to start or invest in steel companies; to a much lesser extent, that may be how people feel toward universities.

It should be briefly noted that colleges and universities have increasingly contracted with private for-profit companies for educational services. Large companies like Pearson have helped develop online programs for schools. Others handle various business services, including technical computer-related tasks. Schools good at teaching English or business administration are not necessarily adept at managing and marketing non-instructional tasks.

Non-University Approaches to Advanced Instruction and Research

Universities are in the business of producing as well as disseminating knowledge. But there are other non-degree-granting ways of doing this, and they have exploded in importance over the past half century. In particular, there has been a large growth in think tanks, centers that produce research and sometimes do some noncredit forms of teaching to a broader public. Some of these are research institutes predating World War II (the Brookings Institution and the Council on Foreign Relations are prime examples). Some have ties to a university but are largely autonomous, such as the Hoover Institution at Stanford. The ultimate example, I suppose, is the Center for Advanced Study at Princeton, completely independent of the university, but home to some of the world's most extraordinary academic achievers, beginning with Albert Einstein. Additionally, a number of federally funded research facilities are administered by universities, such as the Lawrence Livermore National Laboratory, which is historically associated with the University of California but is a separate entity. A number of non-university-related research centers created before World War II are also going strong, perhaps most notably the Battelle Memorial Institute in Columbus, Ohio, which conducts research, manages laboratories, and promotes scientific inquiry. I speak more about these types of institutions in chapter 11.

A large wave of think tanks evolved in the 1970s and since. Some have a national orientation, such as the American Enterprise Institute, Cato Institute, and Heritage Foundation, housed in our nation's capital; and some are regionally oriented ones that have increasingly taken on a national mission, such as the Independent Institute in Oakland, California (producers of this book), the Manhattan Institute, and the Midwest's Heartland Institute. A large number are state-based, fairly small research centers such as the Mackinac Center and Buckeye Institute in the Midwest, the Texas Public Policy Foundation, and the Pacific Research Institute on the West Coast. Most of the state-based think tanks are members of the State Policy Network, which meets regularly to talk about issues of common interest. Some specialize in certain topics: especially relevant here would be the James G. Martin Center in North Carolina, which specializes in research and commentary related to higher education.

Most of the organizations mentioned above have a distinct right-of-center orientation. That is no accident: the feeling that universities have a strong left-of-center bias has led some individuals in the business community to promote organizations with a more market-based libertarian or conservative bent. If universities are going to promote leftish solutions to the problems and issues of the day, then noncollegiate organizations will sprout up to offer more conservative perspectives. Some of these organizations have serious scholars who are doing important research and offer competition to universities in expanding both the creation and the dissemination of knowledge. Indeed, a large proportion of the published research at some of these think tanks is produced by professors at top-flight universities, both in book form or in such respected high-brow magazines as *The Independent Review*, *Cato Journal*, or *City Journal*.[6]

"Necessity Is the Mother of Invention," Plato Once Said (More or Less)[7]

In the real world, innovation is constant, in part to avert creative destruction. The American academic world seemingly faces fewer "necessities" requiring "invention" in large part because of government subsidies. In spite of this, many practitioners of higher education are doing things differently than their competitors: there is some innovation going on in the way we provide services to more advanced students.

Most traditional higher education is heavily subsidized by governments, which reduces both creative destruction and the number of innovative higher education enterprises, and potentially restricts the free flow of ideas. The Platonic notion of necessity being the mother of invention spawned a whole new approach to creating and disseminating knowledge: the modern think tank, which has provided needed competition in the battle to advance the learning of our nation's citizenry. The spirit of innovation that led to the modern-day think tank needs to be extended into traditional higher education in the years ahead, the subject of the next several chapters of this book.

6

Reducing the Government's Role

IN THE FIRST five chapters, we suggested that the world of higher education differs dramatically from the "real world," a place where many exciting things happen, but where great successes are accompanied by losses. Creative destruction is at work. Higher education is woefully inefficient and costly, but mostly because of government support along with some from private philanthropies, it is largely protected from failure. Government subsidies to universities are in a sense a bit like public assistance (welfare) payments to individuals: the subsidies sustain them in the sense that they have enough material sustenance to live, but they also contribute to their failure to strive and to thrive in a vibrant market-based economy. Just as the welfare system reduces incentives to work, to save, and to maintain a traditional two-parent family unit, so higher education "welfare" has similar debilitating effects on American collegiate life. The welfare system of government subsidies of the ivory tower works to prolong mediocrity, inefficiency, and a contempt for excellence.

Governments are not as good at allocating resources as are private businesses, which are incentivized, disciplined, and governed by markets: that is, by the interaction of buyers and sellers of goods and services. Where governments are powerful and make most vital economic decisions, such as contemporary North Korea or the old Soviet Union, the inhabitants tend to have low incomes and limited resources, and they want to flee. They have little incentive to work hard, and the government-owned businesses, largely monopolies, likewise have little need or desire to reduce costs, to deliver a higher-quality product, or to innovate.

In the rest of this book, we will promote a more extensive use of markets in higher education. We point out that profits made by businesses are compensation for the resources they provide others who wish to buy the capital (machines, buildings, and so on) needed for production.[1] We will discuss how to increase the incentives for universities to strive for greater excellence and efficiency and to punish those who cling to their jobs but do little to effect positive change. We will suggest some ideas that make higher education a bit riskier for participants but also increase the probability of future success.

In a perfect world, the optimal situation would be to wipe out overnight the greatest inefficiencies and obstacles to progress in higher education. However, the obstacles to such change have a lot of support; the political milieu in which the nation operates requires less radical, more incremental initiatives. Much of the remaining chapters therefore deal with what some might view as halfway measures—things that will make higher education somewhat cheaper, more efficient, and qualitatively better, but do not change the basic structure of the system. The educationally optimal outcome, the most efficient outcome, and the politically feasible one no doubt differ, and we must seek improvements within that reality. As Winston Churchill supposedly said, "Democracy is the worst form of government—except all others."

Moreover, the political impediments to change may vary in magnitude across the United States. States with, for example, powerful teachers' unions and the tradition of a strong governmental role may be forced to move more cautiously and reluctantly toward reform. But, as we suggested earlier, migration of people and capital can work to nudge the slow-changing states into more aggressive action. If, as I feel pretty certain, enhanced market-based approaches to higher learning and research will make universities better, cheaper, and more effective, then resources (especially people) will move toward them. The word gets out as our "laboratories of democracy" do their experiments to improve our universities.

Getting the Federal Government Mostly out of Higher Education

I think the evidence increasingly suggests that American universities in the long run would benefit from the federal government stopping its involvement.

Until the Civil War, the universities began, thrived, and the nation prospered—with little government involvement in higher education. And where government becomes involved (rightly or wrongly), it tends to operate more efficiently when it is close to the people. When cities do a poor job of cleaning snow-covered streets or when local crime soars, the public makes life uncomfortable for city leaders, who are often literally their neighbors. The leaders in Washington, DC, however, are largely isolated from most of the population. Put into the context of higher education, politicians who formulate public policy are usually more responsive at the state and local levels than at the federal one.

As indicated earlier, the very modest role of the federal government in higher education before World War II expanded significantly in the postwar era and exploded after the passage of the Higher Education Act in 1965 and related federal student financial assistance programs, and again with the creation of the Department of Education in 1978. There is no question in my mind that by most indicators, higher education has gone downhill in the period after this increased federal involvement. As already indicated, it has become much costlier, learning outcomes have stagnated, public support of universities has plummeted, and enrollments have started shrinking for the first sustained length of time (over a decade) in American history.

It is rare if not unprecedented for the secretary of a cabinet department to call for abolishing the unit that he or she recently headed. Yet that is precisely what Betsy DeVos, secretary of education under Donald Trump, did.[2] I would be surprised if at least one previous secretary, Bill Bennett, didn't agree with her.[3] A large variety of Republican politicians have sought to eliminate or radically restructure the Education Department, beginning in 1980 with Ronald Reagan and including Bob Dole, Newt Gingrich, and at least five candidates for the 2024 presidential nomination. As previously indicated, the bill creating the Department of Education narrowly passed Congress and was opposed by many icons of the liberal establishment, including Senator Daniel Patrick Moynihan and the *New York Times*. Since its creation, education in America has deteriorated qualitatively, as indicated at the K–12 level by mediocre scores on standardized tests like the National Assessment of Educational Progress, a deterioration that cannot be blamed solely on the disruptions brought on by the COVID pandemic. Because higher education has worked hard to keep the public from getting objective measures of collegiate academic performance, we will cite only clear market-based evidence: the number of customers has declined consistently for over a decade, a decline that began before the COVID-related disruptions.

One of the strengths—probably the biggest one—of American higher education is its highly decentralized character. Local officials have a better sense of the communities in which colleges largely operate. They understand the local culture, history, and traditions better than bureaucrats headquartered in Washington, DC. Yet the US Department of Education has tried to impose ever more mandates on colleges and universities, in this century most famously and disastrously with its 2011 "Dear Colleague" letter ostensibly offering "guidance" related to enforcing Title IX's provisions of the Education Amendments of 1972, but in reality, imposing mandates on colleges with respect to the handling of allegations of sexual misconduct. The guidelines violated sacred traditions of due process dating back to the Magna Carta in 1215. The 2011 initiative led to a lowering of evidentiary standards for finding guilt of the accused (from "beyond a reasonable doubt" to a "preponderance of evidence"), denying the accused the right to cross-examine those alleging misconduct, sometimes having the prosecutor and determiner of guilt being the same person or office within the university, and so forth. Although the Trump administration sharply diluted the 2011 standards, they were largely revived during the Biden administration.[4] Aside from the issues relating to the substance of the regulations, the frequent altering of regulatory strictures with changing governmental control of the regulative apparatus can lead to huge inequities and inefficiencies. The "bottom line" is worth repeating: the great strengths of American higher education from its competitive, localized character were materially reduced by the federal intrusions of the past half century.

The dangers of an all-powerful education ministry became especially apparent when the Biden administration decided it wanted to forgive vast amounts of federal student loans. After the Supreme Court ruled that the administration lacked the authority to do that, the secretary of education went ahead and did it anyhow, using a different legal justification. Education Secretary Miguel Cardona, a bureaucrat, asserted the authority to make major public policy, contrary to commonly understood mandated procedures under the US Constitution. If there were no Department of Education, this dispute would have been avoided.

The extreme inefficiencies of government regulatory efforts can perhaps be best shown by looking at the efforts to simplify the FAFSA (Free Application for Federal Student Aid) form that anyone wanting federal financial assistance must complete. I attended a meeting at the Department of Education in 2007 chaired by the then secretary of education, Margaret Spellings, where a group gathered for several hours to discuss how to shorten the FAFSA form, then exceeding a hundred questions. Many, especially lower-income Americans, were intimidated by the length and complexity of the form and simply did not apply for assistance. Fast-forward thirteen years: the form was essentially the same length as in 2007, despite renewed appeals to shorten it, culminating in the FAFSA Simplification Act passed by Congress in December 2020. At this writing, over three years after the 2020 legislation passed, the Education Department has badly botched the release of the congressionally mandated revised form, throwing admissions and student financial aid offices of colleges into disarray—nearly two decades after serious efforts to revise the form began (during both Democratic and Republican administrations).

Introducing Markets and Creative Destruction: A Preview

To this point, this book has identified the problems confronting higher education, the broad benefits to the economy of creative destruction and of a competitive market-focused economy, the modest extent of creative destruction in American universities, and examples of current or planned innovative behavior. But we have mostly avoided answering the important question: What can we do to make higher education better, cheaper, more responsive to the needs of society? In this chapter we give a preview, a glimpse, at a path forward in getting potential solutions, which we will then discuss in greater detail in coming chapters.

The Critical Importance of Information

For markets to be efficient and welfare-creating contributors to humankind, the various players—the producers and the consumers, buyers and sellers—need accurate information to determine their optimal strategy. In the real world, buyers of consumer products might consult *Consumer Reports* or look for the UL certification on electrical products. Sellers of goods and services will read government or private sector reports on prices, sales volume, inventories, interest rates, and the like, along with daily publications like the *Wall Street Journal*. In short, they devour market information.

Economists have increasingly stressed the importance of information in a well-functioning economy. Early in the twentieth century, Ludwig von Mises argued that centrally planned and controlled socialist systems could not succeed because central planners lack the information necessary to make optimal decisions about producing and pricing goods and services.[5] His younger Austrian associate (and later winner of the Nobel Prize in Economics) Friedrich Hayek in 1945 argued that knowledge was critical to efficiently functioning markets.[6] In the 1960s, another future Nobel laureate, George Stigler, further strengthened an appreciation of the importance of good market knowledge to the efficient operation of an economy.[7] Since then, many economists have spoken about information, or the lack of it, in their analysis of markets. To this author's knowledge, no important economist has argued "ignorance is bliss" when it comes to the advancement of economic welfare.

Indeed, one of the arguments advanced to subsidize universities is that they are creators and disseminators of knowledge, important in creating the skills needed for innovation and in developing a well-ordered society. Yet universities are loath to collect or release information (knowledge) about *themselves*, about how well they are doing. Their accreditation agencies, which are typically controlled by the universities themselves at least indirectly, either fail to collect or actively hide information from the public on their performance.[8]

At a recent hearing in the House of Representatives, a witness selected by the Democratic minority, Stephanie Cellini of George Washington University, said: "If higher education was a well-functioning competitive market, poor-performing institutions and programs would be forced to close as students discover the program's low value. But the reality is that . . . higher education does not operate like other markets." At the same hearing, Andrew Gillen, then of the Texas Policy Foundation, pointed out that the higher education community sometimes spreads *false* information; it has asserted, for example, that public financial support for higher education has been falling in the early twenty-first century.[9]

What this suggests is that a major part of any market-based reform effort must be to reduce market ignorance in higher education. Universities often criticize the magazines and newspapers providing useful information to potential students with their college rankings, such as *U.S. News & World Report, Forbes, Washington Monthly,* and the *Wall Street Journal*. They also work to keep detailed criticisms of schools that are included in accreditation reports from public view and attention. They do not even administer basic tests on a systematic basis to measure such important things as changes in critical reasoning skills during the college years, or even the acquisition of basic knowledge. Why do they take this curious "ignorance is bliss" approach? To reduce competition and hide embarrassing evidence of mediocre outcomes. The School of Last Resort does not want potential students to know that its seniors know little more than its freshmen, that its top competitors are doing a better job, or even that over half the entrants to the school fail to graduate within six years. Even prestigious elite universities have shown embarrassing levels of performance by graduating students.[10] We make automobile manufacturers reveal the gasoline mileage achieved by their cars—why don't we make knowledge manufacturers (universities) tell us a bit more about what their students accomplish while at school? Elite universities don't want you to know how much more likely you are to get admitted if you are an actual or likely future donor. Do you think Donald Trump got into the Ivy League University of Pennsylvania as a transfer from much less elite Fordham University based on his intellectual prowess or academic achievement? Or, that his son-in-law Jared Kushner got into Harvard strictly on his academic prowess? These kinds of things colleges don't want publicized.

The whole recent Varsity Blues college admissions scandal revealed the sordid reality of preferential treatment in admissions, leading to criminal charges brought against dozens of parents who were accused of paying bribes to get their children into the University of Southern California and other schools through a scheme organized by William Rick Singer. Most parents were ultimately convicted. In most markets, *all* buyers can obtain a product if they pay the price. But in higher education, the price varies from individual to individual. Some potential purchasers of the service are deliberately refused the opportunity. The published, or sticker, price is nearly meaningless, as average discount rates exceed 50 percent. Student A may pay $60,000 in tuition, student B $25,000, and student C only $5,000. If auto dealers or big-box stores like Walmart or Target did that, they would both be sued and bankrupted very quickly. Why don't we try to emulate the practice of discount retailers (charging everyone about the same) in higher education?[11]

To be sure, in the real world, price discrimination sometimes serves a useful purpose. On any given airplane, passengers may be paying five or even ten different fares (even after adjusting for seat quality, first-class service, and so on). It is economically inefficient to fly half-full airplanes, since the cost of flying, say, 150 passengers is only a bit more (maybe 5 percent) than flying half that number. Per passenger operating costs fall sharply as occupancy rises. That is why cruise companies offer very low rates for last-minute bookings on empty ship cabins. Price discrimination can thus promote efficiency. Airlines that in an earlier era of federal price regulation often had flights with 50 percent occupancy, now operate close to 100 percent occupancy routinely in today's less regulated environment with price discrimination. A nontransportation example: bars that are packed at six o'clock may be nearly empty at three in the afternoon, so having "happy hours" to induce some to alter their drinking habits makes sense—better utilizing bar space.

These arguments work less well for higher education, but another one seemingly does: American society largely believes that college should be available for all, rich and poor alike, so we give "scholarships," or tuition discounts, for those unable to pay the sticker price. Colleges then engage in a form of private income redistribution—taking more from the rich than the poor, the Robin Hood approach to college admissions. The FAFSA form gives colleges detailed financial information on customers, improving the ability of schools to price discriminate. This, however, raises an interesting question: Are nongovernment entities, many of them private, the appropriate venue to attempt to redistribute income by denoting some customers as more worthy of low prices than others? Why do they do it but car dealers and Walmart do not?

The Major Players in Market-Based Reform

Colleges and universities have many moving parts and constituencies. Any reform of higher education designed to introduce a more robust set of market incentives into decision-making needs to look at all the major players.

Students

The whole reason universities were created was to increase knowledge, reasoning skills, virtue, and leadership, mostly in young individuals approaching adulthood. Although universities do other things unrelated to their students or instruction, such as running hospitals and clinics, doing massive amounts of research, and even providing community entertainment (through athletic competitions, theaters, musical programs, and the like), without students there would be no university.

Some schools, notably liberal arts colleges, community colleges, and for-profit institutions, are focused almost exclusively on their instructional mission. Yet students are often neglected in campus decision-making, even at schools where perhaps half or more of the revenue is derived from tuition and related fees. At schools with massive research offerings, undergraduate students are regularly treated as second-class members of the campus community. Poorly paid graduate students and adjunct faculty are used to teach so that the most senior faculty can do research or teach a small number of advanced graduate students. Within the university is a redistribution of resources from the undergraduates—who receive fairly low-cost education via large lectures, the internet, and low-paid teaching assistants—to graduate students who study with high-priced senior faculty, or to administrators such as DEI staff or student affairs employees trying to promote woke objectives about which most students have at best a marginal interest. I'll never forget a senior professor at Stanford telling me he was sending his own son to Claremont McKenna College, a fine liberal arts college, instead of to Stanford, even though his son could attend Stanford at virtually no cost. He told me that his son would get much more attention at Claremont than at Stanford, where faculty were obsessed with their research, assisted by a few select graduate students. As someone who has spent some time on both campuses, I suspect my friend was right.

A large portion of the revenues that many schools receive is only tangentially related to students, even though students are the raison d'être for institutional existence. The time has come, perhaps, to treat students as important and valued customers rather than cash cows that justify the public support of higher education. With respect to the majority of students attending public colleges and universities, that could be achieved by converting state government subsidies given to schools to *payments made to the students themselves*— more about that in coming chapters.

Many states have implemented educational choice programs at the K–12 level, providing financial assistance to help cover tuition and other fees for students wishing to attend private elementary and secondary schools (and sometimes, for high school kids taking college courses). By all indications, these programs have proved popular with parents. Why don't we extend that principle more generally to college attendance? Why don't we eliminate subsidy payments made to the producers of educational services and give them to the consumers?

There are numerous other variants on pricing educational services more rationally. Charge higher tuition for students wishing to go to classes in peak hours, when classrooms tend to be jammed. Why don't we charge lower tuition fees for attending summer school to help induce better use of facilities? Should students taking classes from popular but low-paid professors be assessed the same tuition fees as those taking classes from the sometimes higher-paid but less popular professors? Should students taking courses that are relatively cheap to provide because class sizes are large or because junior faculty or teaching assistants are poorly compensated pay the same tuition fees as those attending classes taught by high-paid professors to small numbers of students?

In the competitive, market-based private economy, better, more productive employees are paid better than those who are less productive. Should the same principle apply at colleges? Should students who do well in class and excel pay lower fees than those who do poorly? We already base scholarship aid in part on academic performance, but should we extend that principle? Should we more aggressively reward the best and the brightest?

Should state government funding be related to the likely future productivity of graduates? Mississippi state auditor Shad White made a superb point in a recent *Wall Street Journal* op-ed: "Electrical-engineering majors earn more than $71,000 after graduation in Mississippi . . . whereas sociology majors earn a third of that. The state nevertheless sends our public universities the same amount to educate the engineer as it does the sociologist. This makes no sense."[12]

Maybe colleges should learn a little from schools like Berea College or the College of the Ozarks and employ students more aggressively to provide non-instructional labor to the colleges, for example, by mowing the grass, painting buildings, and doing other chores, giving the colleges relatively dependable and low-priced labor while helping the students as well. Why cannot students both learn and help their schools by performing more semiskilled white-collar chores—for example, why can't senior or graduate journalism or marketing majors help produce materials for the admissions or the development office? Some of that is happening already, but why can't it be expanded?

One last student-related point: Schools spend vast amounts to make the college experience more fun with greater amenities. Crowded bare-bones dormitory rooms are being replaced with apartment-like facilities with more room, private bathroom facilities, and so on. Some campuses build water theme parks to allow students to float down a short "lazy river" while napping, drinking, or doing X-rated activities. I have heard that one college in North Carolina provides valet service to students driving their cars to campus. Some campuses have food-delivery robot carts delivering hot meals to the dorms. Near professional-level athletic teams that have only the remotest connection to the academic enterprise provide entertainment for students and a broader public, but do the students really want it? A case can be made that affluent students should have the opportunity to live at an upscale level, but almost *mandating* that for entire student bodies is inappropriate, particularly when some of the funds directly or indirectly may be coming from tax subsidies, even at so-called private schools.

The Faculty

The other major player at universities that is absolutely critical is the faculty—the ones providing both the instruction benefiting students and the research that potentially benefits society. The incentive system, as manifested by the salaries paid, is seriously flawed. First of all, the publish-or-perish environment at many schools leads to nice salaries and benefits to those writing a lot of academic journal articles, giving them a lighter teaching load. Some who are superb teachers make far less than their well-published colleagues. Why should a professor who published two articles last year in the *Journal of Last Resort* that few people read or cite, while doing a mediocre job of teaching a small number of students, get a higher salary and bigger raises than a professor with fine teaching evaluations who instructs far more students? Particularly if the latter professor also conscientiously advises students on such non-instructional but important things as choosing a career and helps them get jobs via carefully written references and even conversations with potential employers?

Put differently, *the criteria used in determining faculty rewards are largely defined by the faculty themselves to suit their preferences and do not necessarily serve the broader interests of society.* This is furthered by the practice of awarding tenure, or essentially lifetime employment contracts, to faculty after a given number of years (often seven) of service. Although tenure has legitimate benefits, such as insulating faculty against attacks by the administration or fellow faculty based on their views that diverge from that of the majority of the college community, it sometimes comes at a high cost. What if enrollments in the classics plummet, yet the college has three highly paid senior professors in that area when at most one professor of Latin or Greek is needed to meet teaching obligations?

As one who has taught across seven decades, from the 1960s through the current one (2020s), I will probably incur the ire of some colleagues when I say that faculty are on average underutilized. Some work fifty or even sixty hours a week with only short vacation breaks, maybe for a total of twenty-four hundred hours a year, but at many schools some charitably work thirty hours a week for maybe thirty-two to thirty-five weeks a year, roughly eleven hundred hours, far less than the work involvement of the typical nonacademic worker. And what other professional field gives its workers paid "sabbatical leaves"? Typically, doctors and lawyers who work more get paid proportionally more from their patients, clients, or employers: why shouldn't the same principle be applied to faculty? A complication here: a fair amount of faculty instruction today is done by members of labor unions, making change more expensive and difficult.

Why don't we restructure faculty compensation? One crude way: lower every faculty member's salary by 10 percent but allocate all that salary reduction money to bonuses for superior performance. Also mandate that salary increases cannot be proportionally equally distributed to all. At least insist that all salary increase monies be distributed on the basis of merit or recent achievement rather than guaranteed to all employees independent of their individual accomplishments.

For both faculty and students, why is the school "year" seven or at most eight months long of actual work? Students complete a bachelor's degree typically after about twenty-eight months of classroom study and work—over a period of roughly forty-five months, nearly four years. Why not do academic work about nine months a year and get a degree with the same amount of instruction in about three calendar years—allowing graduates to enter the real world of adult work a year earlier, making maybe an extra $40,000 or more in earnings? (This is approximately the Thales College model.) Why does it take three years to get a bachelor's degree at Oxford, German universities, or Thales College, but four years in most US schools?

If we are going to persist in the standard four-year degree, why not concentrate instruction largely into a three-year time frame, with students spending several months (say six) doing two internships in both their junior and senior years? This would help students and employers alike in better matching the labor force requirements of buyers (employers) with the skills of sellers (graduating students) of labor services.

The Administration

Reiterating, I would submit that, on average, American universities today are not much if any better than they were, say, forty to fifty years ago—indeed, they may very well be worse. Teaching quality has certainly not improved, students are studying less, and although faculty research output per person is up somewhat, the practical significance of that is sharply reduced by the unimportance of and even scholarly indifference to much of the published product. But personnel costs per student have risen significantly, even adjusting for inflation. Why? Partly because administrative staffs have exploded. Many schools now employ twice as many "administrators" as faculty, if not more. A few years ago, in 2018, I calculated that if we had maintained the same faculty-administrator ratio as in 1976, we could have lowered tuition fees on average by about 20 percent.[13]

Some administrators are taking up new and likely unconstitutional tasks such as achieving a more desired racial mix—to put it uncharitably but accurately, these DEI apparatchiks have been hired to enforce the administration's racist objectives. Why don't we simply get rid of all of them? Do we need umpteen "sustainability" coordinators? What does "sustainability" have to do with learning? Does every academic unit within a university need its own publicity operation? They didn't used to have one—historically, one modest-size office served the entire institution. What do they do that truly increases the value to students or researchers who are doing the real work of the university?

An area with a big growth in funding over the past generation is development or advancement—the fundraisers. Universities say they are net revenue enhancers—bringing in more revenue than they spend. My own experience is there is a lot of waste: too many luxurious cocktail parties, excessive travel, often on expensive private aircraft, and so on.

Similarly, the student affairs bureaucracy at most schools has grown enormously, often to promote woke ideological objectives as much as to handle legitimate functions relating to students. Should universities even own and run dormitories to house and feed students? Are they in the education business or the food and lodging business? Do students that are allowed more freedom with respect to housing and food consumption gain or suffer as a consequence? What are the academic and disciplinary records of students largely free of student affairs bureaucracies (those who commute or live in fraternities and sororities, for example) relative to those under closer university supervision? Does empirical evidence support current practice? I don't know, but I am highly skeptical.

The growth in bureaucracy ultimately raises the costs of educating college students, and that increase has been sizable. Figure 6.1 shows that the number of administrators per hundred students went from slightly over two in 1976

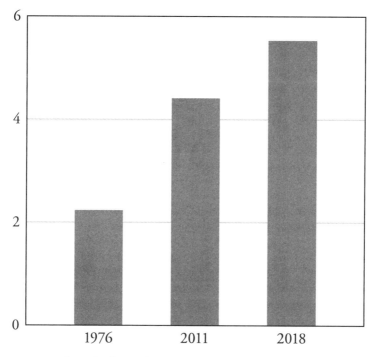

Figure 6.1 Number of college administrators per 100 students

Sources: National Center for Education Statistics, Digest of Education Statistics, 2022, Table 315.10, https://nces.ed.gov/programs/digest/d22/tables/dt22_315.10.asp; National Center for Education Statistics, Digest of Education Statistics, 2022, Table 303.10, https://nces.ed.gov/programs/digest/d22/tables/dt22_303.10.asp.

to well over five in 2018. If each administrator cost $100,000 (salary plus typically generous fringe benefits), administrative costs per student rose well over $3,000 annually per student, or close to $15,000 over a typical period earning a bachelor's degree. Have students gained that much in benefits from having a collegiate nanny state imposed on them? I think not.

Intercollegiate Athletics

Most American universities have moderately extensive intercollegiate athletic programs. To be sure, some prestigious schools have no such programs, or only small operations to facilitate the physical education of students, run at low cost. The University of Chicago, Cal Tech, and MIT do not have big intercollegiate athletic programs, but all are successful universities. Honest accounting techniques suggest that a majority of the larger schools lose money on their intercollegiate ventures. (I work at a university that loses over $20 million annually—roughly $1,000 per student—and a majority of students rarely attend events.) It makes some alumni happy that they have these programs, and a dozen or two collegiate football and basketball powers claim that they break even on their programs, even though I am dubious of those claims since capital costs are usually ignored or grossly understated.[14]

There are other issues. What do big-time college athletic programs have to do with higher education? They are virtually nonexistent elsewhere in the world. Why are they part of our universities? Is it immoral to pay coaches ten times as much as university presidents, largely financed from the underpayment of student athletes who only recently have started getting *any* compensation for their services, and even now collect no salaries? The system is irrational, expensive, morally dubious. It is sustained by the fact that these programs often provide great entertainment.[15] There have been some sensible suggestions as to how to rein in exploding costs without destroying the entertainment value of college athletics.[16] One other aspect of college athletics deserves minimally cursory mention: Title IX's impact. The mandate of rough gender equality has led to the addition of some women's sporting events and teams, but also to the elimination of some so-called "minor" men's sports (e.g., fencing, gymnastics, sometimes even swimming). Also, many believe as I do that the rise of biological males self-identifying as females is working to ruin (or severely damage) the integrity of women's sports such as swimming and track and field.

Other Important Participants (Trustees, Alumni, Political Leaders)

A number of other groups consider themselves part of the university community. Let me briefly mention three of them here, discussing them more in later chapters.

The Governing Board

Most universities have a governing board, with names like board of trustees, board of regents, board of visitors, and the like. These boards are usually empowered to make major decisions for the university, such as who will be the president, what the tuition fees will be, whether new programs should be started or old ones phased out, and so on. Theoretically, these boards have enormous power. Yet the reality is often different. Many boards are rubber stamps for almost anything the university administration wants. As one friend and former student who is on a governing board put it recently, "We are . . . potted plants." Many members are on the board because of a large donation (especially at private schools) or political connections (public schools). Many view board service as a prestigious sinecure and devote little time to university affairs. Yet some trustees are busybodies who try to involve themselves in what are normally administrative decisions—for example, who the next football coach should be.

Many questions arise. How long should trustee terms be? Should trustees be expected to devote a good deal of time to university affairs? Should trustees rely on the president and other key officials exclusively for campus-relevant information? Alternatively, should they have their own independent conduit of news on campus happenings? (Short answer: yes.) Should trustees be rewarded in some fashion for their service?

Alumni and Donors

Graduates of a college sometimes feel they are now *members* of the college community. This is particularly true at private schools with sizable tuition fees. In a sense, they view their university in the same way many also view fraternity or sorority membership, believing their past contributions and continued fondness for the institution give them a right to play some role in campus decision-making. This belief shows up in a variety of contexts. Two that get a good deal of attention relate to athletics and facilities, particularly where alumni are helping to finance new buildings. Alumni at superpower athletic powers think they should minimally have the ability to get tickets to big games and sometimes even a voice on such things as the hiring or firing of an athletic director, the building of a new stadium or practice facility, and so forth. Some alums whose financial contributions are truly monumental (think of Nike founder Phil Knight at the University of Oregon or Michael Bloomberg at Johns Hopkins, both billion-dollar donors to their alma maters) probably feel that since they are paying for a great many university activities, they should have a disproportionate role in decision-making.

Politicians

State universities are subsidized as a result of appropriation decisions made by legislators and governors. As a consequence, sometimes those politicians believe they should have a role in campus decision-making. As public support for colleges and universities has fallen, politicians in some states have become more aggressive in trying to alter the direction in which universities move, both by the way and by the amount they allot subsidies, and by direct regulation. Moreover, these politicians are generally involved in the selection of university trustees. Like the Federal Reserve, which has cherished and largely earned independence from the politicians in Congress or presidents and their aides, state universities in most states in modern times have had a fair amount of freedom to act without heavy-handed political intervention, although the amount of involvement has risen considerably in recent years. What is the optimal amount of involvement? Should the politicians even be subsidizing institutions at all (as opposed to not subsidizing them or providing assistance to students, not institutions)? These questions are addressed extensively in coming chapters. Given the diversity in political cultures among the states, the answers may vary across the country.

Conclusion

American universities need to change. They especially need to develop incentives to do things better and more efficiently. Market mechanisms that produce efficiencies are underused. This chapter sets the stage for a more focused and specific analysis of how to introduce markets more thoroughly into higher education, resulting in both greater successes and greater failures—creative destruction.

One thing that differentiates colleges from private businesses is ownership. We know precisely who owns a private corporation and is thus "the boss." Although many were unhappy, no one doubted after Elon Musk bought Twitter that he was in charge and could make major decisions, firing many and even changing the name of the flagship product. But the ownership and control of universities is far more dubious.[17] A challenge in implementing any reform is figuring out who is in charge. Who makes the decisions? At for-profit schools, the answer is straightforward, as ownership is similar to what it is at other competitive market-based enterprises. But at other schools that dominate higher education delivery, the issue is more ambiguous. Instituting market-based reforms can happen only when there is clarity as to who is in charge. Unfortunately, it is not always clear, and until that issue is resolved, radical market-based reform is unlikely to proceed very far.

7

Reimagining Higher Education: Reducing the Federal Role

GOVERNMENTS ARE THE antithesis of markets. They make decisions centrally rather than rely on the invisible hand of market resource allocation. In the previous chapter, in recognition of this, we called for the elimination of the US Department of Education. Even if government were to be involved, I argued, it should be the government relatively close to the people, particularly given the large cultural and political differences across the vast land that is America.

Yet even under the most ideal of political circumstances, that is not going to happen overnight. The federal involvement in higher education is so extensive that ending it will take time, and the federal government performs some functions, albeit very imperfectly, that need to be addressed. For example, a huge portion of American college students depend at least in part on the federal government to finance their schooling. Should that be ended overnight, or phased out gradually? The legal environment for some innovative private solutions, such as income share agreements, is perhaps a bit murky, so maybe new legislation is needed. Should the actually useful information-providing role that the federal government now plays in helping customers (potential students) assess their college options be continued, expanded, or privatized? In short, simply abolishing the Department of Education is not the only policy issue or solution needing attention in reimagining American universities and making them more responsive to market forces.

Eliminating or Redoing Federal Student Financial Assistance

Inefficient and damaging as the federal student financial aid programs are, eliminating them instantly is politically infeasible and would also cause hardship that would perhaps be avoidable if the transition to new approaches to financial assistance is gradual. Several major reforms of the existing federal student loan and grant programs would make them more responsive to market forces and save money. Although the ideal would be to get the federal government out of the higher education business quickly, a few "second-best" approaches might be more politically doable and would make meaningful progress.

Restricting and Reforming Loan Programs

A significant proportion of funds lent under the federal student loan programs does not even go to directly fund the education of undergraduate students. There are so-called PLUS loans made to the *parents* of students that are only tangentially related to funding student participation in higher education. There are a multitude of smaller programs, some of them going back decades, such as the subsidized Federal Work-Study Program dating from the 1960s. And, of course, there is the large Pell Grant program for several million students. In the interest of simplification and efficiency, why not simply have one or two programs instead of well over a dozen?

Here are a few reforms that would sizably reduce the dollar magnitude of federal obligations while still maintaining the principle that deserving lower-income students could borrow from the federal government. *First, limit program eligibility to four or perhaps five years.* Undergraduate degrees are most often completed in four years, with a few specialized professional programs like architecture sometimes taking five years. Students should be incentivized to finish their programs promptly. And does it make sense to subsidize the perpetual student, one who gets two or three degrees rather than enter the labor force? Why not put a lifetime limit on the number of years of federal subsidy permitted?

Second, put in some performance standards. Stop lending money to students with substandard academic performance who are highly unlikely to obtain their degree in a timely fashion. Students barely hanging on in school on academic or disciplinary probation should be denied loans after a semester or two of substandard performance. Incentivize reasonably high-quality academic excellence, not mere college attendance.

Third, eliminate support for advanced degrees. Why should someone earning an advanced degree that dramatically improves one's income get support from the federal government, particularly when the federal government does not have loan programs for far less educated individuals wanting a year or two of postsecondary school training to get a vocationally specific skill certificate, such as one denoting computer coding expertise or adeptness as a court reporter? Why should a person wanting an MBA from a top school be able to borrow from the federal government when a high school graduate wanting to start an auto body repair shop cannot? Most of the outstanding large-balance student loans (over $100,000) are for students who have pursued advanced degrees—and who on average earn a high income.

Fourth, make a serious effort to collect student loan debts, and stop de facto loan forgiveness programs. To cite just one statistic, outstanding student loan debt owed by borrowers *over the age of 60* more than tripled in the decade 2011 to 2021, while the debt of those under 30 increased by a modest 10 percent.[1] The older borrowers almost certainly borrowed most of their money many years ago—and have just let loan balances accumulate, perhaps expecting that loan forgiveness or death at some point would remove this financial obligation. If loans were administered on a true commercial basis, the program would be less burdensome to the American taxpayer and more equitable, particularly to those Americans unable to borrow cheaply from the federal government or those who have honorably worked to repay their debts.

Demanding "Skin in the Game"

The loan programs are used to entice students to attend college. One can question the propriety of that in a world where at least one-third of attendees do not graduate and at least one-third of those that do are "underemployed" (doing low-skilled jobs) a significant amount of time. Nonetheless, prospective enrollees are told, "Come to our school using federal financing, which you can pay back after you graduate with your enhanced earnings." As mentioned, many students don't graduate at all, and others end up taking jobs they could have received with a high school diploma.[2] Moreover, many colleges knowingly accept students with a low probability of success, based on poor high school grades or admission test scores. Yet the colleges entice the students to come, bringing with them their federally financed tuition fees for a semester or two. If the student drops out or defaults on her loan, the federal government (and the taxpayers and bondholders who finance it) lose, not the school.

Colleges know that the success rate of poor students is low, but they take them anyhow to gain tuition revenue (and sometimes additional state subsidies). This leads to high loan default rates. But what if the colleges had to cosign for the loans, meaning they would end up paying all or part of the loan principal if the student stopped paying? Colleges would be incentivized to accept far fewer marginal students. There would be fewer loan defaults. Universities would have to make a decision: Is student applicant A likely to repay his loan, or are we likely to get stuck with the repayment ourselves? Schools would be forced to act closer to what businesses in the private market sector do all the time—assess probable costs and benefits. Taxpayers would save and federal budget deficits would fall a bit. Given the large amounts of defaults on student loans, the potential liability might be in the many millions of dollars annually, which, at the margin, might force some schools into bankruptcy. But I view that as a *good* outcome: Creative destruction would be at work, stimulated by market forces previously suppressed by government handouts. It would facilitate a needed restructuring of higher education and sharpen the negative consequences of policies that do not serve the public (or even usually private) good.

Assessing Alternatives to Federal Funding

The ideas above would improve a costly and inefficient system of federal support. But why not go all the way—get the federal government completely out of the business of financing college student education? Again, Plato's observation that necessity is the mother of invention applies here. Ingenious people will find better ways of financing student attendance at institutions of higher learning. Some possibilities follow.

Private Loans

If the federal government ceased making loans, the private sector would expand its lending activity. Banks and other lenders already make small and midsize loans to consumers to purchase or remodel houses, to purchase cars or boats, and a multitude of other things. If financial institutions can lend money for purchasing cars, why not for paying college tuition bills? In fact, some of them already do, and private student loans outstanding in recent years approach roughly $100 billion, far from insignificant.

Private loans have been vastly dwarfed in magnitude by the trillion-dollar federal program, so much larger because the interest rates charged on private loans are higher than what the federal government charges, and because the federal government has created a series of special perks for its borrowers not duplicated in the private market, such as generous loan "forbearance" provisions and, even more important, loan repayment programs based on income with generous loan forgiveness provisions after a period of ten years or so. The Biden administration's loan forgiveness effort created a vast moral hazard problem—students no doubt increasingly asked, Why not borrow from the federal government, since there is a high probability that I won't have to pay back anything or perhaps only a part of the loan?

The accounting reality is that the federal loan programs have been operating at a sizable loss, ultimately subsidized by the taxpayers (and often financed by debt issued by a federal government seemingly incapable of balancing its own budget even in good times). The banks and related private financial institutions have probably made an operating profit on their student loans, but not extraordinarily large or more banks would make them (many banks simply don't even make any student loans on a regular basis). Bank lending profits are a legitimate compensation for the capital they use and the risks they take.

Income Share Agreements (ISAs)

Before the 1980s, most students needing outside financial assistance to help pay for college relied on privately owned banks. The explosion in the federal loan programs after 2000, with their low interest rates relative to private lending and the absence of typical commercial standards for assessing risk, has meant that taxpayers are generally responsible for unpaid loans. Yet I think if the federal government appropriately abandoned the student loan market, a modestly used financing method, income share agreements (ISAs), might suddenly become popular. With an ISA, a financing organization makes a deal with the student needing funds. Suppose the student estimates her funding requirements over the four years needed to earn a bachelor's degree to be $80,000 beyond the funds she has available through savings, parental contributions, anticipated earnings while in college, and so on. The funding organization agrees to pay $80,000 to the student, perhaps in four $20,000 annual checks (or, more likely, $10,000 for each of eight semesters). The student, in turn, agrees to pay the funder a percentage of postschool (and hopefully postgraduation) earnings for a negotiated period of time, perhaps ten years. For example, perhaps the student agrees to pay 15 percent of her earnings in excess of $20,000 a year for ten years. Suppose the student graduates and does well, earning on average $100,000 annually over the decade (perhaps starting at $60,000 and rising to $125,000 in the ninth and tenth postgraduation year). Over the decade the student will pay back $120,000, giving the ISA owner a modest but decent positive return on the investment of $80,000. On the students who do especially well in postgraduate employment, the financial investor makes a huge profit, on others who are less successful, they suffer losses—as is generally the case with financial institutions in the private sector.

The neatest thing about ISAs is that they let labor market realities determine the terms of the agreement. An electrical engineering major at a prestigious school like MIT or Georgia Tech will probably have no trouble getting an ISA on reasonable terms, since the probable postcollege earnings are very high, reaching into the six digits before the end of the ISA contract. Similarly, a bright college graduate wanting $100,000 or so to help finance an MBA at Penn's Wharton School, Northwestern, Duke, or UCLA will probably have no trouble getting an ISA on decent terms, since graduates from those programs routinely make six-digit salaries from the moment they get their degree. Similarly, prospective physicians and lawyers might well find ISAs an appealing means of financing their professional education.

But what about the gender studies, sociology, history, art, or keyboard music majors attending mid- or lower-quality institutions where college graduation is more risky and postgraduate earnings are usually meager? Investors either will simply not finance the education of these students on the grounds that it is too risky, or they will impose costly terms—say requiring the student to pay 20 percent of earnings beyond $15,000 a year for twenty-five years after graduation. These terms would discourage many from majoring in these low-paying fields, or even attending less successful colleges, while the demand for engineers, computer scientists, MBAs, accountants, economists, and other relatively high-paying jobs would remain robust and applications to higher-quality schools would soar. Schools with a generally poor record of graduating students with good incomes would suffer, and many would probably close—*creative destruction working beautifully*. Similarly, even without ISAs and their high repayment terms, students are already starting to abandon some woke majors whose graduates have difficulty in obtaining employment—markets again at work. ISAs are potentially an important instrument in making higher education more efficient and a better investment for the nation. Survival of the fittest.

Under the current system, the federal government treats a sociology or gender studies major from Ball State University exactly the same as a computer science major at MIT. As a consequence, the supply of gender studies majors is abundant (many woke progressives wanting to promote a political agenda)— huge supply, low demand for graduates, and, hence, low salaries. We are encouraging and subsidizing these majors (especially since many effectively default or only partially repay their federal student loan obligations) relative to majors that society, working through markets, deems more valuable. The nation needs engineers and computer scientists more than it needs gender studies or sociology majors, and this market-based approach accordingly recognizes that and works to correct the imbalance. Currently, the computer scientist at MIT is almost certainly burdened far more paying for college than the far less needed gender studies major who is implicitly subsidized.

Over time in a world with heavy ISA funding of college education, labor markets would adjust to changes. We would anticipate that a much-needed sharp decline in the supply of low-paying majors would occur initially, and probably an increase in the supply of high-paying ones. Ultimately, of course, this would alleviate the supply-demand imbalance in the labor market, one in which many gender studies graduates end up as baristas or in other low-paying jobs. In the long run, such a rebalancing would lead to far fewer but better-paid sociologists and other currently underemployed majors. We would have a much-needed increase in highly productive individuals in high-demand areas. Also, we would expect that schools whose students have trouble getting decent ISA financing would lose enrollments relative to schools with a better reputation. The academic flight to quality, already occurring in higher education despite massive government subsidies, would accelerate, leading to somewhat fewer, but qualitatively better, colleges providing training more in accord with the actual labor market needs of the nation as reflected in demand-and-supply conditions.

An intriguing possibility: wealthy colleges with large endowments could invest in their own students. Suppose Harvard, Yale, or Princeton had ISA contracts with 15,000 students each averaging $100,000. That would be $1.5 billion for each school, well under 10 percent of the school's endowment (3 percent at this writing at Harvard). Perhaps 10 to 20 percent of the students at these schools could get some ISA financing from their own schools.

A brief digression: I would note, however, that these schools with about $3 million in endowment funds for each student should be able to offer *free* tuition to *all* students, since the schools could easily spend $120,000 annually for each student (including graduate and professional ones) *from endowment funds alone*—that is roughly four times the amount a typical state university spends to fund its operation. In fairness, these ultra-wealthy schools today generally do not charge students from families with annual incomes of less than $100,000 much if anything in fees.

The United States has lots of charitable foundations with large endowments. Many of them, such as the Gates or Lumina foundations, have donated heavily to higher education entities over the years. Why don't they use part of their endowments to help finance ISAs? I think an idea like this would appeal to some philanthropists like Warren Buffett, who has greatly augmented the already substantial resources of the Gates Foundation.

ISAs have not yet caught on big, although some schools (notably Purdue) have used them on a modest scale. Part of the reason may be related to the enforceability of ISA contracts. Federal and possibly state laws may need some revisiting to enable this useful financing mode to gain greater traction. Critics liken ISAs to indentured servitude, and there is a bit of a similarity.

Before the American Revolution, thousands of poor Englishmen came to the American colonies, agreeing to work for very low compensation for a fixed number of years (sometimes seven)—in return for having the costly expense of transportation across the Atlantic covered. As an American economic historian, I think the indentured servitude of the seventeenth and eighteenth centuries was an ingenious solution to a major financing problem, a solution that brought thousands of hardworking new Americans that helped a nation be born and flourish. In a sense, the federal H-1B visa program for skilled immigrants has some dimensions of "indentured servitude" or ISAs.[3] Three hundred years later, ISAs today can help give hardworking and capable Americans (including immigrants) an opportunity to achieve the American dream.

I have one nagging concern about the widespread use of ISAs. The rapacious federal bureaucracy would demand regulatory jurisdiction. I fear organizations like the Consumer Financial Protection Bureau would try to impose constraints that would make ISAs less attractive and probably less responsive to market conditions. The solution in my judgment is not to restrict the use of ISAs but rather to restrain the regulatory agencies, arguably even abolishing them or at least prohibiting them from asserting jurisdiction over ISAs.

Changes in Pell Grants

An exceedingly popular form of federal student financial assistance is the Pell Grant program, dating from the 1970s, providing funds for students from lower-income backgrounds. The existing program has clearly not worked as planned, and as indicated earlier, the proportion of students getting degrees who come from low-income families is, at best, about the same as it was a half century ago, before the federal financial aid programs were inaugurated or, if they had been, were still very small. If it becomes politically infeasible to eliminate Pell Grants, it might be possible, and would certainly be fruitful, to convert them into a voucher program for low-income students.

Under the existing Pell Grant program, college financial aid offices annually receive funds from the federal government designed to cover most anticipated Pell Grant costs for the coming academic year, based on past enrollment trends. The money goes to the schools, not to the students. Why? Why not convert the program into a true voucher that is made payable to the student, exclusively for use for college tuition fees and related expenses? The schools are not then routinely getting a big check from the federal government to be used for student aid. Instead, the students themselves get the money—consumer sovereignty at work. They, not university bureaucrats, have ultimate control over the use of the money. And students can make a last-minute decision to change colleges without bureaucratic hassle. No longer waiting in line at the financial aid office to discuss Pell Grant eligibility for the coming year. The Pell Grant program in recent years has cost roughly $25 billion annually—enough for $5,000 scholarships for five million low-income students. To make the program much more effective, the amount could be varied not only with income but also with student achievement. Give bonuses for high achievement and *reduce* awards for mediocre performance. *Incentivize students to perform well in college.* Limit grants to four years to likewise encourage diligent application to studies. Give students who complete their degree in three years a bonus of perhaps $2,500. Scholarship (Pell Grant) assistance from the federal government should be related more to academic performance rather than merely the number of credit hours earned.

Standardized Testing: The National College Equivalence Exam (NCEE)

Arguably the one potentially useful thing the federal government does now is collect lots of information about students, schools, different majors, and so on, mostly through the IPEDS (Integrated Postsecondary Education Data System) of the National Center for Education Statistics. One critical piece of data that no one collects, however, is the measure of educational achievement during a student's college years. What if we administered a standardized test of general knowledge that highly educated persons should know at the conclusion of high school (or at the beginning of college) and then again late in the last year of schooling right before graduation? This information would be available to a wide variety of audiences: graduate schools and future employers, as well as students assessing which colleges to attend and even organizations like magazines that rank schools.

The proposed National College Equivalence Examination (NCEE) could be administered by existing organizations such as the College Board (formerly the College Entrance Examination Board), which governs the use of the SAT, or by the ACT (the name of both the administrating organization and the test), or directly with the Educational Testing Service, which administers the SAT. Or it could be run by a new nonprofit private organization funded from modest fees collected from those taking the test. Or, less preferable in my judgment, it could be administered by the National Center for Education Statistics, as it is the largest collector and depository of college performance data. One of the few positive things the US Department of Education does is compile data for the College Scorecard, an imperfect but useful source for much sought-after consumer information. It gives potential students data on retention and graduation rates, earnings of students in many majors, and other useful information.

In my opinion, a well-respected NCEE test could substitute for existing accreditation. Every school would be assessed by the same yardstick. Perhaps new private organizations will evolve that would start awarding degrees to students with a high NCEE performance—whether achieved through home-schooling and studying or by attendance at a university. A student could accumulate credits from several institutions and then let the NCEE, not a single school, determine whether he has achieved the equivalent of a college degree. A bonus: the anticompetitive accreditation racket would be weakened, maybe even destroyed.

Other Changes in Federal Higher Education Policies

Although colleges are impacted by federal regulatory policies relating to environmental issues like climate change, those regulations are not targeted specifically to the college community. Some forms of federal regulation, like minimum wage laws, have existed for decades and have occasionally had some impact on college costs. A few regulatory rules, however, significantly affect colleges. An old one relates to legislation regulating research on human subjects, which beginning in the 1970s was subject to federal mandates. It necessitated, for example, that colleges create committees called institutional review boards to evaluate the appropriateness of research efforts involving students in experiments, of the data to be gathered, and so on. I have not seen much serious scholarly work suggesting that human-subject research abuses were previously substantial, or that they have notably declined since that legislation passed, and wonder whether other remedies for abuses, such as private lawsuits, can just as effectively curb them.[4] We return to the research dimension of colleges in chapter 11.

Taxing University Endowments, Donations, and Compensation Payments

The large accumulations in university endowments are given privileged status by governments, especially the federal one. Individuals can lower their income tax or estate tax burden by making gifts to colleges and universities. Colleges can receive massive investment income from dividends or capital gains from the sale of stock or other assets, and that income is not taxed by the federal (or other) governments. But should it be? Why should Microsoft or General Motors or Merck be taxed, but not Harvard and Yale? For that matter, why should some individuals be allowed to lower their tax burden by making gifts to their universities, but not to their own children?

I noted earlier that some evidence suggests big endowments partly go toward making life better for faculty and staff. A sense is growing that giving university endowments special tax status may be inappropriate. Ironically, progressives, typically Democrats, are generally big proponents of "taxing the rich," but they did not push hard to tax the endowments of large private universities, or even some state ones, most notably the University of Texas. Why? I think the answer is simple: universities have been major supporters of progressive causes by providing ideas, personnel, and even money to support left-wing governments. Conservatives, who tend to be anti-tax, have not pushed taxing universities. However, that may be changing a bit. In 2017, the Tax Cuts and Jobs Act imposed a 1.4 percent tax on the investment income of a few dozen universities with endowment assets exceeding $500,000 per student. Another provision of tax law may be susceptible to change. Most private foundations must spend at least 5 percent of their endowment annually to maintain favorable tax status. Universities, however, are exempted, and many universities pay out only 4 percent or so of their endowment principal annually to fund university activities. Why the special treatment of universities compared with that of, say, the Ford, Rockefeller, and Gates Foundations?

At this writing, the 2017 law involves tax reductions expiring in 2025 that will need to be reauthorized or canceled. Decisions made by Congress, probably in 2025, will determine what precisely happens. The liberal elements that would normally work to eliminate the federal endowment tax have been somewhat uneasy or even opposed to the legacy admission preferences shown by many private colleges, which might contribute to a continuance or even expansion of existing endowment taxation.

Indeed, I could see efforts made to flatly prohibit the favorable tax treatment of donations by private donors to universities that have extraordinarily high levels of wealth, which many view as enclaves for the kids of the rich. Also, many believe senior university officials should not be getting multi-million-dollar payments for running these institutions so dependent on tax subsidies and or preferences. Multimillion-dollar severance payments that are occasionally made to university presidents (and especially football or basketball coaches!) could well be subject to less favorable treatment in the future, especially in light of declining public support of higher education among the American public.

Conclusion

The federal government has significantly worsened higher education in America, and eliminating the twin evils of the federal student loan and related assistance programs and the US Department of Education is a much-needed reform. But it may not be obtainable overnight, and political compromise may be necessary. This chapter looks at many "second-best" solutions to the problem of excessive federal involvement in higher education. A good example: if federal student loans are to persist, at least force colleges to have some skin in the game. Perhaps the federal government could make it less risky for financial investors to make more income share agreement contracts. Converting Pell Grants into student-controlled vouchers is probably a good idea. Using the formidable data base of the National Center for Education Statistics more aggressively to improve information for consumers on colleges is another one. However, a majority of students at four-year universities in the United States attend schools owned by state governments, and it is to that topic we now turn.

What Can State Governments Do?

A LARGE MAJORITY of students attending American colleges and universities enroll in schools that state governments subsidize and usually, in fact, "own." Most college-educated Americans identify with public state universities, not elite private enclaves serving a small minority of students.

To be sure, most of the top schools as measured by media outlets like *U.S. News & World Report* are private. At this writing, the two best universities according to *U.S. News*, two campuses of the University of California (Berkeley and Los Angeles), are tied for the fifteenth best national university—fourteen private schools are ranked higher. In the *Wall Street Journal*'s latest rankings, done by College Pulse, the University of Florida is the top state school, ranked fifteenth among all universities. Still, a very large portion of the human capital created in America is formed at our state universities. Three presidents of the modern era (Lyndon Johnson, Gerald Ford, and Joe Biden) are state university graduates and two others (Dwight Eisenhower and Jimmy Carter), also attended public universities: West Point and the Naval Academy. Of the thirty CEOs of the companies in the Dow Jones Industrial Average at this writing, twenty-five had bachelor's degrees from American universities (others came from India, Britain, or Sweden)—nine of them public state universities. Far more CEOs were American public university graduates than were graduates of all eight Ivy League schools combined.

Historically, state governments have had far more to do with the advanced education of Americans than has the federal government. The states set most of the rules for how universities are governed and provide a majority of the critical outside funding. Still, as outlined earlier, there is a good deal of diversity in the way states decide how to handle the institutions of higher education under their control.

As our earlier analysis indicates, the case for *any* public funding of education, especially higher education, is problematic. If this author were czar, we would completely eliminate public funding of collegiate academic instruction. But that is not politically doable, so below we offer some "second-best" alternatives that would increase competition and efficiency.

Privatizing State Universities

The most dramatic thing state governments could do to alter the higher education landscape for the better is privatize state universities. Doing that would involve a healthy increase in the role that markets play in allocating higher education resources—and not cost a penny of public funds beyond what is already being spent. Indeed, it might involve spending *fewer* public dollars. Today, state governments give money to the *producers* of higher education services, state universities. Why not instead give the money to the *consumers* of those services, the students?

In other words, extend into higher education an idea that has proven increasingly popular in K–12 schooling. Beginning around thirty years ago, states, first Wisconsin and then others, notably Ohio, began to give vouchers to students usable for private primary and secondary school tuition fees, picking up on an idea suggested by Milton Friedman in his seminal libertarian manifesto, *Capitalism and Freedom*, many decades ago. There are many variants on the idea of making standard public schools more "private," such as charter schools, student educational savings accounts, funds for homeschooling, and so on, but the goal was and is to give students choices other than the traditional government school monopolist: that is, to increase competition. The literature on this effort is voluminous, but much of it shows two things: first, these options have been immensely popular with students and their parents; second, on balance, the students have had improved learning outcomes.[1]

The one important experience in state-funded college vouchers occurred in Colorado. Starting in 2005, students there were eligible to obtain College Opportunity Fund (COF) grants. Funds would be given to residents to pay fees at Colorado's state universities and one or two private institutions. Two features made the Colorado experiment of limited national applicability. First, Colorado had probably the strictest limit on state spending growth of any state as a consequence of its TEL (tax and expenditure limitation) amendment adopted in the 1990s. This limit led to a reduction in real state spending on higher education late in the first decade of the twenty-first century, just when the voucher plan was beginning. Second, and no doubt related to the first point, vouchers were modest, not covering all fees. In 2005–06, the initial year, the average voucher was valued at $2,400, but by 2010 it had declined by 45 percent to $1,320—at a time of rising tuition fees. The average COF grant at the beginning covered 36 percent of public four-year tuition for full-time students, but by 2012 it covered only 22 percent.[2] In no way were Colorado's state universities fully "privatized." That said, by 2019, Colorado higher education appropriations per student were 40 percent below the national average, ranking 48th in the nation.[3] Moreover, the political composition of Colorado's government changed considerably, moving from a Republican governor (Bill Owens) sympathetic to vouchers to a Democratic governor (Jared Polis), who was distinctly more hostile. The Colorado voucher experiment, never fully funded, simply withered away.

Bottom line: there has never been a full-blown collegiate voucher experiment.[4] One thing many states have done is let high school students take college courses while in high school, reasoning, correctly in my judgment, that a rigid age-determined demarcation of the line between "secondary" and "college-level" learning is educationally inappropriate. This point was resoundingly demonstrated to me when Virin, my eighth-grade son, successfully completed a freshman composition course at Ohio University. Thomas Jefferson, who certainly developed a way with words (e.g., the Declaration of Independence) managed to graduate from the College of William and Mary at 18. Students attending state colleges while in high school in many states have the tuition for their college courses paid in whole or part by the state. Although not full-blown voucher programs, these are in principle similar— tuition fees arising from the student's college attendance are paid by the state, not the individual college enrollee.

Not only do vouchers increase the clout of students and make universities more attentive to their interests, but they can also be a means of increasing competition and intellectual diversity, particularly if accompanied by the removal of barriers to transfer schools. Take a student from Illinois. She could spend her freshman and sophomore years at Illinois State University getting a sound general education, and her junior and senior years at the University of Illinois, which may have demonstrated superior expertise in a specialized area of study vocationally relevant to the student after graduation.

Done optimally, after a transition period of perhaps three or four years, current "state" universities would no longer receive any state subsidies. With that, they would gain freedom from state regulations and could, for example, charge whatever tuition fees they want. They could determine the composition and powers of their own governing board, establish the courses needed for graduation, and set aside collective bargaining agreements for state employees. Essentially, they would be privatized. Because of the potential financial trauma caused by such a major change, perhaps initially the vouchers would be good only for students attending the existing state universities. In time, however, competition and choice could (and should) be enhanced by allowing students to choose any college in state, including traditional private schools, and possibly even allow for attendance at out-of-state or even international universities—good students attending Indiana University might decide to spend a year at the University of Toronto or even Oxford, or at Ohio State University or Michigan State, broadening not only their academic but also their social and cultural background, widening their perspective on the world in which we live.

Considerations of merit and income could easily be introduced into the voucher system, making it both more effective and possibly even politically more popular. Democrats generally have opposed vouchers at primary and secondary schools, usually heavily swayed by teacher union opposition. To win initial support from Democrats for collegiate vouchers, advocates (usually Republicans, independents, or libertarians) could offer to make them somewhat progressive. The standard voucher for students with a family income between $60,000 and $100,000 a year might be $8,000. However, those vouchers could be reduced for higher-income students, perhaps to $4,000 for those from families with an income above $200,000 a year (implying a reduction equal to about 4 cents for each dollar of income earned between $100,000 and $200,000). Similarly, they could be increased for those from households with an income less than $60,000, up to perhaps a $12,000 maximum. Colleges would become much more accessible to the poor. How could liberals and progressives oppose that?

In general, good students currently get no government support for superb academic performance, nor penalties for poor grades. To be sure, even under existing policies both in-state and out-of-state students receive some state subsidy, since their tuition fees are typically less than the cost of their attendance. However, why not promote academic productivity the way the private sector promotes superb occupational performance with higher salaries and bonuses? Why not give an extra amount to entering students ranking in the top 10 percent of their high school class as well as to top college students? And to discourage collegiate lingering (fifth- and even sixth-year seniors), simply stop the vouchers after four years. Georgia pioneered merit-based scholarships akin to vouchers with its HOPE scholarship program beginning in 1993, and several other states have begun similar efforts, but on the whole the merit-based voucher approach is still uncommon.

Some creative things can be done with vouchers to address other deficiencies in higher education. To cite one example, the state government could reduce the voucher amount per student at a given institution if the overall undergraduate grade point average at that school exceeds 2.50, in order to curtail somewhat the grade inflation that has mightily contributed to a lower work effort among American students and to less creation of human capital. Suppose XYZ University's overall undergraduate GPA is 2.90 (slightly below a B average). The baseline voucher, $8,000 in the example above, could be altered downward for students at XYZ to as low as a $5,000 minimum (a $75 reduction for each 0.01 the campus GPA exceeds 2.50). To lower the effective cost to incoming students, colleges would start penalizing faculty members or academic units engaging in excessive grade inflation. In a similar way, schools that charge their students massive participation fees to support intercollegiate athletics could be penalized by reducing voucher funds. In short, vouchers could be used adroitly to address a variety of problems endemic to higher education.

Another issue relates to graduate and professional education, where per-student costs tend to be inherently higher—smaller classes, higher-paid senior faculty. One approach is simply to have larger vouchers for these students. Typically, however, at such advanced levels of instruction, a much larger proportion of students are from out of state and presumably ineligible for vouchers. Also, by any objective measure we have too many persons getting advanced degrees in some disciplines, say English literature or history, given the current levels of demand. (An aside: I am personally chagrined at the anti-humanities bias prevailing in America today, manifested, for example, in a growing ignorance about our heritage, which is loosening the glue that binds us together as Americans.) Certainly, vouchers should not be given to a student who takes six or eight years to get a PhD. Here, perhaps I am biased: I got such a degree in less than three years and felt well prepared then for a fruitful career. The law of diminishing returns strongly applies in academia— the fourth or fifth year of advanced study adds less to one's knowledge and skill base than the first or second year. If all government aid to doctoral students ceased after four years, we would likely get needed reforms that forced students to learn more expeditiously and not spend three years writing a dissertation on some obscure topic of interest to almost no one except the student's thesis adviser. And what is the utility on cost-benefit grounds of a growing number of postdoctoral fellowships? Moreover, a strong case can be made for simply not giving vouchers at all for professional programs leading to high-paying positions, such as MBAs getting jobs with major Wall Street firms or lawyers or physicians earning six-digit salaries—why should this financial investment be subsidized by the state?

Creating Lifetime Educational Spending Accounts

Two deficiencies of current public education funding in the US need attention. First, we tend to compartmentalize education by age-related criteria excessively. We treat the learning of a college freshman aged 18 significantly differently from the learning of a 17-year-old high school senior. Second, at the secondary and higher educational levels, we tend to undervalue forms of learning outside the traditional book-oriented academic disciplines and have become excessively wedded to two- and four-year "degrees" as the norm for postsecondary education. If worker earnings data are any indication, a large part of the human capital formed during a lifetime occurs after formal education ends, through on-the-job work experiences and maturity and wisdom accumulated with age.[5]

One idea that recognizes these deficiencies and incorporates the idea of privatizing higher education using vouchers is to introduce lifetime educational spending accounts. An illustration: give each child at the age of 4 (under the care of a parent or guardian until the age of 18) an educational savings account that allows the holder to use up to $50,000 in educational vouchers over a lifetime. Funds can be used for private elementary or secondary school tuition fees, higher education tuition fees, after-school or summer school enrichment opportunities, vocational training programs (e.g., for computer programmers, welders, beauticians), and so on. Even support for homeschooling instructional materials could be covered (remember, to a considerable extent Abraham Lincoln was essentially "homeschooled"). Perhaps the state could add more funds to the spending accounts for those students who excel academically.

Under such a scheme, students and their parents, not government agencies, would be making choices on how to best use scarce public resources for their own personal benefit. Over time, that might reallocate funds away from uses determined by legislators and governors swayed by lobbyists and other pressure groups toward what the public actually prefers. One form of education that is comparatively neglected is vocational training. Earlier federal programs like the Job Training Partnership Act were criticized as being ineffective pork barrel projects, but the concept of providing skills training with direct vocational relevance is highly appropriate: we need bricklayers and welders as well as accountants and engineers.

New legislation would have to address all sorts of other issues. The educational spending accounts would likely be invalidated if the holder left the state, a provision that might restrict some interstate movement. Inflation and other factors would almost certainly lead to increasing the magnitude of the spending accounts. And given changing preferences, a new political regime could simply phase out educational savings account balances, although that would no doubt be hugely controversial.

Nonetheless, the idea has a great deal of appeal. It gives parents and students an alternative to the existing monopoly of public schools, including universities. It increases choice and competition. It supports a more market-based approach to allocating educational resources. It is an idea whose time has come.

Tinkering with the Public Higher Education System

The complete privatization of American state universities and community colleges through a publicly financed voucher plan is a great idea, but it is not politically feasible now, particularly in blue states with a strong progressive tradition skeptical of market-based solutions and powerful teachers' unions fiercely opposed to major changes in the status quo. Nonetheless, a number of reforms can be implemented within the current system of state-owned and state-regulated universities that might enhance benefits to the citizenry. Moreover, there are compromised or blended models—for example, one that gradually reduces traditional state university appropriations while increasing the number and size of vouchers or HOPE-type scholarships. In other words, moving toward a full voucher model may be the ideal politically in some states. A number of potentially useful reforms within the context of the current state university model are worth exploring.

The Governing Board

I am not alone in believing that university governing boards are often disappointments.[6] They often rubber-stamp administrative spending desires, even those involving expenditures that are more aspirational than practical and economical. Boards are chosen in all kinds of ways: by governors, by election, by legislative and executive branch concurrence, and so on. Too many university trustees look at their appointment as a sinecure for past service or for political contributions, enjoying the perks (getting free tickets to high-profile athletic events, meeting distinguished individuals at campus cocktail parties, taking trips with university officials to posh conferences in resorts), but not doing the homework needed to be on top of major issues.

At the same time, a tradition of "shared governance" in higher education, strongly enunciated by faculty groups like the American Association of University Professors, has often circumscribed the willingness of trustees to "take charge" and mandate certain changes they view as desirable. Implicitly, governing boards have often ceded control over university policy, leading to the domination of many institutions by woke activists whose viewpoints are often wildly out of sync with both public opinion and sound university governance. I sense (and some university presidents I know agree) that elected boards are usually disappointments, in part because voter knowledge about candidates is usually nonexistent. Staggered board terms are a must: chaos can erupt (as it has at New College in Florida) when a new government comes in and completely replaces an existing board, often to impose a radically different philosophy of governing that causes further institutional turmoil.

Boards of more than a dozen members are generally unwieldly, too large to act decisively and quickly when needed, and they require a lot of university resources just to be kept fully informed. Private university boards of fifty or more, not uncommon, are farcical, and are typically rubber-stamping groups of rich alumni donors. By contrast, a board of fewer than seven members risks failing to consider important perspectives, and arguably vests too much power in a small number of persons. In most institutions, the optimal board size is probably between seven and twelve, possibly also with a small number of nonvoting member participants.

The terms of board members vary widely nationally. I always thought that the worst situation was in Virginia. The Board of Visitors of the University of Virginia is both somewhat too large (sixteen members) and has far-too-short terms—four years. Compounding the matter, Virginia's governor appoints the board and is also limited to one four-year term (without some non-gubernatorial intervening service). Thus Board of Visitors' terms expire just as members are getting good at knowing their job—and the new governor wants to appoint his or her own persons. Many Ohio public universities have had nine-person boards (along with some nonvoting honorary members) serving nine-year terms, about right I think, although that state is now moving to six-year board terms with the possibility of a four-year extension, also a reasonable approach.

Often board members are rich donors to the governor or the prevailing political party in the state. To gain diversity in thinking, perhaps it should be mandated that no more than two-thirds of the board members can belong to the same political party (I am thinking of the brouhahas over leadership in Florida and North Carolina here). Arguably, it is inappropriate to do as Governor Ron DeSantis did at New College in Florida, replacing the entire existing board with a highly conservative board that held a wildly different perspective on institutional direction than the existing board. To me, however, even more important than board composition and political diversity is providing board members with objective, unbiased information. Too often, boards get nearly all their information from the president's office or those of his or her close subordinates, which often fails to disclose alternative perspectives on issues and papering over campus scandals that embroil students and faculty. The huge sex scandal involving gymnastics team physician Larry Nassar at Michigan State occurred without the governing board immediately knowing about it, clearly wrong. And more recently, a sexual harassment matter involving the same university's football coach, Mel Tucker, was not immediately brought to board attention. More often, board members are not provided detailed financial information about new campus initiatives.

University leaders depend on the governing board for their appointment and salary. They want the boards to get only good news. Therefore, boards should have their own person, maybe called the board secretary, whose pay and evaluation are controlled directly by the board and who should even be physically separated from the locus of campus political power (that is, not in or near the president's office). That person should see to it that the board hears about different perspectives on issues, learns about incipient campus scandals, and knows which academic units are languishing, either in enrollment or quality.

The cost of higher education has risen sharply, even allowing for overall inflation. Why? In part, because *university governing boards have let them rise.* They have allowed administrations to acquiesce to the demands of campus constituencies to increase spending to meet pet desires. In some states, a university president is able to persuade the governor or others who appoint the trustees to name powerful friends and allies to the governing board.[7] For a full decade from 2012 through 2022, Mitch Daniels did not raise tuition at Purdue University by a dime, because he concentrated single-mindedly on keeping costs under control, and he had a board that supported this objective. Other universities, by contrast, had presidents who were controlled by their own rent-seeking constituents, and boards that acquiesced in spending for expensive projects, such as building marginally needed luxurious facilities financed by borrowing. In the 2010s, many campuses went on building sprees for luxury housing that has become an albatross as enrollments failed to rise.

Should Legislatures or Governors Dictate Campus Policies?

As disenchantment with American universities has risen, so politicians have found it desirable to advocate government restraints on some university activities. In the last few years, I have heard serious political discussions about such questions as:

- Should state universities be required to teach a course in critical race theory to all undergraduates?
- Should state universities be *prohibited* from teaching critical race theory?
- Should diversity-affirming statements be required of students, faculty, and administrative staff?
- Should mandatory diversity-affirming statements be *prohibited* at state universities?
- Should diversity, equity, and inclusion (DEI) offices be abolished?
- Should faculty at state universities be prohibited from going on strike during the academic year (thereby depriving tuition-paying students of expected courses)?
- Should state universities be required to accept all transfer credits from other accredited state universities?
- Should tenure be abolished at state universities?
- Should full-time non-administrative faculty be required to teach at least one (or two) courses each academic year or semester?
- Should state universities be required to adopt and enforce standards of freedom of expression like those in the Chicago principles of the University of Chicago?
- Should state universities be required to have an "institutional neutrality" policy prohibiting official university opinions on controversial issues?
- Should the flagship state university be required to accept for admission any student in the top 10 percent of his or her high school graduating class?

- Should construction workers be required to be paid "prevailing wages" (usually union-negotiated rates) on state university building projects?
- Should state universities be required to publish online the salaries and teaching loads of all faculty and salaries of all other staff?
- Should tuition fees be frozen at existing levels for two years?
- Should the hazing of students lead to the dismissal of the students responsible?
- Should serious campus disciplinary actions against students always be deliberated in open hearings with the accused student facing standard American judicial procedures, including the right to cross-examine and to be represented by an attorney?
- Should university subsidies of intercollegiate athletics from student fees or institutional resources be limited to 5 percent (3 percent?) of the amount of state appropriations?
- Should state-supported community colleges be prohibited from offering bachelor's or professional degrees?
- Should state-supported universities be prohibited from raising tuition or fees more than the rate of inflation?

That list of twenty proposals is illustrative but far from inclusive of issues that receive legislative or gubernatorial scrutiny. Lots of legislators have their own ideas about how universities should be run, and occasionally they can get enough traction to see their ideas incorporated into legislation signed by the governor.

Personally, I happen to agree with a few of the ideas above and have even testified before the Ohio legislature to that effect. But I am wary of legislative imposition of university standards. For one thing, the political composition of a government changes, and perhaps this year's conservative majority would prohibit mandatory diversity statements while next year's progressive majority might mandate them. It is not optimal to have university policies that change frequently with the whims of the electorate and its politicians. For libertarian and conservative types to clamor for the government regulation of universities is also philosophically inconsistent with their general disdain for government control over people's lives. That is why I think the privatization and voucher approach is often a superior way to reform the behavior of our state universities, without politicians getting into the details of specific policy matters.

Providing Students and Taxpayers with Better Information

I have stressed the critical role of information and the fact that many participants in higher education don't know much about our colleges and universities. State governments can alleviate this problem in various ways. For example, they could mandate tests at state universities at the beginning and the end of the college experience—for example, the previously mentioned National College Equivalence Examination (NCEE) or the existing Collegiate Learning Assessment (CLA)—to measure changes in critical-thinking skills and writing ability during the college years. Then widely publicize the results. How much on average did the students learn in their college years at the University of Oklahoma as opposed to students at rival state institutions like Oklahoma State?

States can also publish data on professor teaching loads, research grants, publications, and salaries to get measures of faculty productivity. I once authored a somewhat embarrassing study using such data for the faculty of the University of Texas. Such information can usually provide data on per student administrative costs by campus. If, as arguably is the case at the present, the federal government is doing an inadequate job of gathering vocational information on college graduates, each state could do it, or perhaps join with neighboring states to get statistical information on student job success by region. Having accurate information about schools and the performance of their students and faculty would help students make informed choices and possibly even lead to a more rational allocation of government higher education resources by states.

State Coordinating Boards: Good or Bad?

Virtually every state has one or more boards with oversight of public state universities. California effectively has *three* such boards: one for the University of California, one for the California State University system (the other four-year universities), and one for community colleges. The Office of the President of the University of California, the nation's most prominent state university, employs two thousand or so employees—and doesn't itself teach a single student or perform much research. I often wondered what would happen if that entire apparatus were wiped out and administrative control were divested to each of the individual campuses of the university. Maybe more typical than California would be Texas, which has a single Higher Education Coordinating Board with some oversight responsibilities over the entire university system, although, complicating things a bit, some of the individual universities (such as the University of Texas or Texas A&M) have several campuses themselves. Such coordinating boards have historically tried to prevent excessive duplication (e.g., having too many schools offering PhD degrees in English). They can also be the agency to do the useful statewide data gathering mentioned above.

The issue is this: Are state coordinating boards a desirable and useful means of reducing wasteful duplication of effort and gathering vital information, or are they themselves another inefficient layer of bureaucracy that raises the cost of higher education? The answer may well vary by state. I have often wondered why small states with fewer than two million residents and perhaps only three to five truly independent state-supported schools need such a coordinating board. In those cases, aren't the boards needless but costly regulators duplicating the administrative functions largely provided by the individual institutions?

Performance Funding

Traditionally, in many states, subsidies for public universities have been based at least in part on some enrollment-based formula, with larger amounts for expensive graduate and professional students than for beginning under-graduates. In the past generation, however, there have been greater calls for performance-based funding, where schools are rewarded for improvements in student achievement, research output, or operating efficiencies.

Let me give an example. Suppose a school has a freshman-to-sophomore retention rate of 60 percent. Suppose the state legislature or the state coordinating board says it will increase the university subsidy by 5 percent if it increases the retention rate between the freshman and sophomore year to

65 percent within two years. There is a good chance the university will try to do it. Suppose it is successful. Does that mean that student satisfaction with the school is rising? Maybe, but what if the school engages in dramatic grade inflation to increase the number of poorly performing students continuing for a second year? Is that good? I doubt it.

Sometimes schools will game the system so it can report better performance that in reality is illusionary. Thus, the great gains in efficiency and outcomes promised by performance-based funding have not always been realized. The concept of incentivizing participants in higher education to perform better is a good one, but the devil is in the execution, which recent history has not suggested has been good (witness the falling enrollments and declining public support generally for higher education in recent years despite increased performance-based funding).

Conclusion: The Invisible Hand of Markets or the Iron Fist of Government?

Governments, rightly or wrongly, are likely to subsidize higher education for the foreseeable future, because universities, despite their inefficiencies and arrogance, provide services that, on balance, the public thinks have positive spillover effects. Badly imitating Winston Churchill, I could say that universities are the worst form of providing advanced education to the citizenry—except all others. Thus we are going to continue to subsidize schools with taxpayer-provided resources for the next few years and probably longer.

In this chapter, I suggest two approaches to higher education subsidization, one that has a much more market orientation than the other. Government vouchers to students, not schools, offer a way to introduce more competition and market forces into higher education. The alternative approach—maintaining the current funding system but introducing some reforms—is a distinctly second-best solution. For example, attempts to cut wasteful duplication have had mixed results, sometimes merely introducing another layer of bureaucracy. Similarly, efforts at enhancing performance funding have not led to noticeable boosts in productivity, the amount of learning, or cost efficiencies its advocates hoped for. Privatizing state universities is probably the best path to successful reform.

9

Inside Job:
Reforming Universities Within

FOR THE UMPTEENTH time: colleges and universities have become expensive, do an inadequate job of disbursing knowledge, are increasingly intolerant of diverse viewpoints, and are increasingly viewed with hostility by the public. The sins are many and seemingly growing. Does that mean, however, that they are totally incapable of reform, of eradicating some of their biggest obstacles to positive transformation? I don't think so. Several schools have made important improvements over the past decade without much external coercion; look at Purdue University, where inflation-adjusted costs to students were *reduced* around 20 percent without any loss of quality, indeed with signs of improvement, all because of uncommonly good leadership by President Mitch Daniels and his staff. With resolute leadership, positive change *is* possible.

As external forces mount, more universities may well feel forced to do things that were previously unthinkable. That may make cost reductions feasible that were previously politically impossible, arising from a desperate fight for survival rather than from a newly developed desire to reform. The mere threat of creative destruction might lead to positive change. Reform is often more palatable than bankruptcy, and even internally disliked changes are likely to be preferable to ones dictated from outside, for example, by state politicians and bureaucrats. In this chapter, we will look at several reforms that colleges and universities can undertake to make themselves leaner and more productive, incorporating to a greater extent the principles of market resource allocation and rewarding merit over longevity, positive change over stultifying tradition.

Three areas of reform are worth our exploration. First, the biggest cost universities face is for personnel. Administrative staffs have exploded, and my offhand guess is that at least 20 percent of administrative positions could be eliminated on most campuses without any appreciable deterioration in the quality of university services. Faculty jobs likewise need reassessing: Are professors working enough, and doing the *right kind* of work in order to achieve institutional goals regarding the creation and dissemination of knowledge? Is tenure an outmoded concept? Should the faculty play a big or small role in campus decision-making? Second, there is a scandalous waste of space on campuses. Can schools reduce future capital costs by reimaging and intensifying the use of buildings, backing away from an edifice complex involving elaborate new construction that is expensive and detracts from the central purposes of universities? In making needed changes, can we utilize both personnel and facilities twelve months a year, as is common in almost all other human endeavors? Third, campuses often inefficiently carry out a lot of auxiliary activities that perhaps others should be performing, everything from running dormitories and food services to managing heating, cooling, and sometimes even power plants. For example, as previously asked, should we pay students to mow grass and paint buildings rather than using expensive unionized labor?

Still other issues arise. Are campus intercollegiate athletics really a way of providing students with needed campus recreation that also contributes to attributes like leadership and discipline, or are they an embarrassing and often costly non-academic distraction? Should hospitals be run by universities or by administratively separate institutions specializing in health care? Is it really the job of universities to devote significant resources to broader social issues like mitigating climate change or promoting sustainability or other environmentally related goals?

Another big issue: Who should be the prime mover in instituting campus change? The president and the senior staff? the faculty? the governing board? And what is the role of key donors or alumni? The answer here may be *all* are important, but the precise role of each of the many actors within a university varies with the campus culture and traditions, its form of institution (public, not-for-profit private, and for-profit private), and so on.[1]

One final introductory thought: we repeat that there are vast differences in colleges and universities in America. What works on a campus with fifty thousand students may not work well on one with five thousand or five hundred, or even, in a few cases, less than a hundred. Some schools value a relatively homogenous student body, often students with a similar religious perspective, while others revel in their diversity. It is certainly not true that for American institutions of higher education that one size fits all, or that there is a single model of efficiency and effectiveness that works well in all settings.

Personnel Issues

In most universities, a majority of expenditures go to pay for the labor needed to run the school. Over half of those personnel costs used to be related to faculty salaries and benefits, but that is generally no longer the case in American higher education. It is typical for faculty to constitute less than one-third of the staff, often considerably less. The most noteworthy personnel change within American universities over the past half century is the vast growth in administrative staff. As noted earlier, you could randomly gather a group of professors from around the country and put them in a room: within a few minutes, they will be complaining about administrative bloat and overreach.

Administrative Bloat

When Socrates taught the youth of Athens, he did not have a director of admissions or a registrar or a dean of students to help him. Socrates *was* the faculty and, along with the students, was the entire Socratic "learning community." But today, some universities have several times as many administrative staff as professors and instructors. As indicated earlier, one important area of growth in administrative staff is in the area of DEI. That concept did not even exist when I began teaching, yet, *even without an administrative bureaucracy consciously stressing diversity, the student body and faculty during the early decades after 1960 nonetheless became markedly more diverse.* In the second half of the last century, women became more numerous on American campuses, the number of black and Hispanic Americans grew, and a growing immigrant presence led to more students from differing ethnicities, religions, and races. We became dramatically more diverse—and this was done without a DEI bureaucracy. Yet today some universities employ over a hundred DEI bureaucrats who are supposed to achieve and enforce some ill-defined optimal diversity. Would horrible mistreatment of minority groups spring up if we simply eliminated this class of administrators? I strongly doubt it.

Moreover, the US Supreme Court in the *Students for Fair Admissions v. Harvard* and the accompanying University of North Carolina cases made it abundantly clear that race should not be considered in making admissions decisions. As Chief Justice Roberts put it in the 2023 decisions, "Racial classifications are simply too pernicious," echoing a 2007 statement of his that "the way to stop discrimination on the basis of race is to stop discrimination based on race."[2] There is no question that DEI programs were created *predominantly* to promote minority racial participation in universities, most notably by black students. Gender is no longer mentioned much in extolling the virtues of "diversity," probably because women overwhelmingly outnumber males on campus and no one seems much interested in the decidedly nonwoke objective of achieving rough gender equality.[3] If even considering race is illegal, why do we still have massive DEI bureaucracies that reach into the triple digits at some schools?

Some administrative bureaucracies have exploded in size because of dubious reasoning or false premises. I once heard a college development (sometimes called "advancement") officer say, "We are a net plus to the university because the fundraising revenues we procure exceed the cost of the development efforts—we make a 'profit.'" What he was saying, in effect, is that "we raise enough money to cover our staff costs and a bit more." That is, administrative costs (fundraising efforts) approached 100 percent of the revenue procured. But a good charity should keep its administrative costs low—probably no more than 10 percent or so of its budget. Fundraising should primarily be about expanding scholarships for students, obtaining research grants for faculty, financing building construction, and so forth. As indicated earlier, my research with Justin Strehle has shown that a large portion of endowment funds raised via development efforts seem to fund staff salary and numeric expansion, not broader university objectives. Moreover, money raised on capital campaigns often funds elaborate buildings that are not only costly but can also contribute to a mismatch between space needs and enrollment.

What if we told a vice president for university advancement, "If you keep the costs of fundraising to less than 15 percent of the funds raised (actually received, not promised), we will give you a bonus of 5 percent of the amount below 15 percent that you achieved"? Incentivize the administrative staff to *both* raise money and keep administrative costs down!

Administrative staffs have grown so large that one rapidly growing category of administrative employees is *chief of staff*. When staffs were small, the senior administrator of a university or major administrative unit could easily delegate the responsibilities of subordinates himself or herself. For two-thirds of my teaching career at Ohio University, there were *no* chiefs of staff, because the staffs themselves were small, often five or fewer. Now not only the president and provost have a chief of staff, but other administrators do as well. The number of "assistant provosts," "associate provosts," "assistant department chairs," "vice presidents," and "administrative assistants" has exploded as well.

Some areas of administrative staff growth are concerning not only on financial grounds. In particular, I have been disturbed at how bureaucrats associated with the student affairs or dean of students staff have often harassed students to promote their own personal woke ideological agenda. On two occasions I have personally disrupted student disciplinary hearings because administrators wanted to punish students for perfectly legal behavior. (One example: an administrator tried to punish a student for stating on his personal website his religiously based objection to same-sex marriages; the administrator thought that was a punishable offense.) Even more than faculty, administrators often seem to be insensitive to the notion that universities are supposed to be havens for the peaceful and civil free expression of ideas.

Some areas of campus administration—for example, information technology, housing, food operations, and policing—arguably should be farmed out to more efficient private sector specialists. Should universities run parking garages and lots, not only for students and faculty, but for outsiders using university medical facilities and attending athletic events? Why don't universities sell them or engage in a long-term lease with private entrepreneurs for the use and management of those facilities? Ohio State enhanced its endowment by hundreds of millions doing that—why don't other schools? Why don't private transportation companies run the bus systems on large campuses? Why not generally outsource virtually all non-educational dimensions of university activities to private sector specialists?

Another issue, as much concerned with management philosophy as finances, relates to whether the university administration should be highly centralized, with most major policy and budgetary decisions emanating from the office of the president, provost, or chief financial administrator, or decentralized, with most decisions controlled at the level of individual departments or other administrative units like schools or colleges. There is probably no "one size fits all" optimal solution, although my own sense is that on average colleges and universities have become overcentralized—decision-making is increasingly made by persons less intimately involved in the real purposes of universities: teaching and research. I wonder what would happen if governing boards insisted that the ratio of administrative staff to either students or faculty not exceed what existed in, say, 2000. Typically, that would involve the reallocation of resources from administrative personnel to other purposes, in most cases probably a good thing.

Universities occasionally go on binges to try to implement a rational campuswide set of rules to govern resource allocation. For example, one concept that gained popularity on many campuses in the second decade of this century was responsibility-centered management (RCM). Conceptually, with RCM an attempt is made to measure the contribution and costs of each administrative unit in the university, then using that information to reallocate resources toward those units that seem to develop more bang for the buck. This sounds appealing. A huge problem: very often the "output" or contribution a unit makes is difficult to fully measure. For example, we can measure the number of credit hours that students in the physics department took, but can we relate that to what they really learned? Or even, how do you evaluate the contributions of the physics faculty and staff to important research? In areas where "research" comprises creative activities like writing symphonies, poems, or giving piano recitals, the measurement of outcomes is even more tricky. In the private sector, there is a profit bottom line that is nonexistent in higher education.

Faculty and Other Teaching Staff

Faculty salaries are still a huge portion of personnel costs, especially at community colleges and traditional liberal arts colleges offering only bachelor's degrees. But they do the critical, absolutely essential work of scholarly institutions, teaching students and performing research. I know faculty members at multiple colleges and universities who work about 1,000 hours a year—thirty or so hours weekly for thirty-two to thirty-three weeks a year when school is in session (and probably less in years when the faculty member is on "sabbatical leave") and not at all in the summer and holiday-break months. However, I also know those who work 2,500 hours a year—fifty hours or more weekly for fifty weeks a year. To be sure, the hard worker typically makes more money—but not necessarily so on an hourly basis.[4] With tenure in place, the costs of being lazy in higher education are less than they are in the broader economy.

Here are ten questions that schools would do well to consider regarding the faculty:

- Is there an excessive publish-or-perish emphasis, since much research, especially outside the hard sciences, has a minimal or even nonexistent payoff to society?

- Does distance or computerized learning offer possibilities for big savings on instructional costs, or did the pandemic experience demonstrate that traditional in-class instruction is usually superior?

- Are the advantages of tenure—job security for faculty, protection against attacks on faculty based on political views, and so on—greater than the costs?

- Teaching loads on average fell in the late twentieth century and into the early present one. Why? Have the research gains from that outweighed the quality issues related to adjunct faculty teaching many classes? Are costs per journal article published exorbitantly high?

- If we went to three-year bachelor's degrees and paid professors perhaps 20 percent more than at present to work year-round, would faculty, students, and society benefit?

- What is the faculty's role in the "shared governance" of universities? Should it be confined to curricular and instructional issues, where the faculty role is appropriately strong?
- Should faculty work as independent contractors selling teaching services to multiple schools or "degree aggregators" rather than working for a single university?
- Are we overly rigid in degree requirements for college teachers? For example, should good high school teachers with MA degrees be allowed to teach college freshman English courses often taught by PhDs?
- Should professors going on strike during an academic term, disrupting their students' education, be fired?
- Should post-tenure faculty review with the potential for dismissal be more widely implemented?

Very appropriately, I think, at most colleges and universities, professors are treated as respected professionals and are given a good deal of discretion in how they do their work and even a fair amount over what kind of work they do—what advanced courses they teach, for example, or what research projects they work on. When I started switching the orientation of my research from economic history and labor economics to higher education a quarter of a century ago, I did not ask anyone for permission—I just did it. That is pretty typical. In some instances where faculty unions exist, a lot of the interaction between faculty and the administration is highly formalized via the collective bargaining unit. But the evaluation of the success of a professor is always somewhat murky because the "output" is rarely precisely quantifiable. To cite one important example: student teaching evaluations give us a pretty good feel for how popular professors are but say nothing about how much students have really learned. And, to me at least, in part the measure of my success as a teacher is how my students fare in later life, and how much of their success is attributable to me. Some of the "output" of a professor is obvious only after a long and variable lag.

Some discussion of a few of the questions raised above is desirable here. Research is discussed more explicitly in chapter 11, so I will defer discussing that for now. The role of technology in teaching, however, merits commentary.

From the time of Socrates to the middle of the twentieth century, there were few changes in the way we taught students. The advent of radio, movies, and especially television opened up the possibilities of "distance learning." I can recall in the early 1980s pioneering at my university by simultaneously lecturing students from a classroom at the main Athens, Ohio, campus and via television at three branch campus locations up to a hundred miles away. It seemed like such a great idea, and even today we do some of that kind of instruction, but in general both the students and faculty felt the lack of the traditional closeness that provides a chemistry that prods students to learn and faculty to want to spur them on via out-of-class interaction. The pandemic drove that point home forcefully as students rightly complained that they were learning less in class and missing out on vital peer interaction that enhances the transition from adolescence to adulthood.

A big issue is how much professors should teach. Some are truly brilliant researchers who truly expand the frontiers of our knowledge and should be spending most of their time in the lab or other research space rather than in the classroom. But they are found mostly at the few institutions designated as R1 universities (which conduct "very high research activity"). Most of the faculty at the overwhelming majority of schools should have teaching-intensive work responsibilities that involve a large number of students in a typical year. A professor at a midquality school today might teach five classes a year (three one semester, two the other), perhaps two survey courses averaging fifty students each, and three smaller specialized classes averaging twenty each—for a total of 160 students per year. If he or she costs $100,000 (salary plus fringe benefits), that amounts to $625 per student.

But what if we went to a year with three 15-week semesters, and each professor taught ten classes (four one semester, three each of the other two)? Suppose one is a survey lecture for two hundred students, three are classes of fifty, and six are smaller upper-division courses averaging twenty students—for a total of 470 students. Suppose we increase the professor's annual pay and fringe benefits by 25 percent and give her two student graduate assistants each $5,000 one semester to offer help for struggling students and to grade the one large lecture class. The total cost is $135,000—$287 per student. We have cut instructional costs per student by 54 percent, and the professor still has at least five weeks of paid vacation a year, rather generous for a professional worker. Without any technological change or other transformative alteration, we have cut instructional costs dramatically.

Would there be a qualitative decline in learning? Probably not. Teaching a lecture section of two hundred students has not been shown to result in a sizable loss of learning. As faculty age, they may lose some of their zeal to learn and teach, leading to their becoming boring teachers doing no research. A post-tenure review process, which some universities have already implemented, can perhaps lead to dismissing professors who show an egregious productivity decline, giving them first a warning and a chance to reverse their downward slide.

Adam Smith's Intriguing Idea

As indicated earlier, in his magisterial *Wealth of Nations*, Adam Smith, writing at the very time that the American colonies declared their independence nearly 250 years ago, suggested that when the professors charged their students tuition fees, rather than charging the university (Oxford University in his example), the quality of the teaching and learning was much higher. Why doesn't some entrepreneurial school and group of faculty do just that? Realistically, it would have to be a small school, perhaps one just starting.

There are variants on the "pay the professor" scheme. Here is one possible plan: Tuition per student credit hour remains uniform for all undergraduate instruction, with students paying $1,000 per credit hour (a $30,000 annual tuition for a student taking ten 3-credit-hour courses). The professor collects the fees for each course. Suppose a professor of average teaching quality or popularity teaches 150 students a year in five 3-credit-hour courses: one large survey course lecture with fifty students, and four advanced undergraduate classes averaging twenty-five students each. Suppose the professor keeps 40 percent of the money, forwarding the other 60 percent to the university for providing teaching and office space as well as administrative support services (the registrar's office, admissions office, library resources, an academic officer to handling scheduling, and so on). The university could even use some of its revenues to support research. The faculty member will collect $450,000 a year and retains $180,000, perhaps $135,000 in salary plus $45,000 in various other benefits (retirement and health insurance protection).

But now suppose a charismatic teacher lures 300 students annually—180 (room capacity) for the big survey course lecture and thirty in each of four advanced classes. With the same fees as above, the professor will collect $900,000 a year, clearing 40 percent of that ($360,000) , more than $250,000 in salary before generous fringe benefits. Suppose a third, boring and weak professor with the same teaching load gets only forty-five students in the big lecture and fifteen in each advanced class, or 105 students total, meaning he or she collects only $315,000 in revenue, allowing payments of $90,000 for salary and $36,000 for benefits. (This example tends to provide more for professors and less for the university administration than is currently the case.)

There are lots of variations on the idea and some issues that need to be addressed. For example, professors may try to "buy" high enrollments by engaging in excessive grade inflation. To prevent this, the university could decree that the class grade point average cannot exceed 2.50 or 2.70. Professors should be forbidden to offer booze, drugs, or sexual enticements to lure students. (I once had a colleague who somehow brought a sizable portion of the university marching band to perform at the beginning of class! The students loved it.) Where do you draw the line on acceptable behavior? Under another variation on the model described above, the professor could set the fee for each class, and popular professors can enhance their income by charging higher fees than professorial dullards.

What about nationally recognized research-oriented individuals? Those with outside grants could teach less, using research grant money instead of fees earned from students. Grant proposals would request salary funds to allow researchers to avoid substantial teaching. A higher rate of per student teaching compensation could also be used for graduate-level courses. Well-known researchers also typically earn funds from honoraria for visiting lectures or even royalties from patents arising out of work in university labs. The university administration would subsist not only on its share of the tuition fees, but also on state subsidies, donations, endowment funds, and the like. Need-based scholarships could ensure that admission is not based predominantly on family financial status. But, in general, the publish-or-perish environment on many campuses would move closer to a teach-well-or-perish one. And market forces would play a large role as well.

The Student Role in Internal Reform: Where Is Consumer Sovereignty?

As we noted earlier, and especially emphasized in chapter 7, the customer is king in a truly market-based environment—indeed, several prominent economists such as W. H. Hutt have popularized the concept of "consumer sovereignty."[5] Where students pay nearly all the bills through high tuition and other fees, universities ignore or denigrate them at their peril. Even in today's environment, where the role of students has been muted by government subsidies paid direct to universities, a school can be in trouble when large numbers of students vote with their feet not to attend it. If we initiated a robust student voucher system, that role would be enhanced, and I feel certain universities would work much harder to attract and keep students. Significant ethical issues are involved here, such as schools forcing students to take dubiously beneficial classes in order to get another semester or two of tuition monies (and sometimes accompanying state subsidies) in return for the all-important diploma.

Universities require students in order to exist. Nonstudent groupings of scholars may work at think tanks or research institutes, but they are not truly universities as conventionally defined. Aside from paying fees, students can do more than passively go to class and socialize with their fellow classmates. As indicated, they can help maintain the campus with their physical labor. They can conduct campus tours for prospective new students. They can augment their campus learning with internships that integrate book learning with practical experience. A hugely important dimension of student life comes with a big lag—as alumni, former students are often critical in providing donations and serving in leadership roles, such as university trustees, as well as serving the broader society.

Moreover, I think students legitimately have a fairly important, albeit modest, role in campus decision-making. Should intercollegiate athletics be partially financed from student activity fees? That happens on lots of campuses, but it is a non-academic expenditure on which students should be consulted—and listened to. They certainly should play a significant role in deciding on issues that directly impact student life, including issues regarding living and eating in campus facilities and rules on student behavior. Membership of mature advanced students on disciplinary bodies seems appropriate in most instances. I think some student input into decisions of the university's governing board is also appropriate, perhaps merely by having a nonvoting member or two on the board. Input from a student senate or similarly named organization should be considered seriously. Often, however, student senate elections have no substantive effects, and student input reflects a youthful lack of maturity and experience. Don't depend on the students to run the university!

At the same time, input should be in accordance with the rule of law, where that term encompasses the "laws" governing campus behavior as determined most importantly by the governing board of the institution. Protests designed to disrupt normal campus activities—classes, public lectures, athletic events—should be dealt with harshly. The right to express oneself should be secure, but not the right to forcefully enact change. First Amendment transgressions that prevent viewpoints from being expressed should be treated severely, just as such physical transgressions as assault, arson, or rape.

Debates and Lecture Series: Increasing the Diversity of Expression

Although universities are scandalously inefficient and teach too little, the biggest contemporary problem on campuses is often the lack of a diversity of ideas and robust discussion of alternative perspectives on the issues of the day. As indicated earlier, the overwhelming majority of faculty on most campuses are at least liberal, with the number of far-left progressive firebrands often far outnumbering the conservatives and libertarians. Moreover, the intolerance of alternative perspectives is sometimes frightening, threatening to destroy the intellectual vitality of campus communities across the land. To be sure, this is not universally true. Hillsdale and Grove City colleges, for example, probably have as many conservative and libertarian professors as liberal and progressive ones, and maybe many more. Extreme wokeness at a college can have devastating market effects—for example, Evergreen State College in Washington had a dramatic decline (roughly 50 percent over a period of four years) in enrollment following the school engaging in woke-inspired excesses, like forbidding white students to enter the campus on one day.

Still the overwhelming majority of colleges have an ideological imbalance that cannot be erased overnight without hiring and firing many faculty and administrators, a move that would cause serious other problems and is neither legally nor financially feasible. But schools can do at least one thing to partially right the imbalance and increase the diverse flow of ideas: institute a highly visible (arguably with compulsory attendance) major campus lecture or, even better, debate series, where the intent is to present alternative points of view.

Suppose XYZ University creates an Athenian Dialogue lecture series, perhaps giving it a budget of $500,000, a small fraction of 1 percent of the school's budget. Suppose six campuswide debates are scheduled in a large space (auditorium, gymnasium, theater, concert hall), three each semester with local or campus police providing crowd control. Debaters would take an issue of the day with distinct alternative views. A few examples: Pro or con?

- "Taxes Should Be Raised and Government Spending Slashed to Prevent a Looming Fiscal Armageddon."
- "America's Vitality and World Leadership Are Being Reduced by Our Irrational Immigration Policy—We Need More, Not Fewer, Productive Immigrants."
- "American Should Stop Trying to Be the World's Policeman: We Should Stop Interfering in Ukraine, the Middle East, and Asia."
- "We Should Privatize and Rationalize Our Social Security System, Giving Individuals Their Own Private IRA Accounts Instead."
- "An Amendment to the US Constitution Is Needed to Protect LGBTQ Minorities from Persecution."
- "A Balanced Budget Amendment to the Constitution Is Needed to Restore Fiscal Sanity."
- "Our Borders Should Not Be Uncontrolled; Keep Asylum Seekers out of the Country until Approved for Admission."
- "The US Department of Education Should Be Abolished and Its Functions Returned to the States and/or Private Organizations."

- "If North Korea or Iran Were to Utilize Nuclear Weapons, We Must Retaliate by Massive Counterattacks to Deter Their Future Use."
- "Nations Possessing Nuclear Weapons Should Work Together to Eliminate Those Weapons, including, If Necessary, a Commitment to Annihilate Any Initiator of Nuclear Attack."
- "Reparations Should Be Paid to Descendants of American Slaves."
- "Federal Taxes Should Be Limited to 15 Percent of National Output Unless a Supermajority of Congress in an Emergency Approves an Exception."

Obviously, this list is merely illustrative, not exhaustive.

Using Markets More in Campus Decision-Making

To more rationally make decisions on campus, colleges and universities could introduce internal markets to allocate resources. Suppose the central administration added a nice chunk of funds to the budget of each unit within the institution—but then required that those units have to pay for the use of space and personnel. For example, the Economics Department is given $50,000, but is told it needs to rent the classrooms it uses, with many of the rents being low, maybe even zero for undesirable rooms and times. However, a popular classroom at 10 a.m. might rent for the semester for $1,000 an hour, but at 8 a.m. or in the evening for only $250. If a big auditorium is desired at 10 a.m. or 1 p.m. by the psychology, history, and political science departments for a lecture class, the central administration could hold an auction for that space.

The concept could be carried further, to the level of each faculty member. Suppose each full professor is given a budget of $12,000, each associate professor a budget of $9,000, and each instructor or assistant professor a $5,000 allocation. From those funds the professor must rent an office and parking place, and pay student research or teaching assistants. Big offices with windows and a nice view might rent for $6,000 a year, a smaller interior office for only $1,500. Parking next to one's office building might cost $2,000 annually, but a spot at the stadium located six blocks away would be only $250 or even be free.[6]

To be sure, diminishing returns can set in with this approach. If the school charges for the paper used to copy things as well as a per-page service fee, the costs of administering the system might outweigh the benefits. But for the big things, such as office and classroom space, the concept is a workable one.

One area where activities tend to be *underfunded* is preventive maintenance. The faculty, students, and athletic department clamor for new buildings, so administrators seeking to be popular (and maintain their job security) will try to fulfill their needs. But almost no one is clamoring for routine painting or roof repair. The faculty demand resources, as do administrators and even students—but the buildings are silent, unable to advocate for their needs. This is one area where the trustees can actually play a constructive role—surveying unmet maintenance needs and adequately budgeting for them before the deterioration of facilities requires costly replacement or major renovation.

Conclusion

For decades, universities have increasingly failed or underperformed in terms of positive contributions to American society. Yet the urgency for fundamental change has grown, so institutions from within may be able to effect positive improvements. Making university communities more cognizant of the costs of wokelike and intransigent behavior is good, and instilling some dimensions of market-type thinking into university operations is useful. Why can't we incentivize professors to pay more attention to their students, as Smith suggested could be done? Why can't we use the price mechanism and budgets to better use campus physical resources? Why can't we use relatively low-cost means such as campus debates to increase campus intellectual diversity, circumventing the obstacles posed by tenure and lifetime employment contracts?

10

Other Reforms:
Thinking outside the Box

To this point, this critique of American higher education has focused on the universities themselves, along with their owners and financiers (including governments), managers, and employees. But there are other outside forces that could have a positive impact on American post-secondary education, making it cheaper, more effective both academically and vocationally, and less ideological, more interested in acquiring the truth amid an environment of unfettered civil free expression. This chapter looks at a few of them.

Revive for-Profit Education

The ultimate expression of a purely market-oriented approach to higher education that allows for the full operation of the virtues of creative destruction is for-profit schools. As noted earlier, they grew rapidly in the first decade of this century before declining precipitously in the second decade. There is no question that the decline occurred because of a hostile environment toward proprietary education developed during the Obama years and—after a pause and a slight reversal in the Trump era—renewed in the Biden years. Although never explicitly stated by government officialdom, recent Democratic administrations have clearly sought to eliminate the for-profit mode of higher education delivery.

It must be made clear, however, that the for-profit university expansion of the early years of this century was largely *indirectly financed by the federal government*, so in one sense even the private for-profit schools were very real wards of the state. The overwhelming majority of students in for-profit institutions borrowed funds from the federal government through its student loan program. However, any comprehensive reform of American higher education would involve, almost as its first order of business, the end to federal student loans for the reasons discussed earlier.

Could for-profit schools, operating without government subsidies, and even having to pay taxes that help fund subsidies to their competitors, survive? I think the answer is yes, although not likely in huge magnitudes. I think of primary and secondary public school education, which even more than higher education is dependent (almost 100 percent so) on government subsidies. Yet private primary and secondary education exists (although on a not-for-profit basis) and even seems to be growing in recent years, both through traditional schools and via homeschooling. The public wants choices and competition—alternatives to public schools. Besides, without bureaucratic government restraints, the for-profits are generally more efficient—offering "more bang for the buck."

A key to the revival of for-profit colleges could be a government voucher system that allows students to attend *any* approved (currently, "accredited") postsecondary institution, private or public. These voucher payments, however, would likely cover only part of the cost of schooling. It is doubtful states would give many vouchers for over $10,000 a year, necessitating students having to pay part of the instructional and living costs out of their own pockets (as well as those of their parents and possibly private lenders or investors by way of income share agreements). [1] If the federal Pell Grants were converted to genuine vouchers usable at for-profit private institutions, those, along with some state assistance, could cover most costs, particularly because for-profits have avoided many of the expenses of traditional not-for-profit higher education. Typically, they have lower capital costs (since they don't have the edifice complex afflicting most traditional schools), don't subsidize intercollegiate athletics, don't support large burdensome DEI bureaucracies, and so on.

As indicated earlier, one big problem with *any* governmentally involved solution was outlined decades ago by former education secretary William Bennett: Every dollar of government student aid increases the demand for higher education and leads to higher tuition fees. The *colleges* (and their staffs) capture a majority of funds intended for students. Dropping government money in the form of vouchers out of airplanes (or the equivalent) may create more problems than it solves. For example, price controls on private institutions would largely destroy the ability of entrepreneurs to forge a presumably successful and profitable approach to business expansion.

Kill Off Accreditation

The rationale behind accreditation may have once made sense—say, in 1950—when it was legitimate to have an agency identify unscrupulous performers in the higher education industry—the so-called diploma mills that offered dubious pieces of paper called "diplomas" for students who had allegedly but not really "learned" something. In recent decades, accreditation has been critical for one dominant reason: it is required to get access to federal aid for students and research grants for faculty. But even that justification is eliminated if the federal government completely exits the higher education business.

Accreditation agencies are numerous. Six are large regional accreditors offering general institutional accreditation, while hundreds of others serve a single academic discipline, such as law or business. As discussed elsewhere, the defects of accreditation are many: it is costly, provides little real consumer information, restricts competition, and is riddled with conflicts of interest.

In short, accreditation is an expensive, crude way of certifying competence. Moreover, if we instituted reforms such as a testing standard (the proposed National College Equivalence Examination), it would be easy to measure the learning outcomes of students. Other data, including an expanded College Scorecard (hopefully no longer run by the US Department of Education), could provide useful profiles of the quality of colleges, with organizations like *U.S. News & World Report* providing convenient consumer information to interested students: What do typical graduates earn? What proportion of students fail to graduate, or even make it to the second year? Which majors provide the highest-paying jobs at the school of interest? You don't need a regional accreditor like the Higher Learning Commission to make that determination: *U.S. News, Forbes,* the *Wall Street Journal,* maybe even *Consumer Reports,* can do this for you. Perhaps the state of Nebraska will have a voucher program for its residents, and the Nebraska State Board of Education can deny vouchers to students who attend schools with lower than a stated composite score that is based on factors such as graduation rates, postgraduate earnings, retention rates, and scores on the NCEE test administered near graduation. Perhaps the College Board, ACT, or similar organization will develop an Indicator of Collegiate Quality Index that could be used nationally.

Earlier we listed a plethora of problems with the existing accreditation procedures. Of growing concern, however, has been the notion that accreditation can be used to achieve ideological goals that reduce institutional autonomy, stifle intellectual diversity, and threaten unbridled but civil and peaceful expression of ideas. The notion, for example, that in order for a college to be accredited, its students must affirm some commitment to racial diversity or other goal is completely inconsistent with a vibrant learning community where individual freedom of expression is not only permitted but encouraged. To be sure, diversity in some learning settings is inappropriate: it is expected, for example, that seminaries run by a Roman Catholic diocese that is training priests will impose a requirement that all students be Catholic and adhere to the fundamental teachings of that church. This is fine and to be expected. But these religious learning communities offering postgraduate educational experiences generally do not receive government funding, nor do they seek accreditation.

An interesting approach to accreditation was successfully implemented in Florida with the blessing of Governor Ron DeSantis. Public schools are required to periodically change their accreditor. That potentially introduces an element of competition among the national accrediting organizations. This is not the preferred radical step (which is to completely eliminate the institutional accreditors) but appears to be an improvement over the status quo.

Competitive Credit Aggregators That Confer Degrees: A New Concept?

Universities reek of monopolistic practices. Students usually take courses from only one provider of educational services, the university they attend. These universities, in turn, are "accredited" by an organization that itself reeks of conflicts of interest and monopolistic practices. But does it have to be that way? Why can't students take courses from several universities, with taking perhaps no more than one-third of them from any one school? Why do we not have "credit aggregators," organizations (with either a profit or a not-for-profit status) that evaluate credits students send in from a variety of schools, accumulated to an established minimum magnitude and distributed in such a way as to meet the aggregator's standards for a bachelor's degree? And why not require students to take the National College Equivalence Examination to certify their mastery of general knowledge, critical thinking, and writing capabilities, and a command of more detailed knowledge in an area of special interest, the student's major? With that accomplished, the aggregator can issue a bachelor's degree. If students from that aggregator subsequently do well in life, the demand for its graduates will become strong.

Although students could still take all their courses at one school, the ease of transferring credits to the aggregator and that agency's conferral of degrees introduces an element of competition currently not present. Students trying to economize might look for courses that are cheap but seem qualitatively the equal of what is offered at their original "home" institution. A student at a fine liberal arts college with a reputation for offering solid general education experiences could in the third and fourth year of study take courses from a second institution with a high reputation in the student's major field of study. The degree could then be conferred by either the original liberal arts college or, if it is unwilling, the second college or even by the college credit aggregator itself.

Some elements of this idea have already been tried relatively successfully, notably by private firms like StraighterLine, but fuller implementation along the lines outlined above have been thwarted by such obstacles as accreditation mandates and government funding restrictions. If accreditation were eliminated or radically revised, along with federal financial assistance programs, that problem would essentially disappear.

At the same time, however, I fully acknowledge that going to college involves more than accumulating knowledge and getting a certificate that enhances vocational opportunities. An old saw is that students usually learn more from their classmates than from their instructors. Much collegiate learning and personal enjoyment come from informal associations with new friends. College is perhaps one-half the accumulation of knowledge and one-half the presence of other things that make the college years worthwhile, including vocationally relevant nonclassroom experiences (via the networking that college attendance and friendships bring and even part-time work while in college). Besides, for many, college is as much a "consumption" good (having fun, getting drunk, and dating) as it is an "investment" good. Many students, perhaps most, consider it a transitory gap of four years between mandatory secondary-level schooling and the real world. For many, attending a single school and making tons of new acquaintances, both academic and social, is a perfectly acceptable way to transition from adolescence to adulthood. There may be synergies, however, in having students attend multiple schools, or from professors selling their services to multiple colleges through instructional companies, with aggregators accumulating the credits earned at multiple providers of educational services.

Think Tanks: Should They Offer College Credit? Degrees?

Earlier we noted that independent, private, not-for-profit research centers have been flourishing, many emphasizing analyses of the issues of the day. Many publish serious research: at least five of the books I have written were sponsored in whole or in part by such think tanks. Much research has been disseminated by right-of-center think tanks created in the 1970s and later to try to offer alternatives to the mostly leftish policy recommendations emanating from universities, although it is also true that a number of left-leaning centers have also long existed (e.g., the Brookings Institution) or evolved in this century (e.g., New America, formerly the New America Foundation).

Couldn't these think tanks expand their mission by offering courses for college credit? Couldn't they have these courses marketed by degree aggregators or associate themselves with existing universities? Why doesn't the Cato Institute offer classes taught by Dr. Andrew Gillen, an employee of theirs who is a former instructor for Johns Hopkins University at its large center in Washington, DC, and an expert on higher education? Or Dr. Graham Walker, president of the Independent Institute, who has served as a professor, administrator, or president at several reputable American colleges and universities, one in the Ivy League? Or his colleague Williamson Evers, a former high-ranking US Department of Education official and Stanford PhD? Or, at the American Enterprise Institute, a whole host of distinguished scholars like education guru Rick Hess or the economist and financial expert Desmond Lachman? Or why can't the Hoover Institution's Summer Policy Boot Camp serve as the basis for instruction?[2]

A slightly wilder idea: Have the State Policy Network (SPN), a coalition of state and regionally centered think tanks, offer a wide variety of courses, possibly even a degree. Since the SPN affiliates have a conservative or libertarian orientation, perhaps they should start the Adam Smith or Milton Friedman University. Students would take many courses online, but perhaps some in person at one or more of the SPN-affiliated think tanks. ALEC, the American Legislative Exchange Council, does some policy analysis relating to higher education that could be expanded into college credit coursework.

Some non-university organizations already do some of this. Take the Ludwig von Mises Institute, a libertarian-oriented center in Auburn, Alabama, located on the edge of the Auburn University campus (but not affiliated with that school). For decades, it has offered each summer a Mises University program, where undergraduate or graduate students from colleges all over the nation come to learn about the mysteries and insights of Austrian economics. I taught there for several years and considered the intellectual quality of the discussions to be outstanding—sometimes dazzlingly so. Students from universities all over the US and, indeed, the entire planet, literally stay up half the night talking about issues raised in the daily lectures. If we wiped away artificial anticompetitive accreditation obstacles, why couldn't the Mises Institute and similar organizations offer credit-level courses marketed to college credit aggregators, if not full-fledged academic degrees? The Mises Institute even has a research component, publishing works with a libertarian orientation, along with offering an annual Austrian Student Scholars Conference where new ideas are vigorously discussed.

Other academic-oriented organizations have programs that enhance the learning and wisdom of college students. One is the Intercollegiate Studies Institute (ISI), headquartered in Delaware, which has a strong conservative orientation (its first president was William F. Buckley). It puts on all sorts of seminars and short courses for college students. In the first decade of this century, ISI conducted valuable surveys of the civic literacy of American college students, showing that most students have spotty knowledge of our history and civic institutions. Tests administered to freshmen and also to graduating seniors showed that the acquisition of what, to borrow from E. D. Hirsch, might be called "core knowledge" during the college years was embarrassingly meager—even at elite American universities.[3] Other conservative groups also promote non-university-affiliated forms of learning, most important perhaps the Liberty Fund, which puts on seminars for both students and professors across the country as well as reprints classic studies in the Western tradition.

One of the most fascinating and high-quality teaching experiences I ever had was at the Economics Institute at the University of Colorado, which once administered a program sponsored by the American Economic Association for foreign students coming for graduate study in the United States. During their time at the institute (much of it during the summer), they became acquainted with English-language instruction by a geographically diverse group of American economics professors. The professors had to be effective teachers, or they would not be asked to return (no tenure, no multiyear contracts). Some were top-flight scholars who came from such schools as Yale or Stanford to lecture for a few days. As a consequence, there was an absolutely first-rate faculty of professors doing a superlative job of teaching—yet no academic degrees were conferred, nor did any accreditor, as far as I know, ever try to stop it. Why can't other professional associations or similar groups enter the competition for students?

Stop the Policing of Free Expression

In recent years, woke college administrators have orchestrated or silently supported suppressions of free speech totally inappropriate for vibrant advanced learning communities. Professors who do not conform to the prevailing campus ethos are harassed, sometimes fired, for sins committed many years earlier that have already been adjudicated. Let me for brevity stress just a few examples here, starting with the shameful treatment by Princeton University of Joshua Katz, a well-known and distinguished classics professor who was fired by the Princeton Board of Trustees at the urging of President Christopher Eisgruber in May 2022.[4] Katz, writing in 2020 in an online publication (*Quillette*), criticized a faculty recommendation to investigate and punish "racist behaviors, incidents, research, and publication" occurring over

Princeton's history (the school had already removed the name of Woodrow Wilson, a former president of both Princeton and the United States, from its public policy school). Katz criticized a black student group that he referred to as a "small terrorist organization" for what he regarded as its inappropriate behavior in the Wilson-renaming controversy. In order to fire Katz for something other than simply exercising his First Amendment rights to free expression, Princeton drudged up a complaint about Katz for sexual misconduct occurring some *sixteen years earlier* that had long been known and previously fully adjudicated by the administration! As Princeton alumnus Edward Yingling put it, "Today the mob at Princeton got its man."

Princeton is far from the only Ivy League school to have had free speech issues. As indicated earlier, the University of Pennsylvania Law School at this writing is in the midst of an effort to fire a distinguished tenured professor, Amy Wax. Her transgression? She said things that made people mad—intolerable to some woke-supremist students, faculty, and administrators. For example, she noted that in her class black students were rarely in the top half of performers, and almost never in the top one-quarter. Penn says that is not true, but a host of national evidence supports the proposition that affirmative action has had some adverse effects on black students admitted to law schools with prior academic achievements below that of most other students.[5]

University attacks on expression are sometimes even directed at prominent donors and former trustees. Northwestern University received over $7 million in donations from longtime trustee Benjamin Slivka, who also devoted thousands of volunteer hours supporting his alma mater (e.g., by meeting with prospective future students). However, he received an email from a DEI apparatchik in Northwestern's Athletics Department saying, "several student-athletes reported . . . that they were upset with comments by you that they deemed racist and/or sexist . . . we . . . would appreciate it if you do not contact student-athletes . . . either by phone, in person or through social media." Slivka informs me that he has been "canceled" by the alma mater for whom he had loyally served and supported for decades and that the president and other key officials refuse to even talk to him.[6]

As indicated earlier, the attacks on free expression and efforts to impose an unquestioned uniform ideology on campuses are not confined to elite college campuses. In what I have called the ne plus ultra of outrageous college attempts at suppressing the freedom of faculty to express themselves, occurred at Ohio Northern University (ONU), at best a midquality liberal arts school in a small Ohio town that has a law school at which Scott Gerber taught for over two decades.[7] Gerber (who has a PhD in addition to a juris doctor degree from the University of Virginia) was teaching class when campus security and the town police came to his classroom and removed him to the dean's office where, in effect, he was told he was being fired and told to sign a separation agreement. Gerber, who has lectured at many prestigious schools, is by far the most distinguished scholar within ONU's otherwise mediocre law faculty and the author of numerous books and articles. His classes are always full and he gets many good reviews of his teaching. He was notified he was not teaching in the fall of 2023—*by a student*! Although not formally notified about why he was being fired, Gerber was noted on campus for having decried the obsession with DEI objectives that did not acknowledge the importance of *intellectual* diversity in the campus environment.

Again, the move to suppress free expression by university professors is not confined to the United States. In neighboring Canada, the famous University of Toronto psychology emeritus professor Jordan Peterson was recently told by the Ontario board regulating psychologists that he was losing his license to practice his profession unless he underwent "reeducation," because Peterson had said things that the licensing board found disturbing. The message: Shape up, or we will put you out of business.[8]

These accounts largely neglect the growing cancel culture where students or other protesters shout down speakers invited to campus whom the protesters view as unacceptable. A representative recent example: Heather Mac Donald, a fellow at the Manhattan Institute with degrees from Yale, the University of Cambridge, and Stanford, was supposed to give a lecture at Claremont McKenna College. She was shouted down by protesters. Unlike most schools, however, the college arranged for her to give her talk to a smaller audience from an alternative site and then live-streamed it to a larger group on the college's website. And, refreshingly, the school suspended a number of the disrupting students and reiterated its strong commitment to freedom of expression. Another well-known modern-day example came with the shouting down of, and protests against, the noted social scientist Charles Murray at Middlebury College, in which some participants suffered physical injury.

Such incidents are commonplace. The conservative columnist Ann Coulter was shouted down at Cornell, and a speaker at the SUNY Albany campus was prevented from giving a lecture, ironically titled "Free Speech on Campus"! However, there seems to be either widespread indifference to or, worse, acceptance of campus mobbing activities shutting down free discourse. A survey by FIRE (see below) of over forty-four thousand students showed 62 percent believed that shouting down of speakers was at least partially acceptable.[9]

The Good Guys: Pressuring Universities to Support Freedom of Expression

Fortunately, universities do not operate in a vacuum; outside watchdog groups call them out on outrageous behavior, often at least minimally forcing colleges to pause and moderate their behavior in attacking professors and students who dare to oppose the woke supremacy that has infested many campuses. Let me enumerate a few of the more prominent of these organizations.

FIRE (Foundation for Individual Rights and Expression) was founded in 1999, led by two prominent civil libertarians, University of Pennsylvania history professor Alan Charles Kors and attorney Harvey Silverglate, both of whom also coauthored a pioneering critique of the constraints on free expression in American higher education.[10] FIRE has been dogged in protecting the right of free expression on campus, filing dozens of lawsuits against universities that have constrained the legal expression of ideas by students or faculty, or violated basic due process in proceedings against students, particularly in sexual harassment cases. FIRE rarely loses lawsuits, and the mere threat of one has on many occasions led universities to back off attacks on student liberties reminiscent of behavior in totalitarian states like the Soviet Union or Nazi Germany. I have been on panels with FIRE president Greg Lukianoff and have been exceedingly impressed with FIRE's dedication, professionalism, and high success rate in legal encounters.

ACTA (American Council of Trustees and Alumni) was founded in the mid-1990s by a politically diverse group of prominent politicians and academics, led in this century primarily by Anne Neal and currently by Michael Poliakoff. As stated previously here, university governing boards tend to be non-activist rubber stamps, and when they do get active, their efforts tend to involve matters tangential to the primary missions of higher education, promoting learning and discovery within an environment that champions free expression and tolerance. In addition to promoting free expression like FIRE, ACTA advocates for a solid liberal arts education at universities and bemoans the decline in course requirements in areas like history or literature. The largest trustee organization, the Association of Governing Boards, seems to me to be an organization more supportive of the status quo, generally telling trustees that they have a limited decision-making role, certainly not an initiator of major policy changes on campus. I testified recently before the Ohio legislature with ACTA president Poliakoff on introducing some major reforms (including the mandatory study of history or civics and the protection of free expression emphasized by FIRE), as well as at a meeting of trustees of all fourteen Ohio public universities that Poliakoff helped organize, trying to make trustees constructively active in promoting free expression and developing an appreciation of our nation's heritage. Numerous studies by ACTA have documented the paucity of knowledge by American college students of our history, the decline in study of Shakespeare and other giants of our literary heritage, and so on.

NAS (National Association of Scholars) is an organization of about three thousand professors and other scholars founded in the late 1980s and run since 2009 by Peter Wood. A group of conservatively oriented intellectuals, NAS has championed many of the same causes as FIRE and ACTA, but other ones as well. For example, it has sounded the alarm about the potential damage to academic integrity and indeed national security by Chinese incursions into American universities through Confucius Institutes. NAS has increasingly played a role in opposing DEI mandates and has supported ACTA's efforts to incorporate a strong liberal arts–based component into college degrees. It includes Amy Wax and Joshua Katz, discussed above, on its board of directors (full disclosure: I am a longtime board member as well). Peter Wood wrote strong and cogent letters protesting the Scott Gerber academic fatwa discussed above (as did ACTA's Michael Poliakoff). NAS's magazine, *Academic Questions*, discusses many of the higher education concerns of the day.

The **Heterodox Academy** is a relatively new organization, founded in 2015. Its mission is single-minded: to fight a lack of viewpoint and intellectual diversity on American college campuses. One of the cofounders, Jonathan

Haidt, a psychologist in the business school at New York University, coauthored with FIRE's Greg Lukianoff an influential 2018 book, *The Coddling of the American Mind*, which argued that American universities are setting up a generation of students and, by extension, our entire nation, for failure by overprotecting our students with such monstrosities as "trigger warnings" and "safe spaces." People on campus are self-censoring, afraid to express themselves—the heart of what universities are about.[11] Heterodox has attracted a sizable membership (several thousand) of persons of varying political persuasions concerned about the deterioration of the American collegiate milieu. It is now run by former Brown University political philosopher John Tomasi.

The James G. Martin Center for Academic Renewal in Raleigh, North Carolina, is devoted primarily to research on higher education issues, with a distinctly libertarian or conservative orientation. While historically the center had a strong North Carolina orientation, today its work largely encompasses the whole American collegiate scene.

The **AAUP** (American Association of University Professors) is the oldest of the groups discussed here, having been founded in 1915 by distinguished academics (including the famed philosopher and psychologist John Dewey). Today, most people think, correctly, of the AAUP as a labor union that engages in collective bargaining for professors at a number of the nation's campuses. Well into the twentieth century, college professors had no guaranteed job security and could, and occasionally were, fired for expressing views not in favor with the university or college administration. The AAUP promoted the concept of "tenure," which came widely accepted by the middle of the last century. Its "statement of principles on academic freedom and tenure" developed in the 1920s and codified in 1940 and updated since, is considered the standard interpretation of faculty rights of expression and even today remains an important feature of American academic life. To this day, the AAUP defends faculty, even non-AAUP members, whose tenure is revoked in an inappropriate fashion (e.g., without a hearing). In the case of Scott Gerber, the Ohio chapter of the AAUP wrote not one, but *five* letters of protest to the Ohio Northern University Board of Trustees and that school's president. That said, however, the AAUP has become essentially a labor union with a distinct leftish orientation, sometimes used to attack those who do not subscribe to its increasingly woke policy prescriptions.

Conclusion: Needed Help Is Coming

Fortunately, American universities do not operate completely independently. Although excessive external interference in the affairs of college campuses would be unfortunate, the universities don't operate in a vacuum. They are very much dependent on external support. With that comes some legitimate monitoring and even supervision. Although some of that, especially for state universities, comes from government entities, there is also a vibrant and important network of NGOs (nongovernmental organizations) that not only work to constrain universities through the mobilization of public opinion, but also offer non-university forms of competing providers of knowledge and ideas. As Chairman Mao once said, "Let a hundred flowers bloom!"[12]

Beyond Instruction: Research and Other Activities

IT IS A rare institution of higher education in the United States that doesn't at least claim to have as one of its missions the expansion of the pool of knowledge that we possess. The one exception, perhaps: community colleges offering two-year degrees. Even four-year liberal arts colleges with no graduate instruction usually profess to have a faculty that is at least somewhat involved in discovery—learning new things about the world in which we live. When I taught at one of those schools (Claremont McKenna College), a majority of the faculty that I knew had research activity that they seriously pursued to some extent. Indeed, it is widely argued that, other things equal, active researchers make better teachers, as they can share insights into the importance of academic research.[1] The act and implementation of discovery is critical to the advancement of civilization, and universities play an important role in achieving that worthy objective.

Of course, universities do other things besides instruct students and expand the stock of knowledge. For many Americans, colleges and universities are best known for their athletic teams, especially football and basketball. Additionally, some colleges run hospitals and clinics and present plays, concerts, and public lectures to both entertain and enlighten the general public.

Public Perception: It Is Research, Not Teaching, That Makes Schools "Great"

Colleges and universities both create and disseminate knowledge and creative ideas. Yet when people assess the quality or accomplishments of institutions, they often give top priority to the research achievements rather than the quality of the teaching and student-learning experience. Look at the rankings of colleges and universities by popular media outlets. Some, particularly those done by non-US assessors like the *Shanghai Ranking* (China) or even the *Times Higher Education* (Britain), give little or no emphasis to teaching, for example, making no attempt to measure student assessments of their instructional or advising experiences.

One reason is simple. Research accomplishment is easier to measure: How many articles did Professor X publish? How many citations has she in reputable journals? Citations show how an author's perspectives receive wider recognition and consequentially impact the world of ideas. Also, how many and how large are the research grants she has received? Moreover, research has a greater *geographic* visibility than does teaching accomplishment. The great teaching of a professor is known locally, but not nationally. Indeed, at some highly ranked institutions, the most famous and renowned professors do very little teaching, often only to small graduate seminars. How many highly regarded professors at schools like these teach large introductory classes? A renowned professor's research is published in journals read by scholars around the world. A great teacher's "output" is recognized by at most a few hundred students in a single college community and perhaps by some appreciative former students.

Compounding things, who gets rewarded the most, the superb teacher or the excellent researcher? Almost invariably, the perceived top-flight researcher. Publish or perish. Great researchers get bigger raises, have an easier time getting tenure, receive grants to travel and speak in exotic locales, get invited to participate as consultants for lucrative fees in private matters (e.g., legal disputes), and so on. As a consequence of all that, they get greater job security, often having competing schools clamoring for their services. This happens far less frequently for great teachers.

I looked at the 2024 *Wall Street Journal*/College Pulse rankings of US colleges and universities. Only one of the top twenty schools was a public university, a category of schools educating roughly three-quarters of American college students. Nearly every one of them offered graduate degrees. The top traditional liberal arts college (Amherst) ranked 8th. The list included several schools receiving among the largest US government research grants.

Personally, I have attended or taught at four of the top thirty-five schools on the *WSJ*/College Pulse list—Northwestern, Washington University in St. Louis, Claremont McKenna College, and the University of Illinois—and I perceived that the best undergraduate learning experience was at Claremont McKenna, a small school offering only bachelor's degrees. Classes were small, professors were expected to have generous office hours, maybe eating lunch once a semester with some of their students (at college expense). Although a highly successful research-oriented (and high-paid) professor might end up at Northwestern or Washington University in St. Louis, you rarely find them at a school like Claremont McKenna unless it offers graduate programs with a strong research emphasis.

How Do You Measure Research Accomplishment?

Is Professor X a good researcher? Often in response, you will be told that "he received over $4 million in research grants over the past five years." Yet that is a measure of *inputs*, not outputs. It is a measure of *resources consumed* rather than a true measure of contributions to society from insights from *research accomplished*.

The other most commonly given response is that "X has a very high number of citations in respected academic journals." Indeed, researchers often talk about the *h*-index, a measure of the magnitude and impact of published works, or they look at the number of citations of major papers as indicated on Google Scholar. Although those are a bit better since they measure an outcome (published papers) rather than an input, they are still a measure of the popularity of a professor's ideas or discoveries more than a tangible measure of how those ideas or discoveries improved the human condition.

To be sure, there are other indicators of research accomplishment. A patent indicates that the federal government acknowledges that the researcher has made a uniquely significant innovation. Even here, things are often muddled. Many patents are essentially worthless—not all unique ideas are valuable. In the modern era, teams of researchers generally work together, so distinguishing who the truly innovative and most impressive member of the team is sometimes not easy. Additionally, the conferring of some awards enhances the probability that an individual is making a real contribution to society, such as the Nobel or Pulitzer Prizes or a MacArthur "genius" grant. Even these awards, however, are often tainted by political considerations (especially true in recent years of the MacArthur grants).

To me, perhaps the ultimate manifestation of true accomplishment from research or other creative activity is provided by *markets*: How much do real human beings pay to consume the product or service arising from academic innovation? If a scientist invents a drug that enhances the quantity or quality of life, he or she has truly accomplished something and deserves to be handsomely rewarded. At my university, a friend of mine invented a human growth hormone marketed by a major pharmaceutical company that produced well over $100 million in royalties for my university—as well as similar bounty to himself, a good example of a win-win arrangement for society. Music professors occasionally strike it rich with a composition that is commercially acclaimed or from a recording that strikes the public's fancy. I have had several English department colleagues who have made a fair amount of money from plays or television adaptations (e.g., the Netflix series *The Queen's Gambit*, which drew on the work of the late Walter Tevis).

Most US Research Is Not Done in Universities

Table 11.1 shows official federal data on research and development expenditures at American universities. Although universities like to convey the perception that most research in the United States is conducted by universities, that is not the case. A large portion of the attempts to create new things is carried out by private firms. Pharmaceutical companies spend vast sums trying to develop new drugs. Companies like SpaceX have spent huge sums to develop superior rockets—so good that the US government's own NASA uses them for space exploration. Moreover, some important federally funded research that the public associates with universities is done at federally owned research centers administered by universities, so that research is university-centered only in a limited sense. The Lawrence Livermore National Laboratory, for example, once primarily associated with the University of California, is now administered by a consortium that includes Cal Berkeley but also other firms, such as the Battelle Memorial Institute and some private companies.

Table 11.1 US spending on university research and development in billions of dollars, 1970–2021

Year	Total	Federal	Institutional	Business	Other
1970	16,307	11,502	1,697	426	2,782
1980	19,938	13,476	2,746	776	2,940
1990	33,773	19,986	6,232	2,337	5,218
2000	47,339	27,613	9,323	3,393	7,010
2010	73,829	45,147	14,387	3,857	10,438
2015	78,535	43,342	19,021	4,583	11,589
2021	86,872	49,228	22,482	5,119	13,043

Sources: National Science Foundation; author's calculations.
Note: Amounts are in 2021 dollars using the consumer price index for all urban consumers (CPI-U).

Note that inflation-adjusted university research spending grew over five-fold in the past half century, an increase of over 3 percent a year, considerably faster than the rate of population growth, and slightly faster than the growth of the total economy. The research component share of total output remained rather constant. Note the dramatic slowdown in federal research support after 2010 and, even more important, the large growth in institutional support, meaning universities are increasingly using their other resources (tuition and state subsidy dollars, endowment funds, private donations) to finance research efforts. However, they are also sharing in royalties that are generated by sponsored research.

Many persons like to draw a distinction between "basic" research and "applied research." Universities are important in achieving scientific discoveries that open up the potential for commercial application. The universities do the basic research, and then private companies apply the new research insights to developing products of use to humankind. In general, universities are too distant from markets to gauge the potential commercial success of products.[2] Private companies aim to make a profit, which they can do only if their products (say new drugs) are successful and in demand. I would add that the government receives significant income from taxes paid by companies that launch significant technological innovations. The universities, by contrast, depend a good deal on federal funding to undertake even basic research. Much of the federal funding supports national security objectives, although many federal agencies such as the National Institutes of Health (NIH) and the National Science Foundation (NSF) support research designed ultimately to extend the quantity or quality of human life.[3]

The statistics incorporated in table 11.1 are not perfect. The dollar amounts for university research expenditures are generally underreported since a fair amount of unfunded research is conducted. Indeed, the general reduction in teaching loads at colleges and universities in the late twentieth and early twenty-first centuries was largely justified as needed to increase the research productivity of faculty. I would guess that of the several hundred scholarly writings I have done over a lifetime, less than 10 percent received any sort of private or public outside funding. And the number of publishing outlets grew enormously in this period, even more so since online publishing in "journals" became popular after about 2010.

Research and the Law of Diminishing Returns

One "law" of economics that is close to universally accepted among economists of all political stripes is the law of diminishing returns. If you add more of a resource, say labor, to fixed amounts of other resources, say land and machinery, output will rise, but by diminishing amounts. A farm with one worker, say the owner, might produce ten thousand bushels of wheat annually. If he adds a second worker, a hired hand, output probably will rise, maybe to fifteen thousand bushels, and to seventeen thousand bushels if a third worker is added. The first farmer was responsible for ten thousand bushels—but the second worker increased that output by only five thousand more bushels and the third worker only two thousand more: diminishing returns.

Diminishing returns are definitely present in academic research. Suppose a political science department with fifteen professors each teaching eight courses a year (four each semester) lowers the teaching load to six courses per year (three per semester) in order to promote research. Suppose that the political science faculty collectively turned out ten academic papers each year, but with the teaching load reduction, that grows to thirteen papers annually. Research productivity seems to be rising in tandem with teaching load reductions: teaching fell by 25 percent (from 120 to 90 courses), while research seemingly rose by a slightly greater 30 percent. No diminishing returns! But what if the three additional papers arising from lighter teaching loads appeared in obscure journals and received no citations in major journals (or *h*-index enhancement), thus no attention in the scholarly community? Then research output, meaningfully evaluated, rose very little—teaching declined more than research increased by objective measures of output. It is my sense that this has happened in modern America with its proliferation of scholarly outputs.

A distinguished English-language scholar, Mark Bauerlein, now retired from Emory University, once did a count of the number of articles written about William Shakespeare at the end of the twentieth century and the beginning of this one. Over a twenty-year period, about twenty thousand articles were written about Shakespeare. I enthusiastically accept the proposition that the Bard was the greatest writer in the English language, certainly someone with whom any college-educated American should have a passing familiarity by reading at least a couple of his plays and attending a theatrical performance or two of them as well. But Shakespeare died over four hundred years ago, and while worthy of being taught and perhaps even worthy of a bit of new research in light of new technologies allowing an analysis of his writings, the output of articles and other writings (books, chapters of books, and so on) is simply overwhelming—roughly three articles a day—every single day of the year. It is almost like you can read a new morning interpretation of the Bard, then get a new afternoon insight, culminating in a third new exploration as a nighttime academic snack—every day!! As Bauerlein suggests, wouldn't the world be better off with a much smaller number of new publications—maybe 90 percent less, or a mere two each week with regard to Shakespeare—with the faculty teaching more classes (potentially lowering student fees) or even, I would argue, doing something else useful in life, maybe selling used cars or writing speeches for marginally literate politicians?

The extent of diminishing returns, of courses, varies with academic discipline and even the subject of academic research. Conceivably, we have a need for more research in some promising fields where new technology (AI?) is opening up new vistas. Because of academic tenure and lifetime appointments, we tend to have a surplus of faculty with expertise in areas already heavily researched, and possibly a shortage of cutting-edge faculty in areas of promising research exploration.

The Growing Scandal of Fraudulent Research and Research Theft

Professorial success increasingly depends on publication and research recognition. Aware of this, a growing number of faculty are simply making up results in order to achieve publication and acclaim. In some cases, where results are mixed, they report the novel, most interesting, and unique findings and bury the more conventional and mundane results. In my research heyday, I might run a hundred regression equations designed to assess the validity of some hypothesis, say that lowering individual income taxes enhances the rate of economic growth. Suppose in ninety regressions, the results show that the hypothesis is confirmed, in nine regressions, that there is no observable relationship between taxes and growth, and in one regression, that the completely opposing hypothesis holds: raising income taxes tends to increase economic growth. An honest researcher (which I believe I was) would accurately summarize the entirety of results, perhaps concluding that "the preponderance of evidence supports the proposition that lowering taxes is growth enhancing." But a person who, maybe for ideological reasons, opposes that interpretation, might simply report and discuss in great detail the single case where the evidence suggests that government spending financed through higher taxes is growth inducing. The growing politicization of the faculty has almost certainly increased this problem. Academic journals have unwittingly published a number of studies later revealed as fraudulent. The president of Stanford University for seven years, Marc Tessier-Lavigne, resigned in the summer of 2023 after it was revealed that an investigation by Stanford's board of trustees showed that several studies he authored contained manipulated data.[4] Reports of plagiarism of articles by Harvard president Claudine Gay showed that ethically dubious research practices—including intellectual theft—pervade even the highest levels of American higher education. The Gay revelations ultimately led to her resignation. Indeed, a few months before the Gay plagiarism allegations, a well-known Harvard professor, Francesca Gino, the Tandon Family Professor of Business Administration, was placed on unpaid administrative leave following an extensive investigation suggesting significant amounts of her research used falsified data.

A large number of new "journals" appear to be questionable paper mills operating for a profit. Authors pay the "journal" to publish their work, which is not subject to rigorous peer review and a large portion of which has dubious or erroneous results. Wiley, an old and reputable publisher, recently closed down nineteen journals riddled with fraudulent papers, having retracted more than 11,300 papers that appeared dubious or fraudulent.[5]

Additionally, fictitious research results are often claimed in highly reputable journals. For example, a large number of papers dealing with cancer research discuss cell lines that intrepid investigators have found recently simply do not exist, potentially literally having life-threatening effects in the long run.[6] The integrity of academic scientific research has been materially negatively impacted.

A related issue, mostly beyond the purview of this book, arises from the theft of scientific research. In particular, there is a growing and serious national security concern over the illegal transfer of technology and scientific ideas to the Chinese, and the universities are increasingly involved in these issues. Should US universities even have relationships with Chinese schools in light of this?

Issues in Research Funding

As previously enunciated, American universities are wards of the state, highly dependent on third parties for funding. This is doubly true of academic research, which gets a lot of funding from the federal government, some occasionally from state governments, and much from private foundations or other charitable organizations. And, as mentioned earlier, schools themselves devote some of their resources from tuition fees, donations, and investments to support their mission of funding research, especially by reducing the teaching expectations of the faculty.

In principle, it may make sense for governments to fund basic research— the exploration of fundamental scientific principles that can then perhaps be further developed by private entrepreneurs to enhance the betterment of humankind. People outside the STEM disciplines often complain that there is little funding of their research, and increasing our understanding and collection of humanistic, social science, and artistic endeavors is important too. For example, we need not only teach about our past but also increase our knowledge of it through new historical research. In can be argued that some of the artistic and non-hard-science research serves the common good—a better understanding of our past, for example, helps us understand what being "American" or even "human" means and, in a sense, provides the glue that binds people together. New forms of creative artistic activities can improve our welfare by providing beautiful new forms of human expression.

Sometimes research funded to increase our base of knowledge in the humanities or social sciences may have a "basic" dimension to it with commercial applications. Artists and their endeavors may attract the public, and their works may sell in galleries for thousands of dollars. Composers write music or playwrights theatrical contributions that are commercially popular. Who should get the benefits of the incomes derived—the artists, composers, or scientists—or the universities that initially funded them, sometimes with outside support (i.e., the federal government)? This is especially an issue in the natural sciences and engineering. I can recall that one of my father's golf partners in the 1960s and 1970s, John Bardeen, was the only man to win two Nobel Prizes in Physics, one for something with monumental commercial applications, the transistor, having a near transformative effect on human behavior. However, I do not recall that Professor Bardeen lived as ostentatiously as the commercial importance of his work would suggest was warranted (although he lived comfortably and belonged to the top local country club). Yet he did his transistor work at a private firm (Bell Labs) and his later work (leading to such medical advances as MRI technology) at the University of Illinois.

Very often, arrangements are made whereby a college and the faculty discoverer or creator share in the spoils. This was codified in 1980 in the Bayh-Dole Act (Patent and Trademark Law Amendments Act), allowing contractors (often universities) to receive royalty incomes from discoveries and inventions. It could be argued that because profit-making firms ultimately benefit from basic research, they should fund it as well, and we should privatize most scientific funding (perhaps outside of research related to the military and national security).

Even if the "common good" dimension of much academic research justifies some government funding, some issues in implementation suggest the system is far from operating optimally. This is most apparent with regard to the issue of overhead on federal grants, almost all for scientific research. Typically, organizations like the National Science Foundation (NSF) or the National Institutes of Health (NIH) provide funds for faculty salaries and benefits, research assistance, travel, supplies, some specialized lab equipment, and so forth. But universities correctly argue that the institution has additional indirect expenses—heating and air-conditioning the facilities where the work occurs, paying maintenance people to keep the facilities in good shape and administrators to help keep account of grants and assure that funds are properly used, and so on.

Consequently, on federal grants universities negotiate a standard overhead rate to be added to the amount needed to compensate the researchers for the project. One with 60 percent overhead might provide $800,000 for the researchers' salaries and research-associated expenses (i.e., lab equipment, travel) plus 60 percent of that, or $480,000 for overhead, for a total grant of $1,280,000. Historically, the overhead amounts have varied a good deal by institution. One researcher said to me, only half-jokingly, that "Harvard gets a big overhead percentage because it has expensive marble floors to maintain, while we have cheap linoleum tile that is cheaper to keep up." The grants administration folks at some schools are few and moderately paid, while at others there is a larger, more richly paid bureaucracy. Why should schools that have more extravagant "overhead" expenses get more richly rewarded?

Moreover, many schools collect enough in overhead money that they give some of it back to the researchers themselves as incentives to get still more research grants. A lot of effort goes into overhead negotiations. Why not have a standardized nonnegotiable national rate of, say, 20 to 25 percent and give more money direct to researchers? If the federal agencies approve $25 billion in proposals for research with a 50 percent average overhead surcharge, the total cost to the government is $37.5 billion. If, however, the overhead rate is 25 percent, they can fund $30 billion in research spending that will cost the same $37.5 billion after adding in overhead. Universities and grant-giving federal agencies could get rid of some costly grant administration staff and actual research would likely increase.

Alternatively, a conceptually superior approach would be to evaluate research proposals mainly on research promise, but secondarily and importantly, on *cost*. Here is a way it might work: Have a score between 1 and 100 for each research proposal. Have 70 points be determined by a committee of peer researchers as is done at the present, evaluated on the potential scientific and social value of the expected research. Have 30 points depend on cost—18 points based on the direct costs of the proposal (the lower the cost, the more points earned), 12 points on the requested overhead amount. A school can claim high overhead allowances and extravagant amounts for travel, summer compensation for researchers (e.g., one-third of the academic year salary as opposed to two-ninths), and so on. Doing so, however, will reduce the total evaluation score and perhaps prevent funding. Seeking a high overhead percentage, for example, could torpedo the entire proposal.

Collaboration with Business and State Economic Development Groups

State and local political leaders and even trustees of private schools often argue that university research should augment efforts for economic development—expanding productive resources that can provide jobs and enhance the lives of residents in the broader community. Community colleges can train moderately high-skilled workers to help produce specialized goods (e.g., computer chips). More importantly, perhaps, researchers could become sufficiently well known to attract businesses utilizing the fruits of high-level university research efforts. Silicon Valley evolved around academic research powerhouses like Stanford and Cal Berkeley and a number of smaller but consequential business expansions have occurred in the vicinity of other universities.

Although that is all true, there is not much evidence suggesting that conscious state efforts to support universities in order to improve the standard of living for the population or to stimulate the migration of capital and highly skilled workers have had positive payoffs. Indeed, using statistical techniques to analyze the correlation between state spending on universities and economic growth, I find either no statistically significant positive relationship or, more often and even worse, a *negative* relationship.[7] To fund universities, we take resources from a highly efficient and market-driven competitive private sector and give them to universities that are much less market driven and distinctly less efficient.

Universities as Entertainment: The Strange World of College Sports

When a large portion of the American population thinks about colleges and universities, it doesn't think about the learning or research outcomes on campus. Instead, it starts talking about the football or basketball teams. American universities—unlike those in every other major nation—are a major source of entertainment for many months a year to millions who follow the two American-invented sports of football (as opposed to European "football," or soccer) and basketball. These have become a multibillion-dollar industry with key figures (especially top coaches) often making many times more than their ostensible boss, the university president.

The importance of college sports varies enormously by school. Most large and midsized schools are members of the National Collegiate Athletics Association (NCAA), and a majority of them are so-called Division II or Division III schools, where the commercial dimension of sports is relatively modest, although even at many Division III liberal arts colleges, participation on athletic teams is still considered an important device for recruiting new students. Roughly 260 midsize to large schools are in the top Division I, divided into two categories, called FCS (Football Championship Subdivision, with 128 schools) and FBS (Football Bowl Subdivision, with 133 schools). The crème de la crème of the schools athletically are about 68 members of four powerful FBS athletic conferences, the Big Ten, Southeastern Conference, Atlantic Coast Conference, and the Big Twelve Conference (the Pacific Coast Conference, or Pac-12, previously powerful, was apparently squeezed out of existence in a conference realignment in 2023).

Dozens of the athletic departments at the top FBS schools have annual budgets in the $100–$200 million range. Top football and basketball coaches routinely earn seven-digit salaries. Until a few years ago, players received "scholarships" that covered their costs of attending college—and almost nothing else, even though the best players on commercially important college teams added literally millions of dollars annually to the school's revenue stream. The suppression of player salaries by the NCAA cartel meant that the best of them were severely exploited by the schools.[8] Recent years have seen a partial retreat from that policy, with players now allowed to collect royalties for the use of their name, image, or likeness in various ways (e.g., on sweatshirts). Because players make less than they contribute to the revenue stream, there are surplus funds that seem largely to end up in the hands of the adults supervising the players— financial child molestation at its greatest. Very recently, however, the NCAA and leading conferences have shown a willingness to begin paying salaries to athletes on a limited basis, a huge shift in position, but one that as this writing has not yet taken effect.[9]

The accounting practices of universities regarding intercollegiate sports would certainly not pass muster with organizations like the Securities and Exchange Commission or the Financial Accounting Standards Board. For example, they do not routinely report as expenses the depreciation on their enormous capital assets—massive stadiums sometimes seating over a hundred thousand persons. Even so, in a typical year fewer than twenty of the big-revenue schools truly break even on sports, even counting alumni donations for sports that the schools might have at least partially received even if there were no big-time sports teams.

Fervent supporters of high-revenue-producing college football and basketball teams argue there are enormous positive spillover effects. The teams solidify loyalty to the schools, enhancing alumni support. Players learn important life lessons, including leadership qualities, discipline, and teamwork.

The opposing view? Big-time college sports are a costly embarrassment that has nothing to do with higher learning. With current "transfer portal" rules, some players change schools nearly every year, further diminishing any remote connection to the notion that team participants are true students with a sideline activity as an amateur athlete. The fall 2023 University of Colorado football team had about 50 (!) newly transferred students, for example. Debilitating injuries among athletes, many of them manifested only later in life, impose enormous costs not measured by standard accounting methods. College football and basketball constitute de facto minor league teams for the National Football League and National Basketball Association.

Solution? One possible idea is to divorce college athletics from the universities. Universities can monetize their name and benefit from traditions, but retreat to the business of education.[10] Schools could sell the rights to use their name, could rent or sell their vast stadiums, basketball arenas, and luxurious practice facilities to private, for-profit entities (theoretically including existing professional teams), perhaps imposing some limits, insisting, for example, that athletes be of college age with some modest affiliation with the relevant university. Some professional teams are selling for billions of dollars these days—surely the University of Texas, Ohio State, or many other football teams would be worth *minimally* a few hundred million dollars each, which could nicely enhance university endowments. Again, I repeat: higher education consists of schools of many different shapes and cultures, so what is best for football powers like the Universities of Michigan, Alabama, or Texas is almost certainly different from what is best for an urban midsize university or a liberal arts college, or schools in the Ivy League, which do not grant athletic scholarships. In any case, the operating environment for college sports seems to be changing substantially and constantly, and likely will be materially different in a few years.

Other Major Operations: Medical Centers and More

As indicated earlier, instructing students to be physicians, nurses, dentists, and other medical-related occupations is a legitimate, indeed important, function of a comprehensive large university. But many of these operations, especially the large medical schools, have chosen to operate within the university auspices large hospital or clinic operations that often rival the rest of the university in their size. Some universities develop clinical facilities serving the general public that are located long distances from the campus where students are taught—why are these not spun off into separate entities? Universities have enough problems doing their core academic mission and have no particular expertise in running large commercial operations. Accordingly, I am not going to delve much into this complex matter.

Similarly, as a byproduct of academic programs in the fine and performing arts, schools put on concerts and plays, make films, and operate art galleries and sometimes museums. These programs sometimes combine visiting professional groups to entertain not only the university community but also the general public with some enhancement of learning opportunities for students. My university, for example, recently had the Columbus Symphony Orchestra perform before a sizable audience, but with students from the Ohio University School of Music joining in performing some pieces—a nice combination of educational enhancement with community enrichment and learning as well.

Reprising a point made earlier, I have long felt schools should foster more civilized debate on the issues of the day, not only for their own students but, room capacity permitting, also for the general public. Again, why don't more schools sponsor "Athenian Dialogues" several times each year, involving debates of the burning issues of the day: optimal immigration policy, changes in our public assistance programs, American involvement in overseas conflicts (Ukraine, Taiwan, the Middle East), and so on. Done appropriately, these could provide great learning opportunities for both town and gown, promote intellectual diversity, and expand the mission of schools in an appropriate and low-cost way.

Finally, in the 1860s and after, the federal government created dozens of "land grant" universities, which had as an initial purpose the support of agricultural extension activities. County extension agents were created to help local farmers and others engage in best practices in their occupations. Does this 150-year-old system still make sense? Are the costs associated with it greater than the benefits? I frankly don't know, but I am somewhat dubious and think it is an area where efficiencies are potentially achievable.

Conclusion

Throughout history, centers of learning have sought to do more than convey existing knowledge and perceived truths (including religious perspectives) to students. That has been increasingly true: the importance of non-instructional activities has expanded over time. The concept of a "research university" arose in Germany in the eighteenth and nineteenth centuries, reached America shortly before 1900, and has expanded dramatically since. It raises lots of questions, none of which have definitively "correct" answers that apply to all schools or places. Should individual faculty both teach and do research, and in what proportions? Should good researchers exercise what we economists call their "comparative advantage" and spend all or most of their time in their labs or other research spaces, assisted by, and mentoring, a small number of advanced graduate students?

The use of incentives to spur efficiency and higher productivity applies in the research as well as the teaching domain. Federal policies of funding research need reexamining—for example, the cumbersome and expensive policy of determining "overhead" financial requirements for grant research. Should more research go to the lowest-priced bidder as is done in most other human endeavors? In medical schools, what is the optimal level of involvement of students in research activities designed to improve the quantity and quality of life? Should the commercial activities of, say, a medical center (with clinics and hospitals) be split off into separate corporations with cooperative arrangements with the universities? Indeed, should universities sell their medical facilities (and associated hospitals, parking garages, cafeterias, and so on) to private firms? Big corporations are constantly spinning off operations that do not fit in well with the core activities—shouldn't universities do the same? That is, shouldn't they concentrate on doing what they have historically done reasonably well—teaching and basic research—and leave the rest to others?

12

Conclusion: Three Key Expressions to Guide Collegiate Reform

THREE EXPRESSIONS, SUMMING to merely twenty words, occasionally voiced or written in everyday contemporary America, provide us with guidance in our efforts to make American higher education cheaper, more efficient, more intellectually diverse, more relevant. They are:

1. "It was the best of times, it was the worst of times." (Charles Dickens, *A Tale of Two Cities*)
2. "Necessity is the mother of invention." (an old proverb)[1]
3. "Creative destruction." (Joseph Schumpeter, *Capitalism, Socialism and Democracy*)

"The Best of Times, the Worst of Times"[2]

American higher education is full of contradictions. If you asked a cross-section of highly educated persons across the planet to name the country with the best colleges and universities in the world, I am fairly confident that the United States would get the most votes. It pioneered the concept of providing higher education to large portions of the adult population. American universities have led the world in advanced research. Students flock to American schools from all over the world—far more than Americans emigrating to other countries to get advanced learning. Hence, these are "the best of times."

Yet American universities are very costly, using far more resources per student taught than other countries, operating well below reasonable levels of capacity and efficiency. Moreover, they have increasingly been ideological and intolerant of free expression, and have lost substantial support from the

American public that finances them, as manifested in falling enrollments. They have become dramatically more left-wing than in the past or than the American people generally.[3] Moreover, there are even signs that America is starting to lose its dominant position in academic research. Hence, these are "the worst of times."

"Necessity Is the Mother of Invention"

American universities, while notoriously "liberal" (in the American progressive left sense of the word), are intensely conservative or even insidiously traditional in another sense: they are slow to change their ways, doing most of the important things the same way in which they were done a generation ago, or even a century ago. Distinctive features of the "peculiar institution" of higher education, such as tenure, make change difficult. As we economists like to say, colleges have huge fixed costs, making the reallocation of resources to more productive uses difficult and problematic. Enormous subsidies, mostly from governments but some from private philanthropies that are often incorporated into endowments, have shielded schools from desired change. But the rising problems provide incentives to try to bring about needed change.

Yet the problems of higher education, along with the worldwide demographic reality of plunging birth rates, are posing existential challenges for college presidents (as manifested in their increasingly short tenures as their problems grow). The threat of closure is looming larger and public universities are facing growing pressures from previously largely contented politicians who typically have legal and a good deal of financial control over their destiny. Previously taboo actions are starting to happen: tenure is getting more scrutinized and losing its dominance, for example. Massive administrative expansion is starting to come under closer scrutiny. Scandals questioning academic integrity (i.e., plagiarism) and the backlash over the congressional testimony of elite college presidents have heightened the amount of public scrutiny. At this writing, two flagship state universities, West Virginia University and the University of Arizona, are facing financial woes requiring large budget cuts. Other universities are facing a Hobson's choice: do certain unpalatable things—or die. I turn to obstacles to innovation more substantially in the last half of this chapter.

"Creative Destruction"

As Joseph Schumpeter astutely pointed out, the success and vibrancy of the private competitive free-market system is that it constantly adjusts to changes—population change, new inventions, changing scarcities of resources, new consumer fads, wars, droughts, pandemics. In a thriving free market, resources are constantly moving to alternative uses, which require some things to "die" in order to allow others to be born. Big mistakes are not only often costly but can also be fatal. Failure to embrace a new technology, for example, can lead to falling sales and rising costs relative to competing firms, sometimes enough to force firms to go bankrupt or sell themselves at a low price to a competitor. It rarely happens, however, in higher education. Incentives are bigger, therefore leading to more corrective actions, in the market-disciplined business world than in the ivory tower. Success can bring great wealth, whereas failure can mean unemployment and bankruptcy in business, but seldom in higher education.

Consequently, in our colleges and universities, the reallocation of resources needed in a changing society has been slow in coming. For example, the top universities today as evaluated by veteran observers are very much the same ones as were at the top a generation ago—there are few if any vibrant new kids on the block, and until very recently, very little creative destruction manifested in colleges and universities closing their doors.

However, as higher education stagnates excessively, that may be changing. In just the first eight months of 2023, for example, ten well-established colleges announced they were closing, about one every three or four weeks: Holy Names University (announced in December 2022), Presentation College (January 18), Finlandia University (March 2), Iowa Wesleyan University (March 28), Cardinal Stritch University (April 12), Medaille University (May 26), Cabrini University (June 26), Alliance University (July 5), Hodges University (August 25), and Alderson Broaddus University (August 31).[4] Is this the beginning of some needed creative destruction accompanied by the survival of the fittest?

It is the theme of this book that while we may mourn the loss of those schools (speaking personally, I once gave an enjoyable presentation at one of them), we should accept this as the inevitable consequence of change. Indeed, to preserve and make more effective American higher education, we should accept *and even rejoice* in more closings in the years ahead as resources shift away from institutions with a declining following toward ones that are fiscally and hopefully educationally stronger institutions. I take comfort from the apparent flight to quality in recent years: the schools with enrollment gains and fiscal stability are generally considered to be better, more solid institutions than the ones that are failing. But even elite schools like Harvard and the University of Pennsylvania are taking huge reputational hits and seeing alumni donations fall. Perceived mediocrity in higher education is proving increasingly costly.

Higher education might take another lesson from American business. Many successful American businesses voluntarily and indeed purposefully engage in a controlled creative destruction of their own in order to strengthen themselves. Companies sometimes become too big to be efficient and responsive to change—they then face what economists call decreasing returns to scale. What is the solution? Divide the company into two or more parts where each can single-mindedly concentrate on providing a smaller number of goods and services well. For example, Kellogg's recently announced it was dividing into two companies, one handling traditional cereal products in the US, Canada, and the Caribbean; the other, snacks and ventures in other geographic locales. Similarly, Hewlett-Packard split into two a few years ago, separating computer and printer operations from other activities such as providing business services. The ultimate company change: General Electric, which once did everything from making appliances and power-generation equipment to running a large financial services operation, has divested itself of many of those activities, most recently, for example, creating GE HealthCare Technologies, GE Aerospace, and GE Vernova as separate firms.

Could universities do similar things? Divest themselves of what are essentially professional sports teams? housing operations? food services? medical centers (but possibly not the medical school that actually teaches students)? bus systems? maybe even remedial educational instruction? Maybe schools should concentrate on the core functions they do well and let others do ancillary things. For example, perhaps research universities with a strong reputation in the natural sciences and engineering should jettison highly politicized departments in the humanities that attract few majors. Big schools might divest themselves of whole campuses. Is it more efficient for a school like the University of Texas to have one flagship campus at Austin and divest its other schools into self-contained entities? For example, should the University of Texas at San Antonio become San Antonio State University? Are there increasing or decreasing returns to scale in campus operations? I don't know for sure (although I believe scale economies, if they exist at all, are certainly limited), but this is the type of question university governing boards and top administrators should be asking.

Are Colleges and Universities Truly a "Public Good"?

Governmental involvement in higher education is primarily predicated on the proposition that colleges are a "public good" that has positive spillover effects or externalities. But is that true? Assertions that this is the case are often based on dubious evidence or arguments. For example, higher education advocates argue that colleges impart qualities to students that make for a better, more orderly, more law-abiding society. To be sure, it is factually correct, for example, that crime rates are higher for non-college graduates than for those who have attended college. But did the colleges *themselves* impart a respect for law and order in their students while they were in school? Possibly once upon a time, in the colonial era when colleges had a strong religious focus. But I think today the low crime rates for college graduates are far more likely to be largely a consequence of factors like family background—having a traditional two-parent family as opposed to a single-parent one, for example—than anything learned in college. It could be argued that universities sometimes emit public "bads" (negative externalities), for example, when underemployed former college students either do not repay their student loans or persuade politicians to forgive them. Higher education also champions such dubious public policies as "environmental, social, and governance (ESG) investing," attempting to force investors to avoid politically incorrect industries such as fossil fuels while favoring wokeish things like solar power.

Recent comments by Brown University philosophy professor Felicia Nimue Ackerman suggest that I am not alone in my view: "My half-century in academic philosophy has made me skeptical of the view that the liberal arts promote personal virtue." She goes further, asking, "How come many humanities professors are self-important, status-conscious jerks?"[5] Academics have a vested interest in using their academic authority to *claim* positive externalities from college that in fact often do not exist. The rapid rise in discord in American society over the past decade, as manifested in such things as rioting, race-themed demonstrations, and the shouting down of speakers, has been strongly aided and abetted by members of the academy. Some "critical theory" academics assert they are promoting "justice" to the aggrieved, when in fact their assertions often promote theft that violates time-honored ethical norms. Is today's America, where roughly one-third of adults have a college degree, a better place, a safer place, a happier place, than it was fifty years ago, when barely one-tenth had such an education?

Privatize! Privatize! Let Nothing Evade Your Eyes!

If in general privately directed resource allocations are far more efficient than governmental direction of the use of productive resources, and if the "positive externalities" of universities are either nonexistent or severely overhyped, then why don't we simply privatize all higher education, be it in the form of not-for-profit privately controlled entities or for-profit businesses?

Although I have written quite favorably of moves to take government completely or at least largely out of the higher education business, I have had two reasons to consider far less radical solutions, such as giving government-financed (ultimately, of course, taxpayer-funded) assistance to private customers (prospective college students) rather than direct to universities, many of which are government owned and controlled. First, some things that universities do could have genuine positive externalities, such as some forms of research. If a vaccine that saves lives is partially or completely discovered in a university setting, there are genuine university-generated positive externalities. This *may* be an argument for limited government funding of universities by organizations like the National Institutes of Health or the National Science Foundation.

Second, some political obstacles to ending government subsidies could perhaps with education and persuasion be reduced over time, but they still exist for now. Within universities, woke administrators will not give up power and economic rent seeking without a fight—and solving this problem cannot be done overnight. Wiping out those political obstacles would certainly be worthwhile, but given the modest scope of this volume, our analysis here must be limited. In the meantime, however, perhaps a second-best but realistic solution would be to at least introduce more market dimensions into an institution that is otherwise largely devoid of many of the incentives motivating productive behavior in competitive private markets.

In short, we can do a lot of "privatizing" or quasi-privatizing higher education within the context of the current political milieu. Universities can usually legally sell their housing facilities to private operators, or at least outsource if not sell their food operations (many do this already). If ESPN and other media outlets can make vast profits off intercollegiate athletics, why can't the nominal providers of those services, the colleges and universities, do the same by selling or leasing the economic value associated with big-time college sports? We see some embryonic moves in that direction. For example, the Big Ten Network provides televised and streaming sports entertainment and is majority owned by a private company (Fox), but with substantial minority ownership by the mostly public universities in the Big Ten conference.

Why can't professors' salaries be based more on the revenues that they bring in rather than on the articles they write that almost no one reads? Why can't we at least partially adopt Adam Smith's suggestion, adapted from an earlier Oxford University practice, of paying professors according to the quantity of high-quality educational services provided, as the customer (student) determines? More students, higher pay. To be sure, care has to be exercised in implementing this. Professors could vie for popularity by giving high grades for little effort, or by titillating students with irrelevant and inappropriate entertainment—short R-rated videos, for example, interspersed between segments of appropriate scholarly materials. Also, powerful professors often use their clout to get their favorite courses mandated for students, artificially inducing high enrollments.

The colleges will need a mechanism to help eliminate inappropriate practices—but most likely not the current ineffective and anticompetitive accreditation organizations. Certainly, we need good information on what students are learning, and, indeed, what they are earning after graduation. Accreditation agencies as they exist today not only fail to perform that function, but also stifle educational innovation and serve as a cartel to try to enforce some sort of non-innovative conformity. They generally frown, for example, on year-round schooling or a more vibrant integration of internships into the educational experience. Maybe a national test (my National College Equivalence Examination) can help measure learning and dramatically reduce the rationale for today's accreditation practices (I return to accreditation shortly).

"All's Well That Ends Well" and "The Ends Justify the Means"

As we approach the end of this discussion of the future of higher education, let's evoke two thoughts from the sixteenth (Machiavelli) and early seventeenth (Shakespeare) centuries. The primary goal of higher education is to improve the human condition by producing a more enlightened and prosperous population through the dissemination of both knowledge and innovative discoveries. Those are "the ends" that Machiavelli contemplated.

But "the ends" that maximize social welfare (and thus "end well") are not, even with respect to knowledge dissemination and discovery, necessarily achievable through traditional higher education. Skills learned in coding camps, vocational high schools, short-course training academies, business-run classes for employees in new technologies, and the like are valuable, and on cost-benefit grounds they may often be more effective than expensive four-year degree programs involving much material of little utility to the student learner. Diminishing returns set in regarding higher education, and sometimes the third and fourth years of schooling add less useful knowledge than the first or second. For some a two-year degree plus a specialized short-course certificate program is better career preparation than a traditional bachelor's degree. Even within traditional four-year schools, given the dramatic difference in the workplace productivity of graduates in many (but not all) STEM and business majors compared with those in the woke-infested, politically correct but vocationally near useless majors like gender studies, perhaps colleges should put more teaching and scholarship resources into the high-productivity disciplines and reduce funding for the less productive ones, which also often implies tenure reform to more readily allow staffing changes.

In recent years, there has been a proliferation of nondegree postsecondary schools that provide certificates for skilled training in narrow vocational areas. If colleges are nonreformable, the solution may be to go around them and create quasi-collegiate vocational training enclaves. Dr. Barbara Gellman-Danley, the president of one large regional accreditor, the Higher Learning Commission, put it recently, "We have directly witnessed the rapid expansion of alternative credentials," announcing a new Credential Lab to assess the "quality assurance needs in a chaotic credential landscape."[6]

As an economic historian, I would note that in the past technological innovation has favored the highly educated population relative to workers with minimal skills. The Industrial Revolution was mostly about replacing unskilled workers with machines, be it the spinning jenny more than two hundred years ago in England or the automotive assembly line in early twentieth-century America. However, it may be that the newest technology, most specifically artificial intelligence (AI), will ultimately involve substituting machine (computer)-based technology for highly skilled college-educated workers—this was a big issue in the strike of the mostly college-trained Hollywood writers in 2023. Technological progress may become more threatening to the denizens of academia. It is already doing so to some extent, as some online providers of academic credit have found it is much cheaper to find capable STEM-intensive instructors in lower-wage India than in high-wage America. Technology, previously a friend of the American academic class, may become distinctly less so in the future. (Things might not "end well.")

Obstacles to Reform: Colleges Are Quasi Governments (Public Choice Insights)

In talking with Phil Magness, now of the Independent Institute, I realized how much universities have many of the characteristics of governments; indeed, they are like mini or quasi governments of their own. They have large bureaucracies, are to some extent shielded from market forces, and especially do not have a well-defined bottom line such as profits or stock prices. Public Choice economics has long analyzed government decision-making, providing insights into how governmental solutions often do not serve the greater public good, analysis that I think largely applies to universities as well. Let's look at how three insights from Public Choice economics apply to universities—and add to their costs.[7]

Concentrated Benefits and Dispersed Costs

Nearly a generation ago, powerful members of Congress from Alaska managed to secure federal agreement to fund what became immortalized as the "bridge to nowhere," connecting the town of Ketchikan (2000 Census population of 7,922) with Gravina Island (home to the local airport and about fifty residents). The slated cost was $398 million. There were perhaps ten thousand citizens fervently in favor of the project. Let us suppose it would have on average conferred $10,000 in benefits on each one of those Alaskans. The other 282 million Americans, mostly living in the lower forty-eight states, DC, and Hawaii, would have received no benefits but incurred the $398 million cost—an average of $1.41 a person. The beneficiaries no doubt made lots of phone calls, even several visits, to Alaska's three members of Congress—after all, they had a lot to gain. The other 282 million Americans were "rationally ignorant" of the project—its impact was small, so on cost-benefit grounds it was not even worth learning about it and getting agitated. So the project was approved and would have been built except for a rash of national publicity about a bridge costing nearly $8 million for every resident of the island that it primarily benefited. A project nearly went through that on national cost-benefit grounds made absolutely no sense.

Sometimes public universities benefit from a similar situation—a stadium is supported by taxpayers for a local state university, which benefits a few thousand but imposes costs on millions of taxpayers. But the bigger point here is regarding the quasi government operating *within* a university. Suppose $10 million is allocated by the university administration (rubber-stamped by the governing board) to remodel and make more luxurious offices for fifty high-level university apparatchiks housed in the main administration building, financed by a $50 tuition fee increase for twenty thousand students for fifteen years. Students who are now small children but will be attending the university in 2035 will still be paying for it. The benefits are concentrated on the fifty university apparatchiks, a few who will get decorative fireplaces and mahogany conference tables installed in their offices along with other creature comforts. Benefits are concentrated on well-connected administrators who successfully lobby university trustees to fund it, the students and the broader public be damned.

Rent Seeking

It is human nature for people to try to get more income through little or no effort. As indicated earlier, when workers are compensated more for their services than necessary to secure their employment, we say they are collecting economic rent—an unnecessary payment. In university employment, rent seeking is everywhere. Except in revenue-producing activities like big-time collegiate sports, higher education has few ways to precisely measure in dollars the contributions of individual workers (in business, one can often more precisely do so because of a financial bottom line). Thus within universities there is a concentrated and continuous effort to improve one's compensation—higher salaries, bigger pension benefits, more sick leave, tuition remission for spouses, more vacation time, and so on. Sometimes the push for these things is organized by faculty or student labor unions (and, now apparently at Dartmouth, basketball players).

Although rent seeking occurs in the private sector too, the ivory tower environment increases its effectiveness. The most obvious example of that is tenure for faculty and long-term contracts for key administrators. Faculty can afford to offend bosses and other ostensible superiors in maneuvering to get larger salaries, lighter teaching loads, more graduate assistants to help with routine chores, or other types of perks. Important national political leaders such as the late Henry Kissinger or former House majority leader Dick Armey, both former college professors, observed that university politics is *far* more ruthless than real-world political activity, precisely because professors can take more daring and even outrageous actions to get their way. Tenure protects them from major negative consequences, whereas politicians periodically have to face the voters to retain their job. Kissinger, channeling earlier writers on the subject, once put it cleverly: "The reason that university politics is so vicious is because the stakes are so small."[8]

In most ways, big-time college sports programs are like private businesses, highly dependent on market forces. Successful coaches win more games and increase school revenues from ticket sales, television payouts, parking lot fees, alumni donations, and more. Yet even they can explore rent seeking big time. The poster child as of this writing is Jimbo Fisher, the football coach at Texas A&M University, who was fired at the end of the 2023 season—but who will collect some $76 million (!!) in additional salary payments from A&M over a number of years as the result of an income security ("buyout") provision in his contract, even though he may well be coaching at an A&M competitor trying to defeat the Aggies. The money to pay him (far more than $1,000 per student attending the main College Station campus) for his forced idleness has to come from *somewhere,* likely within Texas A&M itself, most likely in large part from big-time donors who instead could be financing student scholarships or other more traditional academic functions.

Logrolling

The nation's founders were at an impasse over key aspects of our constitution. Alexander Hamilton wanted the national capital to remain in New York, while Thomas Jefferson, James Madison, and George Washington all wanted it on the Potomac River, near their beloved Virginia. Hamilton wanted the new federal government to assume the debts of the states—the Virginians opposed it because state-level indebtedness was trivial, so federal debt assumption provided little benefit. So Jefferson got Hamilton and Madison to meet for dinner. Madison said he would get enough votes in the US House of Representatives (of which he was then serving as a leading member) to pass Hamilton's debt assumption proposal—*if* Hamilton would go along with the Virginian's desire for a capital on the Potomac. "You scratch my back, I'll scratch yours." Hamilton agreed. A great early example of logrolling.

Universities, similar to governments, use logrolling all the time. Usually decisions are made by small groups—the university president and his cabinet of senior administrators, department chairs in a college within a large university, boards of trustees and their various committees, curriculum committees, and, occasionally, faculty senates. Suppose the chair of the political science department fervently wants a new faculty hire approved, but he faces strong opposition from the head of the English department, who wants to continue to require a junior-level English composition course that the university is threatening to eliminate. The two individuals join forces: The English department chair argues forcefully to approve the new position in political science, in return for which the head of the political science department eloquently says that the junior writing requirement is critical to turning out highly literate and marketable graduates.

External Obstacles to Change: Politicians and Donors

Federal Political Obstacles

I again assert: the biggest single problem for American higher education in recent decades has been the growing centralization of power in the federal government, specifically the US Department of Education. Putting aside the specifics of federal actions, a huge problem arises from the occasional abrupt changes in the philosophical and political orientation of that department. The most striking modern example came when the Obama-appointed Education Department bureaucracy issued the disastrous and arguably illegal "Dear Colleague" letter in 2011, in which it demanded that colleges implement draconian Star Chamber justice to deal with an asserted pandemic of sexual assault cases on campuses. In early 2017, the new secretary of education, Betsy DeVos, ordered a rolling back of many of the Obama rules. Fast-forward to the 2020s, and the Biden administration's Education Department leadership tried to reinstall most of the Obama-era rules (which have already led to universities losing a number of court challenges from badly treated male students). The ever-changing political environment leads to inconsistent and costly policy revisions. The unwieldly bureaucracy is notoriously slow to move in the best of times; witness its botched implementation of a 2019 federal law requiring a simplified FAFSA (Free Application for Federal Student Aid) form by the end of 2023—ending an effort dating back at least fifteen years to prepare a simple form that a bright young financial aid administrator could probably do in a couple of hours. At this writing, in March 2024, failure to issue the new FAFSA form, seriously overdue, and make it readily available to students is causing serious problems regarding providing financial aid information to students entering in the fall of 2024.

Incidentally, the impact of the fallout of the department's sexual assault rules are hard to underestimate. Some 87 percent of the substantial (over one million) student enrollment drop between 2015 and 2020 occurred among men. I believe that the overzealous and likely illegal war on young male students by student affairs' warriors enforcing legally dubious Title IX interpretations has made college seem like a hostile environment for many men, so they are fleeing the colleges where they feel unwanted.

Federal or State and Local Taxation of Universities?

As indicated earlier, in 2003, at age 90, the great Nobel Prize–winning economist Milton Friedman, once an advocate of public subsidies for universities, emailed me suggesting that a case could probably be made that the optimal policy would be to tax universities rather than subsidize them.[9] The economics are simple: if a school exhibits "positive externalities" (spillover effects), it deserves a government subsidy, but if it has negative externalities, it should be taxed. Starting in 2017 amid growing disenchantment with universities, Congress adopted a modest federal endowment tax that applies to only thirty-five or so wealthy private schools.

Since then, however, the perceived negative spillover effects of colleges have grown, especially after the demonstrations, riots, and university presidential testimony following the Hamas attack on Israel on October 7, 2023. Student demonstrations on prominent campuses where threats of killing Jews (genocide) occurred were more than normal peaceful discourse about the issues of the day, but potentially dangerous rioting that threatened the public peace and tranquility. In short, a sharp increase in the perceived negative externalities of higher education ensued.

As of this writing, several important legislators, including House Ways and Means Committee chair Jason Smith and Senator J. D. Vance have called publicly for major increases in federal endowment taxes. Several tax increases are scheduled to happen after 2025, so tax policy is likely to undergo increased scrutiny. I looked at the Foundation for Individual Rights and Expression (FIRE) rankings of 248 colleges regarding their commitment to freedom of expression, specifically the rankings for twenty-three highly ranked (and generally very well endowed) private schools. A strong majority of them (61 percent) ranked in the bottom one-third of schools in terms of commitment to free speech principles, with the three absolutely lowest-ranked schools being Harvard (the worst), Columbia, and Penn in the Ivy League, and only three schools (Chicago, Brown, and Johns Hopkins) ranking in the top one-third of the institutions surveyed by FIRE. So, the high-endowment private schools are special hotbeds of the suppression of speech, possibly an argument for an endowment tax. Moreover, these wealthy so-called private universities are often the largest recipients of federal grant money for research. FIRE's highest-ranked schools were all public universities—schools like Michigan Technological University and Auburn.

Perhaps state and local governments should consider taxing the non-academic activities of universities. Private property owners pay taxes on buildings housing college students, but generally universities owning similar housing do not. Why? Similarly, restaurants or cafeterias serving students in most states must pay sales taxes on food purchased by students, but university-owned cafeterias do not. Why? It makes little sense on either academic or equity grounds to me. Public universities are effectively incentivized to engage in funding expensive amenities like luxury dorms and sports facilities. The case for taxation is even stronger regarding university-held properties supporting concerts or sporting events whose prime activities have little or nothing to do with disseminating or creating knowledge or creative ideas.

Kill the Accreditors!

I have previously argued that not only is college accreditation costly and inefficient, but that it also fails to achieve the worthy goal of providing customers (students and their parents) with useful information about education providers. But the rise in attacks by state governments on collegiate practices like operating large DEI offices will likely lead to more counterattacks by the forces opposing higher education reform. For example, several state governments have essentially closed DEI offices that promote racial preferences or force students to sign what are essentially loyalty oaths pledging fealty to a DEI agenda.

One way woke university officials will try to fight those efforts is by having the six major regional accrediting organizations as well as some subject-specific accreditors (for example, the American Bar Association and the American Medical Association) to in effect mandate DEI offices, diversity statements, or other violations of free inquiry: "You will do as we say or we will remove your accreditation." As earlier indicated, the accreditation agencies themselves are best regarded as cartels enforcing specific modes of operation. For example, three-year bachelor's degrees make great sense and can save lots of money and better use resources, but generally have been frowned upon by accreditors who are "owned" and controlled by the very universities they regulate. To me, the only issue is, Do we abolish the accreditors, or do we attempt to radically reform them? The single most important reason colleges today need accreditation is because the federal government will provide student financial assistance only to accredited institutions of higher learning. But the federal government should leave the financial assistance business to others, as advocated previously. The main original purpose of accreditation—to provide students with information on a school's competencies, could be provided in other ways, such as by standardized entrance and exit examinations taken by all students.

Sometimes, perhaps most notably regarding professional licenses, the right to obtain the necessary certificate is controlled by accreditation organizations. The psychology profession has been notorious in threatening to revoke certificates for alleged accreditation violations, most blatantly in Canada with Professor Jordan Peterson.[10]

Judicial Remedies: State Attorneys General and Private Public Interest Law Efforts

One approach to stopping discrimination in favor of or against students on the basis of race or other attributes is for state attorneys general—relying on both federal and state legal precedents—to start filing lawsuits against schools who continue to make admissions decisions on a constitutionally dubious basis. Historically, states have largely left the public universities alone—even though they are owned, at least nominally, by the resident taxpayers. But state attorneys general and related officials can illegitimately and inappropriately attack colleges in nonmeritorious ways to promote ideological agendas or racial or gender discrimination. Another emerging trend in which I have become personally involved: private public interest law firms are beginning to file lawsuits against prominent schools that discriminate against applicants for faculty positions in order to meet DEI objectives. Also, state-based think tanks could file suits. Groups like the Institute for Justice, the Pacific Legal Foundation, and the Buckeye Institute have had success in promoting consumer and taxpayer interests.

Is Higher Education Impervious to Change?

With all the obstacles discussed above, is serious change in higher education nearly impossible? Brian Rosenberg, a former longtime president of a respected liberal arts college, Macalester, has eloquently decried the resistance of higher education to major change.[11] In his view, all the major internal players in the academy (professors, administrators, students, trustees, big donors) blame other participants for the ailments of higher education and fiercely resist change. I agree. Big changes will be forced on colleges largely from the outside, often involving actual creative destruction, and the realization that "necessity is the mother of invention" will finally force colleges to change their ways, aided and abetted perhaps by some new actors of the University of Austin or Thales College variety.

Although I applaud efforts by governors like Ron DeSantis to stir things up and introduce an element of constructive change, I am dubious that this type of move will be the prime mover in positive change. Politicians are not fully conversant with the problems of higher education, are vulnerable to political pressure, and above all, *are constantly leaving office.* The strength of American higher education comes from its diversity and its *lack* of central direction, not from politically directed uniformity, be it from Washington, DC, or a state capital.

An idea: What would happen if ten or twenty of the nation's wealthiest citizens and philanthropists committed $25 billion to major transformational change in higher education, perhaps including the creation of five midsize schools, including one or two in each of the nation's four major geographic regions (Northeast, South, Midwest, and West), each adopting radical new approaches—three-year degrees, a healthy respect for the discovery of knowledge but with less of a publish-or-perish orientation, a rabid commitment to the Chicago principles (including those in the Kalven Report on institutional non-involvement in the political issues of the day), and so on? What if they refuse to bend to the demands of the accreditation cartel and say, "Don't accredit us—we will let the student and research outcomes we produce inform the public as to the quality of our educational offerings"?

Nearly everyone agrees great leaders make a difference. Look for leadership from a future Mitch Daniels, Michael Crow, Paul LeBlanc. For leadership, cultivate those rare individuals who flourish in *all* the relevant worlds surrounding academia, people like former University of Florida president Ben Sasse, who in his lifetime has combined a Yale PhD in history with service as a US senator and major university president, or in Daniels's case, being a pharmaceutical executive, US budget director, and governor as well as a Big Ten university president. All of this, along with getting the federal government completely out of the higher education business and implementing some of the reforms discussed in this volume, could lead us to restoring a vibrant and effective higher education system in the United States.

More Optimistic Final Thoughts

Remember that college serves two functions for students: First is the investment function stressed above. Second is the consumption function: providing an enjoyable way of maturing and preparing for the transition from childhood to adulthood, somewhat like a lengthy and expensive expansion of the Jewish bar or bat mitzvah—a coming-of-age experience. For many, the college years are fun years, and there is nothing inherently wrong with that. Indeed, if economic growth persists, perhaps an increasingly affluent population will view college in the same way they view taking cruises or buying a vacation home. But it is certainly inappropriate to expect governments or even private philanthropists deriving special tax benefits to use taxpayer funds to subsidize the enjoyment of persons approaching adulthood (by financing such things as collegiate "lazy rivers") any more than, for example, it is for them to subsidize cruises for senior citizens.

Finally, and sadly, by many indicators America is in decline—in terms of its economy, morality, and national cohesion. It has some eerily similar characteristics to life in the later Roman Empire, with its bread and circuses (the ancient version of today's welfare state), deteriorating national leadership, debased currency (today's inflation and massive national debts), and decline in a cohesive national identity.[12] Higher education's failure may have contributed to this decline, but is perhaps as likely a consequence as a cause of it.

To end on a positive note, a revitalization, a renaissance, in American higher education could be the catalyst for a broader national revival. The fads and teachings of higher education tend to permeate into the broader society, which may well have served the nation poorly over the past generation or so, but in the future could work to help spur a national revival. Our universities, then, are almost certainly worth saving, reviving, and restoring to a treasured place in our lives.

Notes

Introduction

1. Joseph A. Schumpeter, *Capitalism, Socialism and Democracy* (New York: Harper & Brothers, 1942).

2. Andy Smarick, "The Turnaround Fallacy," *Education Next* 24, no. 3 (November 12, 2009): https:///www.educationnext.org/the-turnaround-fallacy/.

Chapter 1: Higher Education Is Failing! Ten Cardinal Sins

1. Richard Vedder, *Restoring the Promise: Higher Education in America* (Oakland, CA: Independent Institute, 2019).

2. Harriet Torry, "More High-School Grads Forgo College in Hot Labor Market," *Wall Street Journal*, May 29, 2023.

3. Data are from the US Department of Health and Human Services, National Center for Health Statistics (https://www.cdc.gov/nchs/index.htm).

4. Doug Lederman, "Majority of Americans Lack Confidence in Value of 4-Year Degree," *Inside Higher Ed*, April 3, 2023.

5. Meghan Brink, "Public Opinion on the Value of Higher Education Remains Mixed," *Inside Higher Ed*, July 11, 2022.

6. Readers interested in reading some of the author's personal observations on this topic can read Richard Vedder, "Muzzling Free Expression on Campus Causes Self-Censorship," *American Spectator*, March 27, 2023, https://spectator.org/muzzling-free-expression-on-campus-causes-self-censorship/.

7. For a lengthier treatment of this example, see Richard Vedder, "University of Pennsylvania versus Amy Wax," *American Spectator*, Summer 2023, 27–29.

8. See Scott Gerber, "DEI Brings Kafka to My Law School," *Wall Street Journal*, May 10, 2023. The episode has led to numerous protests by various academic groups. For my own short comment, see Richard Vedder, "A Campus Outrage That We Should Not Let Pass," *Wall Street Journal*, May 17, 2023.

9. See, for example, Conor Friedersdorf, "Evidence That Conservative Students Really Do Self-Censor," *The Atlantic,* February 16, 2020, https://www.theatlantic.com/ideas/

archive/2020/02/evidence-conservative-students-really-do-self-censor/606559/.

10. Voluminous studies have documented this. One good one is by Jon A. Shields and Joshua M. Dunn, *Passing on the Right: Conservative Professors in the Progressive University* (New York: Oxford University Press, 2016).

11. Buckley Institute, *A Report of Faculty Political Diversity at Yale*, faculty research report (New Haven, CT: Buckley Institute, May 2023).

12. Eric Kaufmann, "Academic Freedom Is Withering," *Wall Street Journal*, February 28, 2021.

13. The original popularizers of this idea were William Baumol and William Bowen in their book *The Performing Arts: The Economic Dilemma: A Study of Problems Common to Theater, Opera, Music and Dance* (Cambridge, MA: MIT Press, 1966). It took as many performers in 2024 to perform Shakespeare's *Hamlet* as it did when it was originally written more than four hundred years earlier. College teaching is much like theater. A more recent defense of the Baumol effect is in Robert B. Archibald and David H. Feldman, *Federal Financial Aid Policy and College Behavior* (Washington, DC: American Council on Education, 2016).

14. The best single source for data on higher education enrollments and other important variables (cost data, size of faculty, degree attainment, and so on) is the National Center for Education Statistics' annual *Digest of Education Statistics*.

15. William J. Bennett, "Our Greedy Colleges," *New York Times*, February 18, 1987.

16. See the pioneering study by David O. Lucca, Taylor Nadauld, and Karen Shen, *Credit Supply and the Rise in College Tuition: Evidence from the Expansion in Federal Student Aid Programs*, Staff Report no. 733 (Federal Reserve Bank of New York, March 2016).

17. See, for example, Philip Babcock and Mindy Marks, "The Falling Time Cost of College: Evidence from a Half Century of Time Use Data," *Review of Economics and Statistics* 93 (May 2011): 468–78.

18. See Richard Arum and Josipa Roksa, *Academically Adrift: Limited Learning on College Campuses* (Chicago: University of Chicago Press, 2011).

19. This point was made first in extensive detail by Benjamin Ginsberg, *The Fall of the Faculty: The Rise of the All-Administrative University and Why It Matters* (New York: Oxford University Press, 2011).

20. Jay Greene and James Paul, *Diversity University: DEI Bloat in the Academy*, Report July 27, 2021 (Washington, DC: Heritage Foundation).

21. The definitive study here is KC Johnson and Stuart Taylor Jr., *The Campus Rape Frenzy: The Attack on Due Process at America's Universities* (New York: Encounter Books, 2017).

22. The studies by Chetty and his associates are numerous and often cited. One representative study can be found in Raj Chetty, David Grusky, Maximilian Hell, Nathaniel Hendren, and Jimmy Narang, "The Fading American Dream: Trends in Absolute Income Mobility since 1940," *Science*, April 2017, 356:398–406.

23. See Bureau of Census historical income data at http://www.census.gov/data/tables/time-series/demo/income-poverty/historical-income-people.html.

24. For an analysis of data released by the US Department of Education on April 25, 2023, see *The HEA Group* (blog), "Which College Majors Pay the Most?" by Michael Itz-

kowitz, posted May 18, 2023, https://www.theheagroup.com/blog/college-majors-pay-most.

25. Website for the Federal Reserve Bank of St. Louis, *On the Economy* (blog), "The College Boost: Why Are Wealth Returns from a Degree Falling?" by William R. Emmons, Ana Hernandez Kent, and Lowell R. Ricketts, posted July 19, 2018.

26. See my article with Braden Colegrove, "Why Men Are Disappearing on Campus," *Wall Street Journal*, September 20, 2021, A17.

27. US Bureau of Labor Statistics, "College Enrollment and Work Activity of Recent High School and College Graduates," news release, April 26, 2023.

Chapter 2: Capitalism Succeeds by Allowing Failures via Creative Destruction

1. Joseph Schumpeter, *Capitalism, Socialism and Democracy* (New York: Harper & Brothers, 1942).

2. Adam Smith, *Wealth of Nations* (Oxford: Clarendon Press, 1979). First published 1776.

3. Smith, *Wealth of Nations*, 760.

4. Smith, *Wealth of Nations*, 761.

5. Richard Vedder and Justin Strehle, *University Endowments: Do They Promote Social Welfare?* (Washington, DC: Center for College Affordability and Productivity, February 2016.)

6. One private company, Aramco, was dropped from the list because it is largely owned by the government of Saudi Arabia and is only nominally a "private" company.

7. The migration statistics come from the US Bureau of the Census and are estimates, not direct enumerations of peoples such as done in the decennial census. Other groups also keep tabs on migration, most notably the National Association of Realtors, which uses ingenious methods to measure migration trends, including change-of-address requests filed with the US Postal Service. Another indicator of movement trends is provided by data collected by rental haul companies. For example, at this writing it cost $3,432 to rent a 26-foot U-Haul truck in New York City to go to Austin, Texas, but only $2,092 to rent the same truck to make the same trip in the opposite direction, from Austin to New York. Traveling to Austin is popular, so U-Haul trucks accumulate there. They are relatively scarce in New York (since not many people want to move there from Texas), so U-Haul offers reduced rates to get trucks back to New York from hot locales like Austin.

8. Calculating productivity changes involves many issues, especially within higher education, that are not considered here. For a more detailed discussion, see Richard Vedder, *Restoring the Promise: Higher Education in America* (Oakland, CA: Independent Institute, 2019), 178–83.

Chapter 3: Why Are Universities Subsidized, but Firms Taxed?

1. For a good account of the role of migration, see Ilya Somin, *Free to Move: Foot Voting, Migration, and Political Freedom*, rev. ed. (New York: Oxford University Press, 2022).

2. This chapter draws heavily upon my earlier work *Going Broke by Degree: Why College Costs Too Much* (Washington, DC: AEI Press, 2004), especially chapter 7. Adapted with

permission from AEI Press.

3. John Henry Newman, *The Idea of a University* (Notre Dame, IN: University of Notre Dame Press, 1982), 134–35.

4. Milton Friedman, *Capitalism and Freedom* (Chicago: University of Chicago Press, 1962). Other economists, of whom the most noteworthy is James Buchanan, have also provided useful insight.

5. *Capitalism and Freedom*, 118.

6. Email from Milton Friedman to Richard Vedder, September 12, 2003.

7. On the decline of student academic work effort, see Philip Babcock and Mindy Marks, "The Falling Time Cost of Education: Evidence from a Half Century of Time Use Data," *Review of Economics and Statistics* 93 (May 2011): 468–78.

8. This section draws very heavily on my arguments in *Restoring the Promise: Higher Education in America* (Oakland, CA: Independent Institute, 2019), especially 161–71.

9. Richard Vedder, "The Morrill Land-Grant Act: Fact and Mythology," in *Unprofitable Schooling*, edited by Todd J. Zywicki and Neal P. McCluskey (Washington, DC: Cato Institute, 2019), 31–63.

10. The extensive research done by the Equal Opportunity Project of Raj Chetty and associates tends to confirm this, showing that the more prestigious schools, both public and private, are usually dominated by students from moderately to very affluent families.

11. Richard Vedder, "Biden's College-Loan Writeoffs Are Unfair, Irresponsible—and Illegal," *New York Post*, May 26, 2023.

12. See Phillip W. Magness, "For-Profit Universities and the Roots of Adjunctification in US Higher Education," *Liberal Education* 102, no. 2 (2016): 50–59.

13. Jayme S. Lemke and William F. Shughart II, "Assessing For-Profit Colleges," in *Unprofitable Schooling*, edited by Todd J. Zywicki and Neal P. McCluskey (Washington, DC.: Cato Institute, 2019), 201–44.

14. For example, see Josh Kosman, "Obama's Pal Catches Major Break in For-Profit College Deal," *New York Post*, January 3, 2017, updated January 4, 2017, https://nypost.com/2017/01/03/obamas-pal-catches-major-break-in-for-profit-college-deal.

15. Katherine Knott, "New, Stronger Gainful Employment Regs Released," *Inside Higher Ed*, May 18, 2023.

Chapter 4: Creative Destruction and Laboratories of Democracy

1. *New State Ice Co. v. Liebmann*, 285 U.S. 262 (1932).

2. The state of Pennsylvania still makes some appointments to the Penn governing board, and provides some financial assistance, but it operates outside the regulatory and subsidy regime of other truly "state" schools.

3. *Trustees of Dartmouth College v. Woodward* 17 U.S. (4 Wheat.) 518 (1819).

4. A very few schools, perhaps most notably Michigan's Hillsdale College and Pennsylvania's Grove City College, refuse to accept federal financial assistance in any form, including student aid. This makes it legally impossible for the federal government to claim any meaningful regulatory control.

5. Probably the top authority on this is Nathan Grawe. See his *Demographics and the Demand for Higher Education* (Baltimore: Johns Hopkins University Press, 2018).

6. See Liam Knox, "Fighting for Scraps in Pennsylvania," *Inside Higher Ed*, July 12, 2023. For example, the Commonwealth University of Pennsylvania was created by merging Lock Haven University and Mansfield University of Pennsylvania.

7. Additionally, large private research universities such as Johns Hopkins, Duke, the University of Chicago, or Stanford usually derive hundreds of millions of dollars or more annually in federal research grants.

8. Gordon C. Winston, "Subsidies, Hierarchy, and Peers: The Awkward Economics of Higher Education," *Journal of Economic Perspectives* 13 (Winter 1999): 13–26.

9. Charles M. Tiebout, "A Pure Theory of Local Expenditures," *Journal of Political Economy* 64 (October 1956): 416–24.

10. For a rather extensive example of my migration research, see my paper with Lowell Gallaway, "The Mobility of Native Americans," *Journal of Economic History* 31, no. 3 (September 1971): 615–49.

11. We considered Senators Bernie Sanders, Kyrsten Sinema, and Angus King to be Democrats, as they all sit with the Democratic caucus.

12. Jessica Blake, "American Confidence in Higher Ed Hits Historic Low," *Inside Higher Ed*, July 11, 2023.

13. Pew Charitable Trusts, "Two Decades of Change in Federal and State Higher Education Funding," issue brief, October 15, 2019, https://www.pcwtrusts.org/en/re search-and-analysis/issue-briefs/2019/10/two-decades-of-change-in-federal-and-state-higher-education-funding.

Chapter 5: Recent Innovations in Higher Education: Good, but Not Enough

1. For more on the Thales educational initiatives, see Bob Luddy, *The Thales Way* (Raleigh, NC: Thales Press, 2023).

2. Mike LaChance, "University of Florida to Establish Hamilton Center for Classical and Civic Education," *Legal Insurrection*, April 4, 2022.

3. For more information about the act, see Ethics and Public Policy Center, "General Education Act: Model Legislation," November 12, 2023, https://eppc.org/publication/general-education-act-model-legislation/.

4. I served on the Spellings Commission on the Future of Higher Education with Bob Mendenhall, the longtime president of WGU (1999–2016), a man of great integrity and common sense.

5. The COVID-19 pandemic provided abundant evidence that online learning often leads to inferior academic results. See, for example, Michael S. Kofoed, Lucas Gebhart, Dallas Gilmore, and Ryan Moschitto, *Zooming to Class: Experimental Evidence on College Students Online Learning during COVID-19*, Discussion Paper Series, DP 14356 (Bonn: IZA Institute of Labor Economics, May 2021); forthcoming in an American Economic Association journal. The study shows West Point students who studied online performed worse than those receiving in-person instruction.

6. Also, many of the most vibrant discussions of the issues of the day occur at small conferences sponsored by non-university-related think tanks. The only time I interacted with multiple Nobel Prize–winning scholars in one session was at a conference sponsored by the Council on Foreign Relations in New York.

7. Plato, *The Republic*, trans. Benjamin Jowett, book II, 369c, https://www.gutenberg.org/files/55201/55201-h/55201-h#BookII.

Chapter 6: Reducing the Government's Role

1. This is not the first effort to examine the role that profits play in higher education. Indeed, some of the best minds on the topic have come from Britain, the home of Adam Smith, who clearly admired the role of markets and incentives. One such study in which I contributed an essay is James B. Stanfield, ed., *The Profit Motive in Education: Continuing the Revolution* (London: Institute of Economic Affairs, 2012). A classic earlier study is E. G. West, *Education and the State: A Study in Political Economy*, 3rd ed. (Indianapolis: Liberty Fund, 1994).

2. Julia Shapero, "Betsy DeVos Calls for Abolishing the Department of Education," *Axios*, July 17, 2022.

3. This assessment is based on numerous personal conversations, media appearances with Bill Bennett, and on his book with David Wilezol, *Is College Worth It?* (New York: Thomas Nelson, 2013).

4. For a more comprehensive analysis, see KC Johnson and Stuart Taylor Jr., *The Campus Rape Frenzy: The Attack on Due Process at America's Universities* (New York: Encounter Books, 2017).

5. Ludwig von Mises, *Economic Calculation in the Socialist Commonwealth* (Auburn, AL: Ludwig von Mises Institute, 1990). First published 1920.

6. Friedrich A. Hayek, "The Use of Knowledge in Society," *American Economic Review* 35 (September 1945): 519–30.

7. George J. Stigler, "The Economics of Information," *Journal of Political Economy* 69 (June 1961): 213–25, and also his "Information and the Labor Market," *Journal of Political Economy* 70 (October 1962): part 2, 94–105.

8. I have written extensively on the problems with accreditation. See *Restoring the Promise: Higher Education in America* (Oakland, CA: Independent Institute, 2019), chap. 14, for a fuller account. See also a July 2023 article for the James G. Martin Center at https://www.jamesgmartin.center/2023/07/does-college-accreditation-work/.

9. See Katherine Knott, "House Subcommittee Members Disagree over Higher Ed's Value," *Inside Higher Ed*, July 28, 2023.

10. See Richard Arum and Josipa Roksa, *Academically Adrift: Limited Learning on College Campuses* (Chicago: University of Chicago Press, 2011).

11. Two wonderful but arguably slightly dated books are Daniel Golden, *The Price of Admission: How America's Ruling Class Buys Its Way into Elite Colleges—and Who Gets Left outside the Gates* (New York: Three Rivers Press, 2007) and Jerome Karabel, *The Chosen: The Hidden History of Admission and Exclusion at Harvard, Yale, and Princeton* (Boston: Hough-

ton Mifflin, 2005).

12. Shad White, "Jimmy Buffett Didn't Need a Music Degree," *Wall Street Journal*, September 19, 2023.

13. My book *Restoring the Promise: Higher Education in America* (Oakland, CA: Independent Institute, 2019) is filled with data showing how the administrator-student and administrator-faculty ratios have soared over time, materially contributing to the rising labor costs that necessitate large tuition increases. I am indebted to Vivek Ramaswamy for reminding me of the specific statistic cited here. See his *Woke, Inc.* (New York: Center Street, 2021), 100–101.

14. Five schools in 2021–22 had total athletic department revenue exceeding $200 million (Ohio State University and the universities of Texas, Alabama, Michigan, and Georgia), and forty-four other schools had over $100 million in revenue. But much of the "revenue" at many schools comes in the form of student activity fees or direct subsidy payments to athletic departments financed from institutional revenues. See "NCAA Finances: Revenue and Expenses by School," *USA Today*, June 13, 2023.

15. For more of my thoughts on this, see Richard Vedder, "For Whom Does the Ball Roll?" *American Spectator*, September 16, 2023.

16. One excellent set of suggestions was provided by William Shughart II. See his "Cost Inflation in Intercollegiate Athletics: And Some Modest Proposals for Controlling It," in *Doing More With Less: Making Colleges Work Better*, edited by Joshua C. Hall (New York: Springer, 2010), 71–93. In the same volume, the paper by Matthew Denhart and Richard Vedder, "The Academic-Athletics Trade-Off: Universities and Intercollegiate Athletics" (95–136), covers a lot of the issues, albeit both papers are somewhat dated by significant changes in the milieu in which college sports operate.

17. See my article "Who Owns the University?" *Wall Street Journal*, March 16, 2023, for some elaboration on this point.

Chapter 7: Reimagining Higher Education: Reducing the Federal Role

1. Data are from the Consumer Credit Panel and published by the New York Federal Reserve Bank, Center for Microeconomic Data. See "2022 Student Loan Update" at https://www.newyorkfed.org/medialibrary/Interactives/householdcredit/data/xls/Student-loan_update_2022_mangrum.xlsx?sc_lang=en.

2. For the latest study demonstrating high levels of underemployment among recent college graduates, see the Burning Glass Institute and Strada Education Foundation, *Talent Disrupted: College Graduates, Underemployment, and the Way Forward*, February 2024.

3. Under the H-1B visa program, US employers bring in upward of a hundred thousand highly skilled foreign workers for a limited time period, typically three years but often extended to six years. The visa enables the student to enter the country working for a specific employer, who typically covers the cost of the move. At some point, however, the worker must obtain a visa through other means (e.g., marrying an American citizen) or return to their home country.

4. In my own field of economics, there has been an explosion of human subject experi-

mentation. Vernon Smith shared the 2002 Nobel Prize in Economic Sciences for his work in experimental economics.

Chapter 8: What Can State Governments Do?

1. The literature on school vouchers is voluminous. It varies in its assessments, but most of the studies I examined show minimally some positive effects of vouchers on student achievement. Two examples: Cecilia Rouse, "Private School Vouchers and Student Achievement: An Evaluation of the Milwaukee Parental Choice Program," *Quarterly Journal of Economics* 113 (May 1998), 553–602, and Patrick J. Wolf et al., "School Vouchers and Student Outcomes: Experimental Evidence from Washington, DC," *Journal of Policy Analysis and Management* 32 (February 2013): 246–70.

2. Nicholas W. Hillman, David A. Tandberg, and Jacob P. K. Gross, "Market-Based Higher Education: Does Colorado's Voucher Model Improve Higher Education Access and Efficiency?" *Research in Higher Education* 55 (January 2014): 601–25.

3. Colorado Commission on Higher Education, "Recommendation on the Funding Allocation Formula for FY 2022–2023," n.d., https://cdhe.colorado.gov/sites/highered/files/documents/CCHE_Budget_Context_and_Recommendation_Statement_Oct_22_2021_FINAL.pdf.

4. The George HOPE scholarship has a voucher-like quality, but is not a traditional voucher. It is discussed again in a later chapter. Similarly, the original GI Bill had voucher-like characteristics, with the government generally covering the tuition fees of eligible veterans.

5. Earnings vary with both age and educational attainment. Among those with low levels of educational attainment who are working unskilled jobs, older workers make little more than younger ones, but for college graduates, the typical worker in his or her fifties typically makes perhaps double the wages of newly hired college graduates, as workers gain more leadership responsibilities with experience.

6. The role of governing boards has been pondered by many. A study I found thoughtful and useful was by a group headed by former Yale president Benno C. Schmidt, *Governance for a New Era: A Blueprint for Higher Education Trustees* (Washington, DC: American Council of Trustees and Alumni, August 2014). I like its assertion that "shared governance . . . cannot and must not be an excuse for board inaction."

7. See Melissa Korn, Andrea Fuller, and Jennifer S. Forsyth, "Colleges Spend Like There's No Tomorrow. 'These Places Are Just Devouring Money,'" *Wall Street Journal*, August 10, 2023.

Chapter 9: Inside Job: Reforming Universities Within

1. I immodestly reference here my op-ed, "Who Owns the University?" *Wall Street Journal*, March 17, 2023.

2. Joan Biskupic, "John Roberts Doesn't Want Race to Matter as He Ends Affirmative Action for College Admissions Programs," CNN, June 29, 2023, https://www.cnn.com/2023/06/29/politics/john-roberts-affirmative-action-race/index.html.

3. For more on this, see my op-ed with Braden Colegrove, "Why Men Are Disappearing

on Campus," *Wall Street Journal*, September 10, 2023.

4. I have been making this argument about some underworked professors for many years. See, for example, my "Time to Make Professors Teach," *Wall Street Journal*, June 8, 2011, or my "Colleges Wouldn't Cost So Much If Students and Faculty Worked Harder," *Wall Street Journal*, April 11, 2019.

5. William H. Hutt, *Economists and the Public: A Study of Competition and Opinion* (London: Jonathan Cape, 1936), 257.

6. A reviewer points out that a similar plan announced at Clemson University led to an uproar among faculty. Faculty opposition to such a plan can be expected to be severe, and leadership by the governing board in this area might be necessary to effect change.

Chapter 10: Other Reforms: Thinking outside the Box

1. The federal GI Bill program beginning in 1944 has paid tuition fees for eligible veterans.

2. For more information about the Hoover Institute program, see https://www.hoover.org/hoover-institution-summer-policy-boot-camp.

3. See E. D. Hirsch, *Cultural Literacy: What Every American Needs to Know* (New York: Vintage Books, 1988).

4. Melissa Korn and Douglas Belkin, "Princeton Board Fires Tenured Professor Joshua Katz, Citing Sexual Misconduct Investigation," *Wall Street Journal*, May 23, 2022. See also Anemona Hartocollis, "After Campus Uproar, Princeton Proposes to Fire Tenured Professor," *New York Times*, May 19, 2022 (updated May 23, 2022).

5. Richard Sander and Stuart Taylor Jr., *Mismatch: How Affirmative Action Hurts Students It's Intended to Help, and Why Universities Won't Admit It* (New York: Basic Books, 2012). See also the many works of Thomas Sowell, for example, his *Ethnic America: A History* (New York: Basic Books, 1981).

6. Slivka's account is more fully told in his post at Ben Slivka, "Northwestern Cancels Former Trustee," *My Thoughts on Your Future* (blog), October 5, 2023, https://benslivka.com/2023/10/05/northwestern-cancels-former-trustee.

7. Richard Vedder, "The Ne Plus Ultra of Collegiate Wokeness," James G. Martin Center, August 25, 2023. See also Scott Gerber, "DEI Brings Kafka to My Law School," *Wall Street Journal*, May 9, 2023.

8. Micaiah Bilger, "Jordan Peterson Will Appeal 'Re-education Mandate,'" *The College Fix*, August 29, 2023.

9. See College Pulse and FIRE, *2022–2023 College Free Speech Rankings*, https://5666503.fs1.hubspotusercontent-na1.net/hubfs/5666503/CFSR_2022_Report.pdf, and also Nick Perrino, "Opinion: College Campus Hecklers, Your Disruptions Don't Count as Free Speech," *Los Angeles Times*, April 14, 2023.

10. Alan C. Kors and Harvey A. Silverglate, *The Shadow University: The Betrayal of Liberty on America's Campuses* (New York: Simon & Schuster, 1999).

11. Greg Lukianoff and Jonathan Haidt, *The Coddling of the American Mind: How Good Intentions and Bad Ideas Are Setting Up a Generation for Failure* (New York: Penguin Books,

2018).

12. See Mao's speech of 1957, "On the Correct Handling of Contradictions among the People," in *Selected Works of Mao Tse-Tung* vol. 5, 2nd ed. (Paris: Foreign Languages Press, 2021): 368–405, posted on https://www.marxists.org/reference/archive/mao/selected-works/volume-5/mswv5_58.htm.

Chapter 11: Beyond Instruction: Research and Other Activities

1. However, David Figlio and Morton Schapiro, exploring student learning at Northwestern University (where Schapiro was president), found no statistically significant relationship between research accomplishment and teaching effectiveness. See their "Staffing the Higher Education Classroom," *Journal of Economic Perspectives* 35, no. 1 (Winter 2021): 143–62. See also Ali Palali et al., "Are Good Researchers Also Good Teachers? The Relationship between Research Quality and Teaching Quality," *Economics of Education Review* 64 (June 2018): 40–49. My guess is that good researchers tend to neglect teaching, so the positive effects of their research on teaching are often offset by the lack of time they spend on the teaching function.

2. See the writings of Terence Kealey, notably his book *The Economic Laws of Scientific Research* (London: Macmillan, 1996).

3. The experiences of federal research authorities during the 2020–22 COVID-19 crisis showed that not all federal research interventions and policy pronouncements were beneficial, as the costs of complying with some rules (e.g., long periods of business and school closures) dramatically outweighed any health benefits, which were often grossly misstated. See, for example, Wayne Winegarden and McKenzie Richards, *No Solutions, Only Trade-Offs: An Evaluation of the Benefits and Consequences from COVID-19 Restrictions*, issue brief (Pasadena, CA: Pacific Research Institute, 2023).

4. Ayana Archie, "Stanford President Resigns after Fallout from Falsified Data in His Research," *NPR*, July 20, 2023.

5. Nidhi Subbaraman, "Flood of Fake Science Forces Multiple Journal Closures," *Wall Street Journal*, May 14, 2024, https://www.wsj.com/science/academic-studies-research-paper-mills-journals-publishing-f5a3d4bc.

6. Jeffrey Brainard, "Hundreds of Cancer Papers Mention Cell Lines That Don't Seem to Exist," *Science*, May 21, 2024.

7. Although statistical results showing my research on the relationship between higher education spending and economic growth have appeared in several places, perhaps the most accessible and detailed is in my *Going Broke by Degree: Why College Costs Too Much* (Washington, DC: AEI Press, 2004), especially chapter 7.

8. As a scholar on the economics of slavery, I can say confidently that the economic exploitation of top male football and basketball players is by most measures greater than that of slaves in the antebellum South. For one article, see Richard Vedder and Matthew Denhart, "The Real March Madness," *Wall Street Journal*, March 20, 2009. Slaves on average "earned" 40 percent or so of what their wages would have been in competitive labor markets. See my "The Slave Exploitation (Expropriation) Rate," *Explorations in Economic History* 12 (Fall 1975), 453–57.

9. Laine Higgins and Jared Diamond, "NCAA Agrees to Share Revenue with Athletes in Landmark $2.8 Billion Settlement," *Wall Street Journal*, May 23, 2024.

10. Ideas along these lines have been around for a long time. See, for example, Brian Goff and William Shughart II, "Fields of Dreams: On the Construction of Professional Baseball Talent in Colleges and the Minor Leagues," in *Advances in the Economics of Sports*, edited by Gerald W. Scully, vol. 1 (Greenwich, CT: JAI Press, 1992), 91–114.

Chapter 12: Conclusion: Three Key Expressions to Guide Collegiate Reform

1. Earlier in the book, I attributed the statement to Plato, who certainly popularized the expression. However, it dates back even earlier to Aesop's fable "The Crow and the Pitcher," written somewhere in the first half of the sixth century BCE.

2. Here I am plagiarizing not only from Dickens, but myself! See my "The Best of Times, The Worst of Times . . . ," *The Independent Review* 27, no. 3 (Winter 2022–23): 335–42.

3. One survey shows that about 60 percent of full-time university faculty identify themselves as "liberal," about six times the proportion self-identified as "far right or conservative." By contrast, in 1990 the ratio of liberals to conservatives was about two to one (40 percent liberal, 20 percent conservative, 40 percent moderate). "See "Poison Ivy: America's Elite Universities Are Bloated, Complacent, and Illiberal," *The Economist,* March 9, 2024, 56.

4. Josh Moody, "Fitch Ratings Predicts More Closures, Mergers," *Inside Higher Ed*, September 21, 2023. The list does not cover some other near-death experiences involving the merger of a dying college with a stronger entity. Mills College in California merged into Northeastern University in Massachusetts, for example.

5. "Where Did All Those Virtuous Professors Go?" *Wall Street Journal*, September 23, 2023, A12.

6. Higher Learning Commission, September 18, 2023, as reported in the *Chronicle of Higher Education* on September 28, 2023.

7. While many scholars are associated with the founding and evolution of Public Choice economics (e.g., Anthony Downs, Mancur Olson, Duncan Black, William Riker, and William Niskanen), the two individuals who did the most to advance the field were James Buchanan and Gordon Tullock; Buchanan received the 1986 Nobel Prize. Their most famous book was *The Calculus of Consent* (Ann Arbor: University of Michigan Press, 1962).

8. See Quote Investigator, "Academic Politics Are So Vicious Because the Stakes Are So Small," August 18, 2013.

9. See Richard Vedder, "Harvard Should Pay Its Fair Share," *Wall Street Journal*, December 23–24, 2023, B18. Friedman originally advocated for government subsidies in *Capitalism and Freedom* (Chicago: University of Chicago Press, 1962).

10. See Suzannah Alexander, "Counseling's Political Purity Push: Unveiling the Identity Crisis That Hijacked Accreditation and Shaped a Profession," *Minding the Campus,* January 17, 2024.

11. Brian Rosenberg, "Higher Ed's Ruinous Resistance to Change," *Chronicle of Higher Education*, September 27, 2023. That article is adopted from his new book, *Whatever It Is, I'm Against It: Resistance to Change in Higher Education* (Cambridge, MA: Harvard Education

Press, 2023). Rosenberg and I have similar views on some needed reforms, including a better use of the calendar, allowing for three-year bachelor's degrees.

12. See my "Bread and Circuses: Then and Now: America Mimics Rome's Decline," *American Spectator*, October 6, 2023.

Index